Have You Had Your O.D.E. Today?
O'NEAL'S DAILY EXHORTATIONS

O'Neal Stallworth Porter

Have You Had Your O.D.E. *Today?*
O'NEAL'S DAILY EXHORTATIONS

O'Neal Stallworth Porter

Oh Kneel Publishing

Unless otherwise indicated all Scripture quotations are taken from the King James Version of the Holy Bible. Please note that **Oh Kneel Publishing Company's** publishing style capitalizes pronouns in Scripture that refer to the Father, Son, and Holy Spirit, and may differ from some Bible publishers' styles.

Have You Had Your O.D.E. Today?
O'Neal's Daily Exhortations
ISBN – 978-0-9777329-2-0
Copyright 2012 by Oh Kneel Publishing
P.O. Box 13125
Eight Mile, Alabama 36663
(251) 229-1150
Website: www.OKP4U.com
And www.onealporter.com
Email: okp36663@gmail.com

Cover Design: EMJRDESIGNS.COM

Technical Assistance: Garrett Smith

Printed in the United States of America. All rights reserved under International Copyright Law. Contents and/or cover may not be reproduced in whole or part in any form without the expressed written consent of the Publisher.

TABLE OF CONTENTS

Jan. 1	All The Way New	Matthew 9:17
Jan. 2	CTRL-ALT-DEL	Jeremiah 18:4
Jan. 3	The New – Who I Am	Psalm 51:10
Jan. 4	Another Chance	Psalm 51:10
Jan. 5	Push Back That Plate	Matthew 18:33
Jan. 6	Braggadocious Praise	Psalm 63:5
Jan. 7	People Do Change	Acts 9:26
Jan. 8	There Is Nothing Back There	Luke 9:62
Jan. 9	Holiness Is The Goal	II Corinthians 7:1
Jan. 10	Embrace Change	I John 3:2
Jan. 11	Just Focus On Your Assignment	I Cor. 3:6-7
Jan. 12	Seize The Moment	Matthew 5:6
Jan. 13	Doors and Walls: Know The Difference	Revelation 3:8
Jan. 14	Stop Listening To What: "They Say"	Nehemiah 4:2
Jan. 15	Peace Is A Choice	Philippians 4:8
Jan. 16	His Innumerable Thoughts About You	Psalm 139:17
Jan. 17	Don't Be Shy	Hebrews 4:16
Jan. 18	The God Desire	Psalm 42:1
Jan. 19	Tell Somebody Else	Mark 5:19
Jan. 20	Spiritual GPS: God's Perfecting Service	Ephesians 4:11-12
Jan. 21	Keep Studying His Word	II Timothy 2:15
Jan. 22	God's Working With You	Matthew 18:18
Jan. 23	Are You "In Position"?	Isaiah 45:11

Jan. 24	A Public Blessing	Psalm 23:5
Jan. 25	It's A Snow Day	Isaiah 55:10-11
Jan. 26	Who Will You Encourage Today?	Hebrews 3:13
Jan. 27	Praise Him Before The Enemy	Psalm 27:6
Jan. 28	Nothing! Will Pull Me Away	Romans 8:35-39
Jan. 29	Stop Playing Games	James 2:14-17
Jan. 30	Be Real For Him – Not Them	Colossians 2:23
Jan. 31	God's Plan For Your Destiny	Psalm 23:2
Feb. 1	Love Made Me Do It	II Corinthians 5:14
Feb. 2	Keep Pressing and Pushing	Hebrews 10:36
Feb. 3	Can You Love Like That?	Romans 5:8
Feb. 4	Get Your Own Business	II Corinthians 5:18
Feb. 5	God Lives Through You	II Peter 1:4
Feb. 6	Get Ready For Greater	Haggai 2:9
Feb. 7	Peace In The Midst Of…	Isaiah 54:10
Feb. 8	"Is" and "Can"	Hebrews 11:6
Feb. 9	God Wants The Best For You	Psalm 35:27
Feb. 10	Start On The Inside	II Corinthians 4:16
Feb. 11	Be Selfish	Matthew 7:3
Feb. 12	Faith! Controls Your Miracle	II Kings 6:5-7
Feb. 13	Stop Making Noise	I Corinthians 13:1
Feb. 14	No Greater Love	Romans 5:8
Feb. 15	Love Is The Greatest Thing	I Corinthians 13:8,13
Feb. 16	Love Is Better	Psalm 82:3
Feb. 17	Endure With A Smile	II Thessalonians 1:4

Feb. 18	God's Got You	Isaiah 43:2-4
Feb. 19	Just Be A Blessing	Luke 6:34
Feb. 20	You Gotta Love	Matthew 22:39b
Feb. 21	Every Action Is Seed Sown	Galatians 6:7
Feb. 22	Ministry or Misery	I Corinthians 15:33
Feb. 23	Let Your Smile Welcome God	Psalm 24:7
Feb. 24	Run From The Players	II Timothy 3:5
Feb. 25	A Demand On God's Word	II Corinthians 9:8
Feb. 26	A Good Time To Praise	Psalm 34:1
Feb. 27	Sacrificial Living For His Glory	Romans 8:36
Feb. 28	Treat Them Right	Romans 12:17
Feb. 29	God's Grace Manifest In You	Ephesians 3:7
Mar. 1	Be Straight With God	Psalm 139:23
Mar. 2	You Belong To God	I Corinthians 6:19-20
Mar. 3	Let Mercy Abound	II Corinthians 4:1
Mar. 4	Confusion At The Altar	Colossians 2:8
Mar. 5	Why The Wait?	Ephesians 5:16
Mar. 6	How Big Is Your God?	Psalm 35:27
Mar. 7	Let The Error Go	Matthew 18:33
Mar. 8	God Is Fighting For You	II Chronicles 32:8
Mar. 9	Don't Get Distracted	Luke 8:14
Mar. 10	Following Jesus	Matthew 4:22
Mar. 11	The Awesome Potential Within You	I John 3:2
Mar. 12	You Can Be Better	III John 1:2
Mar. 13	Have Strong Faith	Romans 4:20

Mar. 14	See The Good – Experience The Glory	II Chronicles 20:17
Mar. 15	Today – See His Goodness	Psalm 27:13
Mar. 16	Get Up And Get Busy	Proverbs 12:27
Mar. 17	Stop Focusing On Your Weakness	II Corinthians 12:9
Mar. 18	Sing A Song For Your Enemy	II Chronicles 20:22
Mar. 19	Keep Meeting Together	Hebrews 10:25
Mar. 20	Success Is Yours	Joshua 1:8
Mar. 21	The Lord's House	Psalm 122:1
Mar. 22	God Has A Job Opening For You	Matthew 4:19
Mar. 23	"I Can I Tis" – A Good Condition	Philippians 4:13
Mar. 24	From Bitter To Better	Ruth 1:20
Mar. 25	No Other Choice – But To Wait	Isaiah 40:31
Mar. 26	He Is A Right Now God	Psalm 46:1
Mar. 27	Peace Is God's Blessing	I Corinthians 14:33
Mar. 28	God Is Waiting For You	Hebrews 4:15-16
Mar. 29	Relatives Can't Relate	Matthew 10:36
Mar. 30	Embrace The Fire	Daniel 3:17-18
Mar. 31	The Same Folk	Luke 23:21
Apr. 1	Don't Be Fooled	Ephesians 4:14
Apr. 2	Giving Up = Telling Lies	Hebrews 10:35
Apr. 3	Keep It Real With God	Matthew 15:8
Apr. 4	Lucky or Blessed?	Jeremiah 29:11
Apr. 5	The Blood Of Jesus	Hebrews 9:12
Apr. 6	Your Blessings Have Your Address	Deuteronomy 28:2
Apr. 7	You Will Survive	Acts 27:4

Apr. 8	How Deep Did You Dig?	Luke 6:47-49
Apr. 9	Sanctified Satisfaction	Philippians 4:12
Apr. 10	Keep On Keeping On	Luke 18:1
Apr. 11	Lose Yourself In Him	Philippians 3:9
Apr. 12	Robe-less Ministry	II Corinthians 5:18
Apr. 13	You Can Have What You Say	Job 22:28
Apr. 14	Not Better – Just Different	II Corinthians 6:17
Apr. 15	God Will Make A Way	Genesis 22:5
Apr. 16	Perception Is Powerful	Numbers 13:33
Apr. 17	Just Obey	Deuteronomy 28:1-2
Apr. 18	Fasting For Victory	Matthew 4:2
Apr. 19	What Is Your Decision	Matthew 4:22
Apr. 20	It's Your Turn Now	Romans 6:5-11
Apr. 21	You Might As Well Smile	Proverbs 15:30
Apr. 22	Holler Louder	Mark 10:48
Apr. 23	True Giving	II Corinthians 8:2
Apr. 24	"Dunamis" In Your Life	Acts 1:8
Apr. 25	Hold On To Your Faith	I Peter 1:7
Apr. 26	All For One	I Corinthians 12:25
Apr. 27	God Is Great & Greatly To Be Praised	Exodus 15:2
Apr. 28	Holding On – Is Your Only Option	Acts 27:44
Apr. 29	Reposition Your Tongue	Ephesians 4:29
Apr. 30	What Did Jesus Say?	Luke 8:22
May 1	Favour Is On The Way	Proverbs 3:4
May 2	His Power In Your Life	Acts 1:8

May 3	That's Not Faith	James 2:17-20
May 4	Learn And Do Your Part	Ephesians 4:16
May 5	Go Through And Come Out	Isaiah 43:2
May 6	Obedience Brings Deliverance	John 9:7
May 7	Don't Let People Shut You Up	Matthew 10:48
May 8	Relationship Matters	Ruth 1:16
May 9	Go Get Yours	II Kings 7:3
May 10	Time To Celebrate	Esther 9:22
May 11	Great Things Are Still Coming	Hebrews 10:35
May 12	Help Is Everpresent	Hebrews 2:18
May 13	The Spirit Of A True Mother	Judges 5:7
May 14	Get Busy For Others	Galatians 6:10
May 15	Kingdom Blessings	Luke 5:7
May 16	Talk To Your Body	I Thessalonians 4:4
May 17	Conforming To The Christ	Romans 12:2
May 18	A Simple Act Of Obedience	John 2:1-5
May 19	Keep On Keeping On	Luke 18:1
May 20	Get Dressed For Victory	Ephesians 6:10-18
May 21	The Perfect Prayer Partner	Romans 8:26
May 22	God Expects More	Genesis 9:7
May 23	God Honors Faith	Matthew 21:32
May 24	How Much Do You Have In The Bank?	II Kings 20:2-5
May 25	Be Filled With The Holy Ghost	John 7:38
May 26	Duty and Sacrificial Love	I John 3:16
May 27	Live By The Word	Ephesians 5:15

May 28	God Wants To Use You	II Corinthians 4:7
May 29	Tell The Children	I Corinthians 14:33
May 30	His Glory In Your Life	Romans 6:4
May 31	Do You Really Believe?	Matthew 9:28
Jun. 1	Why Are You Not Hungry?	Matthew 5:6
Jun. 2	Who Is Praying For You?	I Samuel 7:8
Jun. 3	Bring Somebody Back	II Corinthians 5:18
Jun. 4	When The Heat Is Turned Up	Daniel 3:17-18
Jun. 5	Disappointments Come	I Samuel 30:6
Jun. 6	God Ain't Sharing His Glory	Isaiah 42:8
Jun. 7	Spirit-Filled Day	Ephesians 5:18
Jun. 8	Blessed With Power – Twice	Romans 8:14-17
Jun. 9	Use The Throne – Not The Phone	Jeremiah 33:3
Jun. 10	Who Is Really In Charge?	Ephesians 5:18
Jun. 11	And It Fell Not!	Matthew 7:25
Jun. 12	Your Life Will Not Perish	Galatians 3:14
Jun. 13	The Holy Spirit: Your Personal Teacher	I John 2:27
Jun. 14	Do You Have A "YES" For God?	Matthew 9:28
Jun. 15	Somebody Needs You	Psalm 82:3
Jun. 16	Reposition For Reward	II Kings 7:3
Jun. 17	The Pursuit Of Peace	Psalm 34:14
Jun. 18	My Soul Is Anchored	I Peter 4:19
Jun. 19	God: The Pattern For Fatherhood	Genesis 1:27
Jun. 20	Heh God! Happy Father's Day	Matthew 7:11
Jun. 21	You Are In His Image	Genesis 3:4-5

Jun. 22	Who Will You Bless Today?	I Peter 4:10
Jun. 23	Blessed And Unmovable	Psalm 1:3
Jun. 24	Let Go And Let God	Luke 12:29
Jun. 25	Make Sure It Counts	Matthew 7:23
Jun. 26	Your Yesterday Helps Somebody Else	Ephesians 2:3
Jun. 27	Act Like Your Daddy	Romans 12:21
Jun. 28	Battle Is His – Victory Yours	II Chronicles 20:22
Jun. 29	The Issue In Your Life	Mark 5:25-34
Jun. 30	Follow The Spirit	John 16:13
Jul. 1	Go Over And Beyond	Matthew 26:7
Jul. 2	Signs That You Are Ready To Be Free	Luke 19:3-4
Jul. 3	Celebrate Your Liberty	Ephesians 2:1-7
Jul. 4	Celebrate Your Dependence On God	Acts 17:28
Jul. 5	Seize The Moment	Matthew 5:6
Jul. 6	God Has A Ram For You	Genesis 22:13
Jul. 7	Ask The Saviour To Help	Isaiah 57:13
Jul. 8	Stop Blinding The Saints	Matthew 5:16
Jul. 9	Are You Ready?	Luke 12:40
Jul. 10	Let God Use You	Matthew 9:8
Jul. 11	Persistence Pays Off	Matthew 9:27
Jul. 12	How Do "You" See You?	Numbers 13:33
Jul. 13	The Struggle Is Not Always Bad	James 3:2
Jul. 14	Don't Twist Your Liberty	I Corinthians 8:9
Jul. 15	Nobody Like The Lord	Psalm 89:6-8
Jul. 16	A Multiple Choice Test	Joshua 24:15

Jul. 17	Deliverance Is In You	Matthew 1:21
Jul. 18	When God Speaks	Luke 5:5
Jul. 19	Don't Complain	Ecclesiastes 7:14
Jul. 20	Run! And Don't Look Back	I Corinthians 10:13
Jul. 21	Walk On Water Again	Matthew 14:28-32
Jul. 22	God Blessing It Right	Haggai 1:6
Jul. 23	Stop Watering Weeds	Psalm 19:14
Jul. 24	Let Your Praise Be Radical	II Samuel 6:14, 20-22
Jul. 25	Say It – Until You See It	Hebrews 10:23
Jul. 26	Endure Until The End	Matthew 24:13
Jul. 27	Don't Stop Believing	Numbers 20:12
Jul. 28	You're Just That Special	Galatians 3:14
Jul. 29	Benefits Of Connection	John 15:5
Jul. 30	The Bad News Ain't News	Mark 13:7
Jul. 31	No More Sad Face	I Kings 18:41
Aug. 1	Your Words Can Make It Happen	Matthew 18:18-19
Aug. 2	Take That Off	I Samuel 17:39
Aug. 3	Be Aware Of The Kiss	Matthew 26:49
Aug. 4	For His Name's Sake	Ezekiel 36:20-25
Aug. 5	Give God Praise	Psalm 34:1
Aug. 6	Conviction Not Condemnation	John 16:8
Aug. 7	An On Time God	Hebrews 10:37
Aug. 8	He Hears And Responds	Psalm 145:19
Aug. 9	Stop Fussing	Proverbs 19:11
Aug. 10	Complete Confidence	Daniel 3:17

Aug. 11	God Will Cheer You Up	Psalm 94:19
Aug. 12	Do The Right Thing For Those You Hurt	Luke 19:8
Aug. 13	Watch God Show Out	Psalm 37:5
Aug. 14	Get Busy Now	John 9:4
Aug. 15	Hallelujah – All Day Long	Hebrews 13:15
Aug. 16	When You Have Changed	I Peter 4:4
Aug. 17	Time For Your Ministry	II Corinthians 9:8
Aug. 18	Worship Must Be Willed	Luke 7:45
Aug. 19	Your Praise Ushers In His Presence	Psalm 22:3
Aug. 20	When Will You Believe?	John 20:29
Aug. 21	Celebrate With Others	Luke 15:9
Aug. 22	Embrace The God Life	Matthew 10:39
Aug. 23	He's Still Working	Philippians 1:6
Aug. 24	Did You Hear The Question?	John 5:6
Aug. 25	Each Victory Will Help	Deuteronomy 7:22
Aug. 26	The Value Of His Name	Psalm 106:8
Aug. 27	Not Yours, But God's	Psalm 24:1
Aug. 28	Living Off The Interest	Galatians 6:7
Aug. 29	Don't Be So Shocked	Habakkuk 1:5
Aug. 30	God: Your Deliverer	Psalm 34:19
Aug. 31	God Is Always There	Deuteronomy 4:31
Sep. 1	Trouble Ain't All That Bad	Matthew 7:25
Sep. 2	You Are Not The Only One	I Corinthians 10:13
Sep. 3	Yes, You Can Be Nice	Romans 12:18
Sep. 4	The Heart Of Worship	Philippians 3:3

Sep. 5	The Living Word Manifest Via You	II Corinthians 3:3
Sep. 6	Daily Living Habits	Romans 12:12
Sep. 7	Simply Forgive	Luke 17:4
Sep. 8	Just Stop	Exodus 16:30
Sep. 9	Don't Let Others Hinder Your Praise	Matthew 26:10
Sep. 10	Keep Up Your Momentum	Hebrews 10:35
Sep. 11	Do You Know The Season?	Ecclesiastes 3:1
Sep. 12	Commit To The Constant	Malachi 3:6
Sep. 13	A Faith Conversation	Genesis 22:5
Sep. 14	Praise Him For Yourself	Luke 8:35-39
Sep. 15	Don't Waste Time Fussing	II Timothy 2:23
Sep. 16	Just What He Said	Numbers 23:19
Sep. 17	Let God Use You – His Way	Romans 9:21
Sep. 18	Holy For Him	II Corinthians 7:1
Sep. 19	God Don't Wanna Hear That	Jeremiah 1:6
Sep. 20	Blessing In Waiting	Isaiah 40:31
Sep. 21	Get Right With God	I Corinthians 11:31-32
Sep. 22	Who Will You Encourage?	Hebrews 3:13
Sep. 23	Glad That Ain't Your God	I Kings 18:27
Sep. 24	No More Hunger	John 6:35
Sep. 25	Let Jesus Lead You	Isaiah 55:8
Sep. 26	What Road Are You On?	Isaiah 35:8
Sep. 27	Ignore The Spectators	I Chronicles 15:29
Sep. 28	God Will Take Care Of You	Galatians 6:7
Sep. 29	What Are You Doing With Your Gift?	Luke 19:13

Sep. 30	Just Be The Original You	Galatians 6:4
Oct. 1	Work The Word	I Corinthians 4:20
Oct. 2	Put Your Praise First	II Chronicles 20:21
Oct. 3	Giving Up Is Not An Option	Luke 18:1-8
Oct. 4	When My Friend Falls	I Peter 4:15
Oct. 5	You Are Not In This Alone	Psalm 23:4
Oct. 6	Don't Stop Doing Good	Galatians 6:9
Oct. 7	God Will Do Even More	Psalm 46:1
Oct. 8	He Will Show Up	Matthew 14:27
Oct. 9	God Gives Green Lights	I Samuel 30:8
Oct. 10	God Gets All The Praise	II Corinthians 4:15
Oct. 11	Another Way He Blesses	Joshua 6:1
Oct. 12	True Believers – Wait	Isaiah 40:31
Oct. 13	Call Jesus Louder	Matthew 20:31
Oct. 14	Getting God's Best	Psalm 37:4
Oct. 15	Don't Rejoice In Others' Mistakes	John 8:7
Oct. 16	Where To Place Your Trust	Psalm 44:6-7
Oct. 17	Forgiving Is Fruitful	Luke 17:4
Oct. 18	God Will Speak Through You	Luke 12:12
Oct. 19	Thank You Lord	Lamentations 3:22
Oct. 20	Just Be The Original You	Galatians 6:4
Oct. 21	Multiply Don't Magnify	Colossians 1:10
Oct. 22	God Deserves More	Romans 6:19
Oct. 23	Minister Don't Mingle	Proverbs 25:26
Oct. 24	Which Eye Are You Using?	II Corinthians 5:7

Oct. 25	Do You Realize What You Have?	II Peter 1:4
Oct. 26	Prepare For Plenty	Proverbs 30:25
Oct. 27	You Don't Need Money	Isaiah 55:1
Oct. 28	You Have A Cross Too	Matthew 16:24
Oct. 29	Now Tell God "Thank Ya"	I Thessalonians 5:18
Oct. 30	Be Proud Of Fellow Believers	II Corinthians 1:14
Oct. 31	Celebrate The God Gifts	II Timothy 1:7
Nov. 1	I Want More Milk	I Peter 2:2
Nov. 2	Go Bless Somebody	Luke 10:33-35
Nov. 3	Everybody Doesn't Need A Mirror	Romans 9:21
Nov. 4	Cease and Desist	Psalm 40:1,10
Nov. 5	The Key To Prevailing Prayer	James 5:16
Nov. 6	When God Speaks	II Chronicles 20:20
Nov. 7	Keep Following The Light	John 8:12
Nov. 8	Don't Be Distracted	Nehemiah 4:3
Nov. 9	The Peace Of God	Philippians 4:7
Nov. 10	Be A Channel Of Blessing	Proverbs 11:25
Nov. 11	The Future Is Still Bright	Jeremiah 29:11
Nov. 12	Walk, Leap and Praise	Acts 3:8
Nov. 13	Focus On Your Function	Luke 10:40
Nov. 14	Choose Your Song Wisely	Ephesians 5:19
Nov. 15	God Is Focused On The Inside	Jeremiah 17:10
Nov. 16	Partnership With God	I Chronicles 19:13
Nov. 17	Your Faith Glorifies God	I Peter 1:7
Nov. 18	Seize The Moment	John 9:4

Nov. 19	Unlikely Help	Luke 10:31-33
Nov. 20	Let Your Joy Be Full	Psalm 16:11
Nov. 21	Don't Be Distracted	II Kings 7:3
Nov. 22	Praise Him For Yourself	Luke 8:35-39
Nov. 23	Gratitude Determines Altitude	II Corinthians 2:14
Nov. 24	The Way To Please God	Hebrews 11:6
Nov. 25	Real Relationship	Proverbs 17:17
Nov. 26	Just Do Your Part	Matthew 10:14
Nov. 27	Today – See His Goodness	Psalm 27:13
Nov. 28	Holy For Him	II Corinthians 7:1
Nov. 29	God's Job Opening Just For You	Matthew 4:19
Nov. 30	It's Not All About You	Romans 12:10
Dec. 1	Neither Do I	John 8:10-11
Dec. 2	How Persistent Is Your Faith?	Acts 9:26
Dec. 3	Why Are You Looking?	Mark 16:6
Dec. 4	Ministry Of Disconnect	Proverbs 1:15
Dec. 5	Your Blessing Will Bless Others	Psalm 23:5
Dec. 6	At The End Of The Day	II Kings 7:3
Dec. 7	Know Who You Are	Acts 28:6
Dec. 8	Watch Your Words	Proverbs 18:21
Dec. 9	It Will Still Happen	Habakkuk 2:3
Dec. 10	God Shows His Awesomeness Via You	Psalm 139:14
Dec. 11	Don't Look Back	Genesis 19:26
Dec. 12	From Bitter To Better	Ruth 1:20
Dec. 13	Concealed From Calamity	Psalm 32:7

Dec. 14	They Need You! Not Your Money!	Acts 3:6
Dec. 15	Keep Giving	Psalm 34:19
Dec. 16	He Will Fight Your Battle	Hebrews 13:6
Dec. 17	Fulfill Your Calling	Isaiah 42:6
Dec. 18	Know The Word For Yourself	Titus 1:9
Dec. 19	Is It A Godly Connect?	Amos 3:3
Dec. 20	Let The Light Shine	Isaiah 60:1
Dec. 21	For Seasoned Saints	Colossians 2:7
Dec. 22	Serve Humanity	Matthew 25:40
Dec. 23	Defeat Is Impossible	Matthew 16:18
Dec. 24	Thank God For The Name	Isaiah 9:6
Dec. 25	A Messy Blessing	Luke 2:11-12
Dec. 26	What Light Do You Have?	John 3:19
Dec. 27	It's Not Too Late!	John 9:4
Dec. 28	Spiritual Rivals	I Timothy 6:8
Dec. 29	Laugh With God	Psalm 2:4
Dec. 30	Freedom From Folk	Proverbs 29:25
Dec. 31	Take Time To Remember	Psalm 77:11
Bonus 1	That Was Yesterday	I Corinthians 12:2
Bonus 2	Bread Of Heaven – Feed Me!	Matthew 6:11
Bonus 3	God's Mercy Is Yours	Psalm 118:1
Bonus 4	Compassion And Understanding	Ephesians 4:2
Bonus 5	Embrace Peace – Victory Is Yours	John 16:33
Bonus 6	Don't Be Duped By The Devil	Isaiah 14:16
Bonus 7	You Won't Drown	Matthew 14:30
Bonus 8	God Is Your Multiplier	Ephesians 3:20
Bonus 9	A Prayer Answering God	Psalm 116:1
Bonus 10	Increase Is En Route	Isaiah 32:15

Acknowledgements

All praise to God who allowed me to go through an awesome season of testing and trial. This season birthed these daily messages to bless others. God truly made all things work together for my good – and for that I praise Him!

To Sabrina. To my children, Kymberly, Brooke, Morgan (son-in-love Tim Martin) and Charles, (granddaughters, Amber, MaKenzi and Madeline) thank you for sharing me with the world. Your continual support and faithfulness to Kingdom work has encouraged and strengthened me to effectively continue to proclaim the gospel in multi-faceted ways.

I honor and acknowledge my parents, Rev. and Mrs. Charles (Joyce) Porter and Sis. Harriet and (Rev. Matthew) Crandle, who bore the responsibility of birthing me into the earth realm and being good stewards by shaping and molding me into who God called and anointed me to be.

To the Pastor S.D. Jackson and the saints of God at Fellowship Christian Church affectionately called "THE SHIP," thank you for allowing me to serve you for over 20 years. I am humbled and blessed for the opportunity to bless God's people.

Dedication

To My O.B.S.

Charles Van James Porter

Daddy Loves You.
I am so proud of the awesome man of God you are becoming.
Always remember, God's Word is your foundation. And if you
build your life on His Word, you will be able to stand!
Stay focused and stay true to God.

Excited About Your Destiny!

From Your E.L.F.

PREFACE

God has an awesome sense of humor. At your lowest moment, He will allow strength to rise from within you when you feel that all hope is gone. He will allow joy to take the place of sadness and sorrow. He will usher in peace and hope in dismal settings and situations. He is simply ensuring that His Word does not fail or come back to Him void. He is truly the "Romans 8:28 God," causing all things to work together for your good because you love Him and you are called according to His purpose.

During one of the most challenging seasons of my earthly existence, God spoke to me and said "Encourage the people." And of course, in my own sheepish way of replying in my mind *(was not going to say it out loud – smile)*: "God, I need encouragement myself!" And, He so wonderfully replied, "O'Neal, you have it. It's on the inside of you. I put it there."

This is the origin of **O.D.E.** – **O**'Neal's **D**aily **E**xhortations! For a year and a half, as led and directed by the Spirit of God, God blessed me to write daily devotionals to encourage, enlighten, empower and edify others' lives. I was under a spiritual mandate to accomplish this. My physical and mental state of being had no say-so in my mission. Whatever was on my schedule or agenda took a back-seat to me fulfilling my mission. I even thank God for a patient family. Many days they were put on hold to allow me to fulfill my mission.

Through this daily process two things occurred. First, I began to hear testimonies of how people were being blessed and encouraged by the words of the daily devotionals. And, secondly, God did a restorative work in me and would not allow me to focus on my own crisis because He had me busy making sure everyone else was alright.

This book has been my medicine and therapy. It has healed hurt and disappointment. It has removed fear and apprehension far away from me. It has restored joy and gladness. It has revealed to me "True Faith." It has blessed my spiritual vision and positioned me for God's greater glory.

As you read this book – be blessed! You may use it as a daily encouragement. Or, you may decide to thumb through the Table of Contents to find a topic that interests you at the moment. Or, you may even just pick it up and read it like a novel, unable to put it down reading page after page. However, as you allow it to minister to you – remember this: The exhortation that you receive from this volume is not just for you, but every day make it your business to find someone to encourage and exhort!

HEBREWS 3:13

For as long as it's still God's Today, keep each other on your toes so sin doesn't slow down your reflexes. – The Message Translation

Encourage each other every day while you have the opportunity. If you do this, none of you will be deceived by sin and become stubborn. – God's Word Translation

Be Blessed TODAY and Everyday!

Have You Had Your O.D.E. *Today?*
O'NEAL'S **D**AILY **E**XHORTATIONS

O'Neal Stallworth Porter

JANUARY 1

All The Way New!

MATTHEW 9:17

"Neither do men put new wine into old bottles: else the bottles break, and the wine runneth out, and the bottles perish: but they put new wine into new bottles, and both are preserved."
– King James Version

"And you don't put your wine in cracked bottles." – The Message Translation

Happy New Year!

God has blessed you to see a new year. So, what is new about you?

Don't get lost in the traditional making of "New Year's Resolutions"! If you yourself have not changed, you are wasting time and deceiving yourself. That's just like putting new wine in old wine skins. It's not going to work or last.

You need more than just new ideas and new plans. You need the Lord to create a new heart and renew the right spirit within you. Then you will be in position to break forth into the new things that God has prepared for you.

That's right! Don't be satisfied with just looking new or sounding new. Search deep within and repent of the old ways and allow God to make you new from the inside out. Be like the clay on the potter's wheel. God can make you over!

As you operate in obedience to the leading of God's Spirit, don't simply get lost in rituals, rules, and resolutions. But, focus each day to practice hearing and obeying God like never before. Remind yourself each time you feel yourself sliding back, that God has made you new!

JANUARY 2
CTRL – ALT – DEL
JEREMIAH 18:4

And the vessel that he made of clay was marred in the hand of the potter: so he made it again another vessel, as seemed good to the potter to make it. – King James Version

Whenever the pot the potter was working on turned out badly, as sometimes happens when you are working with clay, the potter would simply start over and use the same clay to make another pot. – The Message Translation

For those who are not familiar with computer lingo, (CTR – ALT – DEL) are the three keys that you press simultaneously in order to reboot your computer. God does the same thing in your life. There are times that God will restart you in order to help you to function better.

Have you ever cried out, "Lord, make me over!"? The God who extends new mercies every morning will hear your cry. The God who helps a righteous man who has fallen seven times to get back up again will come to your rescue. The God who makes grace abound will cover you.

Life has so many challenges. It is the desire of the enemy to convince you to give up when you have made mistakes or fallen. The devil wants you to throw in the towel. But, you must remember that you serve a loving God who loves you enough to separate your sins as far as the east is from the west.

So, run into the arms of a loving and forgiving God. Allow Him to make you over again. If you need a spiritual makeover, let God have His way. If you need a clean heart created and a right spirit renewed, come to Him as you are – He won't deny you. If your life needs to be rebooted, then step back and let God take control.

JANUARY 3

The New – Who I Am!

PSALM 51:10

Create in me a clean heart, O God; and renew a right spirit within me. – King James Version

God, make a fresh start in me, shape a Genesis week from the chaos of my life. – The Message Translation

The goal and focus is to be more like Jesus. A heart and soul transformation is necessary to be like Him. Sin contaminated the inner man. But the blood of Jesus shed on Calvary is powerful enough to rid us of the contamination and make us brand new creatures. The choice is ours in who and what we desire to be and what we manifest.

The clean heart that pleases God is a heart of new character. You love because that is who you are not because of what someone else does. You forgive and extend mercy because that is your nature not because someone asks your forgiveness. Your pray for your enemies and bless those who say evil things about you because that is your normal mode of operation.

You remind yourself daily that your body is the temple of the Holy Ghost. You disconnect yourself from nouns (people, places, things and ideas) that are not part of your destiny. You realign yourself with those nouns that are advantageous to your moving towards your destiny. The bright light of Christ always shines within you and brightens the world wherever you go!

JANUARY 4
Another Chance!
PSALM 51:10

Create in me a clean heart, O God; and renew a right spirit within me. – King James Version

God, make a fresh start in me, shape a Genesis week from the chaos of my life. – The Message Translation

God is not just the God of a "second chance", but thankfully He is the God of "another chance". His grace and mercy fills your life and gives you an opportunity to regroup and get it together. Every morning you awake to brand new mercies.

As you continue praising God for another day, another year – remember that you don't have to burdened with your yesterday. Whatever you did and whatever happened is over and gone. God has blessed you with the opportunity for a fresh start.

The computer keystroke of "Control-Alt-Delete" reboots your computer and allows it to start over. In the same manner, God will reboot your life and allow you to start over. Just like the clay on the potter's wheel, He will make you over again. Just like the refiner's fire, stay in until you come forth pure and He can see His reflection in your life.

It may not happen overnight, but stay before the throne. Keep praying and praising until the change is complete. It does not matter if your change happens overnight or if it is a process and it occurs little by little. Just be grateful for God's favor upon your life to change.

Don't get satisfied until you see the transformation being made manifest. Yes, see His Word alive in your daily walk and talk. See His Spirit manifest in all of your relationships. See a brand new you that only the power of God could produce!

JANUARY 5

Push Back That Plate!
MATTHEW 18:33

Howbeit this kind goeth not out but by prayer and fasting. – King James Version

But an evil spirit of this kind is only driven out by prayer and fasting. – Weymouth New Testament

There are some instances where your "Faith In Action" is demonstrated by pushing back the plate. More than just words coming out of your mouth, your heart's true belief is demonstrated through your actions. It seems as if the act of "fasting" is a dirty word in the minds of some. However, it is a biblical principle that should be embraced.

In the scripture reference above, the disciples were not successful in their ministry to deliver a possessed man. Jesus revealed that fasting was the missing ingredient in this deliverance session. Ask yourself, "Is anything missing in my spiritual walk"?

Learn to do what it takes for personal deliverance as well as public ministry. Fast AND pray! Fasting should be a regular part of every believer's life. Don't wait for a crisis or critical moment to occur. Stay fasted up and prayed up so you will have spiritual power in your personal life and you will be more beneficial to others.

JANUARY 6

Braggadocious Praise!

PSALM 63:5

My soul shall be satisfied as with marrow and fatness; and my mouth shall praise thee with joyful lips: - King James Version

I will be fully satisfied as with the richest of foods; with singing lips my mouth will praise you. – Today's New International Version

The old saints used to declare: "When I THINK of the goodness of Jesus, my soul cries out hallelujah!" God is just that good. All you have to do is consider who He is and what He has done. Something down on the inside of you will get excited!

The soul is the mind, will and intellect of man. This part of you is satisfied as you embrace who God is. He is the Creator of all things. He is the author and finisher of your faith. He has an awesome plan to bring you to an expected end.

His goodness and mercy made manifest in your life can't help but to illicit praise from your lips. Basking in His presence is consuming and filling. Take this time right now to just open your mouth and begin to brag and boast on WHO He is! That's praise!

JANUARY 7

People Do Change!

ACTS 9:26

And when Saul was come to Jerusalem, he assayed to join himself to the disciples: but they were all afraid of him, and believed not that he was a disciple. – King James Version

Back in Jerusalem he tried to join the disciples, but they were all afraid of him. They didn't trust him one bit. – The Message Translation

The people were afraid of Saul (Paul) because of his past. But, he had an experience with God and he was not the same man. The same man that had tried to destroy the church was now one of the most influential builders of the Christian church.

It is so easy to judge people by their past. What you heard or even know about a person does not determine the destiny that God has prepared for them.

Take a look in the mirror. Have you always had it together, or done the right thing? Of course not! And to be honest – you are still working on you. But, God has changed you hasn't He? Then always remember, that the same God that saved and delivered you has the power to do the same for others too.

JANUARY 8
There Is Nothing Back There!
LUKE 9:62

And Jesus said unto him, No man, having put his hand to the plough, and looking back, is fit for the kingdom of God. – King James Version

Jesus said, "No procrastination. No backward looks. You can't put God's kingdom off till tomorrow. Seize the day." – The Message Translation

If you are reading this – you are without excuse! There is too much work to be done in the kingdom. Stop reminiscing. Quit living in yesterday. Get busy! Whatever you used to do, or whoever you used to be should be put to rest. Get out of the history book. You are a new creature – let the old go!

There is nothing in your past worth holding on to. Paul even declared that he considered his past accomplishments as dung. Basically, whatever he had accomplished or achieved in the past really did not really matter for the present and the goal that was before him!

Focusing on your past disqualifies you from being effective today! Don't get distracted from your present assignment by longing for days gone by. Move on! Hear the voice of God and obey Him. Go and do what God has directed you to do today! Stop looking back!

JANUARY 9
Holiness Is The Goal!
II CORINTHIANS 7:1

Having therefore these promises, dearly beloved, let us cleanse ourselves from all filthiness of the flesh and spirit, perfecting holiness in the fear of God. – King James Version

With promises like this to pull us on, dear friends, let's make a clean break with everything that defiles or distracts us, both within and without. Let's make our entire lives fit and holy temples for the worship of God. More Passionate, More Responsible. – The Message Translation

God has promised great things to you. You need to position yourself to be a vessel of honor unto the King. Every day focus on loving Him more than you did yesterday. Your love must be strong enough to run away from those things that displease Him. Remind your flesh that it is now dead to sin. And communicate to sin that it no longer has power or control over you. Welcome the Holy Spirit to fill every part of your spirit, soul and body.

Holiness is your lifestyle. It is more than how you dress. But don't get it twisted, the Holy Spirit will let you know when your apparel is not godly. Some have used the excuse of liberty to dress in ways that God truly is not glorified. Holiness is also your character and conduct. It is who you are when no one is watching and it is also how you treat others. The conversations that you have demonstrate your commitment to holiness.

Strive daily to be what God called you to be – and that is holy. Command the old man to die daily and allow the new man to be renewed every day. Pattern your life after your big brother Jesus Christ. Remember, you are a joint heir! Be holy even as He is holy!

JANUARY 10
Embrace Change
I JOHN 3:2

Beloved, now are we the sons of God, and it doth not yet appear what we shall be: but we know that, when he shall appear, we shall be like him; for we shall see him as he is. – King James Version

But friends, that's exactly who we are: children of God. And that's only the beginning. Who knows how we'll end up! What we know is that when Christ is openly revealed, we'll see him - and in seeing him, become like him. – The Message Translation

Stop fighting change! According to the Word of God, all are born in sin – however when you are born again you begin a lifelong journey to becoming more like Him! Yes, Jesus Christ is your pattern and model.

Some people make excuses about their actions and choices by saying that's just how they are. But, when you become a believer you have to begin to choose to be different. You are no longer your own, you have been bought with a price. You have to fight your flesh and your mind. Your body is not going to agree with the Spirit of God. The Bible says they are contrary one to another.

Learn to encourage yourself by celebrating small changes. Stop defeating yourself by lying to yourself about what you will or will not do forever. Just start today! Tell yourself that you will have a good attitude "this morning". And when lunch time arrives – celebrate! This will give you strength to do the same thing with the afternoon. All of your little celebrations will provide you with the encouragement needed to successfully embrace change in every area of your life.

JANUARY 11

Just Focus On Your Assignment!

I CORINTHIANS 3:6-7

I have planted, Apollos watered; but God gave the increase. So then neither is he that planteth any thing, neither he that watereth; but God that giveth the increase. – King James Version

I planted the seed, Apollos watered the plants, but God made you grow. It's not the one who plants or the one who waters who is at the center of this process but God, who makes things grow. – The Message Translation

Don't be discouraged when you reach out to help others and it seems that your work is in vain. It is not! Remember, you are only part of the process.

Sometimes your assignment is to simply sow a seed into the life of others. At other times your responsibility is to water the seeds that others have already sown. Sometimes, you may even have the grueling task of being the pruner, to help bring correction to the lives of others. And sometimes, God will bless you to be the harvester to pick the fruit.

But, no matter what your job is don't get the big head. This is all about God. It's not about you. So, do not get frustrated when you set your sights on ministering to others and it seems as if they are not getting it. Step back and learn where you are in the process. God has it all under control.

Just be faithful to your assignment. And continue giving God the glory. And lives will be forever changed because of your obedience to your calling and assignment.

JANUARY 12

Seize The Moment!

MATTHEW 5:6

Let your light so shine before men, that they may see your good works, and glorify your Father which is in heaven. – King James Version

Now that I've put you there on a hilltop, on a light stand - shine! Keep open house; be generous with your lives. By opening up to others, you'll prompt people to open up with God, this generous Father in heaven. – The Message Translation

Take every opportunity to allow the light of Christ to shine in your life. In every walk of life you have the opportunity to allow others to be delivered from darkness by your actions. When you live a transparent life, it gives hope to others. People should be able to see your flesh in its imperfections, yet at the same time see your spirit which illuminates God's glory in everything you do.

The mess that you have gone through in life should become your message. You do not have to be proud of your past, but you also should not be ashamed. For it was God's power, that delivered you. Proudly proclaim that the same power that freed you is still available to deliver others. Let people understand that you may be imperfect, but the God that lives within you is perfect and holy.

When you are doing the right thing, this should point people to Jesus. Let God be glorified in your conversation. In the songs that you sing, in the way that you dress, in the way you treat others – let others see the light of Christ. Don't take credit for doing things

right – give God the glory! Let the world know that it is because of the power of God that you live the life that you do!

JANUARY 13

Doors And Walls: Know The Difference!

REVELATION 3:8

I know thy works: behold, I have set before thee an open door, and no man can shut it: for thou hast a little strength, and hast kept my word, and hast not denied my name. – King James Version

"I see what you've done. Now see what I've done. I've opened a door before you that no one can slam shut. You don't have much strength, I know that; you used what you had to keep my Word. You didn't deny me when times were rough. – The Message Translation

God is a good and faithful God. He is still in control of your situation even when things look challenging. He has the power to open doors that no man can close. And He also has the power to shut doors that no man can open. But, the challenge for you is to know the difference between doors and walls.

Jesus walked through walls. You are not Jesus! His Spirit may reside within you, but God did not create or fashion you to walk through walls. However, He did equip you to walk through doors. You must grow spiritually to the extent of understanding the difference.

God will speak to your heart and let you know when He is leading and guiding you to an opportunity. But, you must also be a good listener and an obedient child to know when He is saying, "No." If

He brings you to a wall, observe the pictures on it and move on. Stop trying to force your way through something God never intended you to go through.

JANUARY 14

Stop Listening To What: "They Say"!

NEHEMIAH 4:2

And he spake before his brethren and the army of Samaria, and said , What do these feeble Jews? Will they fortify themselves? Will they sacrifice? Will they make an end in a day? Will they revive the stones out of the heaps of the rubbish which are burned? – King James Version

In the company of his Samaritan cronies and military he let loose: "What are these miserable Jews doing? Do they think they can get everything back to normal overnight? Make building stones out of make-believe?" – The Message Translation

Has God made you a promise? Has God revealed to you His plans for your future? Have you read what God's Word says about your destiny?

Guess what! The devil also heard those promises and will do any and everything he can to distract you and discourage your faith. He cannot change what God said, so his desire is to change what you believe about what God said. If he can get you to not believe then you won't keep trying.

Stop listening to naysayers. People who are always negative and telling you what you can't do and why you can't do it are tools of the enemy. Stop allowing your ears to receive their negativity and do not allow your mind to continue to ponder their words.

Your faith is under fire. But, if you stay focused and keep trusting God's Word you will come out victorious. Everything that God promised is yours and will still come to pass. Stop listening to what "they say" and keep reciting what God Said! God cannot and will not lie!

JANUARY 15
Peace Is A Choice!
PHILIPPIANS 4:8

Those things, which ye have both learned, and received, and heard, and seen in me, do: and the God of peace shall be with you. – King James Version

Put into practice what you learned from me, what you heard and saw and realized. Do that, and God, who makes everything work together, will work you into his most excellent harmonies. – The Message Translation

You are in charge and in control of the peace in your life. Peace is an attitude and disposition of the soul. Because PEACE is a by-product of the soul – it is a CHOICE! You may choose to be anxious, worried and overly concerned, or you may choose to allow the God of peace to consume your life.

You make choices to worry, fret, complain and fear. Peace is not dependent upon your circumstance or condition. You can have peace in the midst of a trial or challenge. You can usher in God's presence and cause Him to manifest as Jehovah Shalom!

Paul encouraged the saints at Philippi to

1. What you have learned – DO / God's Word
2. What you have received – DO / God's Spirit
3. What you have heard – DO / God's Voice
4. What you have seen – DO / God's Manifestation

And the promise of God's Word is that the God of peace will be with you. If you DO God's Word – your attitude / soul / emotions – undergo a change. And this presence of the Prince of Peace is nothing that the world can offer or compare. This presence of Jehovah Shalom will supersede any challenge or crisis that you are enduring.

JANUARY 16

His Innumerable Thoughts About You!

PSALM 139:17

How precious also are thy thoughts unto me, O God! how great is the sum of them! – King James Version

Your thoughts - how rare, how beautiful! God, I'll never comprehend them! – The Message Translation

God, your thoughts about me are priceless. No one can possibly add them all up. – New International Reader's Version

Don't allow the enemy to fill your mind with negative thoughts about yourself. Don't allow your current status or situation to get you down. Always remember, God has great thoughts concerning you.

His promises are good and they will come to pass in your life. Even when it seems as if your destiny is being delayed, just know it is not denied. God's grace and mercy come to the rescue every time to position you for His glory.

It is impossible for anyone to compute the love of God concerning you. Each morning you wake up with new mercies. Every step you take, He gives you walking companions: goodness and mercy. For waiting upon Him, He fills your mouth with good things and blesses you beyond measure.

So, don't waste time and energy attempting to count your blessings. There are not enough numbers in existence to keep score or tally them. But, live grateful for His awesomeness in your life each day. He's so good!

JANUARY 17

Don't Be Shy!

HEBREWS 4:16

Let us therefore come boldly unto the throne of grace, that we may obtain mercy, and find grace to help in time of need. – King James Version

So let's walk right up to him and get what he is so ready to give. Take the mercy, accept the help. – The Message Translation

You do not have to be fearful in your approach to God. Because of the sacrifice Christ Jesus made on Calvary you have been granted access to the throne room of God. And Jesus is there making intercession for you daily. He knows the tests, trials, and temptations you face on a daily basis.

You don't have to be afraid to talk to God. First and foremost, He is omniscient. He knows all. He is aware of your struggle. He understands your pain. He knows what you need and He has even promised to give you the desires of your heart as you learn to delight in Him. But, He wants you to communicate with Him.

Run to the throne room and get what God has for you. His grace and mercy are plenteous. He will not deny you. Just go to your spiritual Father in full confidence that He is ready, willing, and able to bless you more than you could ever imagine.

JANUARY 18

The God Desire!

PSALM 42:1

As the hart panteth after the water brooks, so panteth my soul after thee, O God. – King James Version

As a deer longs for a stream of cool water, so I long for you, O God. – Good News Translation

When a desire is present, actions correspond. What you do in life is based primarily on what you have decided is important to you. Whether they are good or bad, actions do not always line up with the confession of the mouth but they can be traced to the intent of the heart and desire of the mind.

If you went to a store to make a purchase, but did not have all the money you needed to complete the transaction – what do you do? You make a decision to put some things back. But what drives that decision? Desire! You might need the bread, but you want the ice cream. So you walk out of the store with your desire met.

You have found someone that interests you and you want to explore a relationship with that person. However, it seems as though they may not have the same intention as you. Does that stop you? Of course not! You begin to woo and charm them because your desire is to get their attention and begin a special friendship or relationship.

Obstacles do not stop desire, they only present delays. When you make up your mind that you want a particular thing – you do what it takes to achieve that. When you have truly decided to "make Jesus your choice", the road can be rough, the going can be tough, and the hills may be hard to climb. But, those are simply roadblocks that you learn to go around because you have already decided that He is your desire.

Run after God today. Pursue His Presence. Long for His voice and His touch so that your day will be complete. Ignore the obstacles that may come. Your mind is made up and your heart is fixed. Long for God – and fulfill your desire! He desires you too!

JANUARY 19

Tell Somebody Else!

MARK 5:19

Howbeit Jesus suffered him not, but saith unto him, Go home to thy friends, and tell them how great things the Lord hath done for thee, and hath had compassion on thee. – King James Version

but he wouldn't let him. Jesus said, "Go home to your own people. Tell them your story - what the Master did, how he had mercy on you." – The Message Translation

Sometimes church time is wasted by people who love to tell everybody at the church how good God is. Testimony services are wonderful but the people who need to hear the message are not there. The people at the church already know that God is good! Yet, there remains a dying world of people who don't know who Jesus is.

Understand that the saints should be aware of what God is doing in your life. But, after you have told them what do you do? They are a light. You are a light. Two lights shining in a place of light (the church). Change needs to come. Your light needs to shine in a dark place.

It is time to thank God for His blessings and then move to the streets! Go to the highways and byways and begin to compel men and women to accept the goodness and mercy of Jesus Christ. Testify of His goodness in your community, in your schools, on your jobs – let the world know who He is.

The saints at the church are people of like-minded faith as you are. They know that God has revealed Himself as Jehovah Rapha – the healer, Jehovah Jireh – the provider, Jehovah Nissi, the banner. But there are people in the world who are struggling with life and have no clue of who God is or what He can do! When God moves in your life, make it your business to go and tell somebody who really needs to hear it!

JANUARY 20
Spiritual GPS – God's Perfecting Service
EPHESIANS 4:11-12

And he gave some, apostles; and some, prophets; and some, evangelists; and some, pastors and teachers; 12 For the perfecting of the saints, for the work of the ministry, for the edifying of the body of Christ: - King James Version

Many people use a GPS in their automobile for navigational purposes. Technology has improved to the extent that this small machine can give you directions visual (and audible) or take you from where you are to where you are trying to go.

God also has a Spiritual GPS. He has a mechanism in place to take you from imperfection to perfection, from immaturity to maturity, from sin to holiness. God has you in His GPS. He knows where you are. And He has already mapped out the best route to get to you. Sometimes people like to do back seat driving when it comes to life. But, God does not need a co-pilot. Your prayer should be as the songwriter wrote: "Jesus, Saviour, Pilot Me."

There is a plan and destiny for your life. Because you are human – you make wrong turns. Because God is good – He forgives you and makes a way out of no way, no matter which way you turn. God is full of mercy and compassion. Whenever you get off track, hear the Spirit of God saying: "Recalculating".
Where you are today is the result of three things...

1. Your obedience to being led by the Spirit of God
2. Your deception by the enemy to get you off course
3. Your submission to your own fleshly desires and mind

But, God – can work with all three and still get you to destiny! That is an awesome God! He can take your life that may be a mess – and still produce a message. He can take you from the pit and raise you to the pulpit! Just allow God to use His Spiritual GPS to take you to your next dimension.

JANUARY 21

Keep Studying HIS Word!

II TIMOTHY 2:15

Study to shew thyself approved unto God, a workman that needeth not to be ashamed, rightly dividing the word of truth. – King James Version

Concentrate on doing your best for God, work you won't be ashamed of, laying out the truth plain and simple. – The Message Translation

The times in which you are living, there are many voices speaking. If you are not careful you will find yourself going in the wrong direction because of the ill advice of others. Your life and your destiny are too important to chance them to the whims and desires of others. God speaks directly to you through His Word. You must study His Word and allow Him to minister to you.

Do not waste time trying to prove yourself to flesh. God wants you to know His Word and that His Word be approved and validated by Him and not by man. When God speaks a Word to you, why are you running to man to get confirmation? Is man greater than God? Often this takes place when people are not rooted and grounded in His Word as they should be and they are uncertain.

God's desire is that you know His Word to such an extent that when you hear His voice or even the voice of another you will know the difference. He wants you to know His will. He is revealing to you His plan for your life. Be still and listen. Learn to spend quality time reading and meditating on His Word. He will bring clarity to your understanding.

When you come into an intimate fellowship with God's Word He will produce the right fruit in your life. And there will not be any shame or embarrassment on your part. You will see Him ordering your steps and causing all things to work together for your good. Keep studying His Word.

JANUARY 22
God's Working With You!
MATTHEW 18:18

Verily I say unto you, Whatsoever ye shall bind on earth shall be bound in heaven: and whatsoever ye shall loose on earth shall be loosed in heaven. – King James Version

"Take this most seriously: A yes on earth is yes in heaven; a no on earth is no in heaven. What you say to one another is eternal. I mean this. – The Message Translation

Don't fool yourself! Your words, thoughts, and actions do matter and have far reaching consequences. God's power operating in you gives you the authority to speak and create your destiny. Basically, He is saying that as you release your faith for a particular thing, He would stand behind your word and agree with you.

Stop limiting yourself. And quit allowing the enemy to distract you. Even if things are not working in your favor at the moment – you have the power to change things. Keep standing on God's Word. Keep believing. Keep hoping. Keep trusting. And most of all, keep speaking into the atmosphere your faith statements so they may go beyond your finiteness and move into the spiritual realm of infinity.

Do not waste time with trivial matters such as what you will eat, wear or how you will lodge. As you seek God's way of doing things and His righteousness, He already promised to add these things to your life. Take spiritual authority over things in your life and decree and declare that all things align themselves with God's Word and God's will. You will be amazed at how God will show up and show out on your behalf.

JANUARY 23
Are You "In Position"?
ISAIAH 45:11

"Thus saith the Lord, the Holy One of Israel, and His Maker, Ask me of things to come concerning my sons, and concerning the work of my hands command ye me." – King James Version

God desires partnership. Yes, He desires to work with you for His glory and for your benefit. Stop listening to people who tell you that you cannot know the will of God. That is foolishness. God wants you to know His will concerning you. He wants you to know His plan so that you can walk therein.

In I Corinthians 3:9, He declares that you are "labourers together". And then in Romans 8:16-17, He says that you are "joint heirs". If that is not partnership, what is? In I Corinthians 2:9, He even tells you that the things that your eyes could not see nor your ears hear, He is revealing to you by His Spirit!

Positioning is so critical. Have you ever seen the rain come down and one side of the street was wet while the other side remained dry? That was interesting because of location, part of the street experienced the rain and part of the street did not. Your life is the same way. You must come to understand your position in God.

God is always speaking. God is always blessing. God is always moving. However, you must be in position to receive what God is doing. Just like a receiver on a football team has to be in the right place to catch the ball thrown by the quarterback. Just like your television or radio has to be tuned to the correct channel in order to receive the program that is already being broadcast. You must be in position to experience what God is saying and doing in the earth realm.

Ephesians 2:6 says that He has raised you up and made you sit in heavenly places in Christ Jesus. If you feel out of joint or out of position, there are some steps you should take...

1. Look back and see exactly what caused your problem.
2. Look down and see where you were in relation to the solution of your problem
3. Allow God to show you what needs to be done to solve your problem

In short: Flee carnality. Pursue spirituality. Stop being emotionally led. Begin being BIBLE led. And get in position and see how God begins to work through you in your life.

JANUARY 24
A Public Blessing!
PSALM 23:5

Thou preparest a table before me in the presence of mine enemies: thou anointest my head with oil; my cup runneth over. – King James Version

You prepare a feast for me in the presence of my enemies. You welcome me as a guest, anointing my head with oil. My cup overflows with blessings. – New Living Translation

You serve me a six-course dinner right in front of my enemies. You revive my drooping head; my cup brims with blessing. – The Message Translation

The Lord is a good shepherd. Even though you have suffered many things, He will turn around and bless you in front of your adversary. You don't have to brag or boast, just humble yourself before God and He will exalt you and lift you up (I Peter 5:6). He will allow His blessing to fill your life to such an extent that you will not be able to contain it all.

God will allow those who talked about you and fought against you to see that you have not been forsaken or left alone. Some of your enemies you thought were your friends. You were deceived because it appeared that they were helping you. But in reality, they rejoiced in your dependence upon them. They are about to get real upset when they see you are not under their control but under God's.

Keep going into your secret closet and pray to your Father. He knows, He hears and most importantly He cares. Your God will bring you into a season of public blessing. So, hold on and keep fighting the good fight of faith. Giving up is not an option. It may look bad, feel bad, or even be bad. But, better days are ahead for you! Get ready to be blessed in front of everybody.

JANUARY 25
It's A Snow Day!
ISAIAH 55:10-11

For as the rain cometh down, and the snow from heaven, and returneth not thither, but watereth the earth, and maketh it bring forth and bud, that it may give seed to the sower, and bread to the eater: So shall my word be that goeth forth out of my mouth: it shall not return unto me void, but it shall accomplish that which I please, and it shall prosper in the thing whereto I sent it. – King James Version

Just as rain and snow descend from the skies and don't go back until they've watered the earth, Doing their work of making things grow and blossom, producing seed for farmers and food for the hungry, So will the words that come out of my mouth not come back empty-handed. They'll do the work I sent them to do, they'll complete the assignment I gave them. – The Message Translation

Snow! Snow! Snow! It has it's purpose as does everything that God allows on the earth. The Bible says that it comes down from heaven and waters the earth. For children it is a free day to run, play and make snowmen. For travelers it's a time of challenge and sometimes delay. It affects different people in so many different ways.

God makes a comparison between snow and His Word. Just like snow comes down and waters the earth without simply returning to the heavens without completing its function or purpose, so is God's Word. God's Word has to do what He sent it to accomplish

before it returns unto Him. It has to be successful where God sends it.

One Word from God will bring different manifestations in different lives. Have you ever been to church and everyone heard the same sermon preached but received different things from that one message? God is like that!

That is so awesome. You need a Word from God. Yes! You need a Word from God that will accomplish what God said. God cannot lie. He won't change His mind. What He promised He will perform. What He said will surely come to pass. What He decreed and declared, He will deliver.

Faith comes by hearing, and hearing by the Word of the Lord. So, hold on to what you heard. Yes, hold on to that Word. It cannot go back to God empty. It has to do what God said it has to do. Stand on God's Word and see your healing. Trust in God's Word and walk in your deliverance. Believe God's Word and rest in your peace and prosperity. Speak God's Word and embrace the favor of God in your life.

JANUARY 26
Who Will You Encourage Today?
HEBREWS 3:13

But exhort one another daily, while it is called Today; lest any of you be hardened through the deceitfulness of sin. – King James Version

For as long as it's still God's Today, keep each other on your toes so sin doesn't slow down your reflexes. – The Message Translation

Life offers daily challenges for everyone. There are many times people don't talk about what they are battling with or dealing with in their personal life. But, God often positions you to intersect in others' lives so that you may be a blessing. Yes, God will use you to encourage someone.

You don't have to pry into people's lives to be an encouragement. Just learn to be sensitive to the Spirit of God and He will not only position you around the people who you need to encourage but He will also tell you what to say to them. But, you must be a willing vessel.

Stop waiting for people to come to you! It is ridiculous if you see your brother fall in a ditch that you would not be proactive and do what you can to assist him. Why would you be so self-centered to wait for him to ask for help if you saw him fall in the ditch? That type of egocentricity is dangerous because it makes you appear to be better than others.

Make time to stay focused in life to be a blessing to someone every day. Tomorrow, you might be the one challenged and need someone to rescue you through a Word from God.

JANUARY 27

Praise Him Before The Enemy!
PSALM 27:6

God holds me head and shoulders above all who try to pull me down. I'm headed for his place to offer anthems that will raise the roof! Already I'm singing God-songs; I'm making music to God. – The Message Translation

Stop focusing on your enemies and what they are doing and saying. Invest your energies in giving God praise. His Word does not fail. Pretty soon they will become footstools and not long after that shall wither away. But for now, just give God praise.

The fact that you are alive and have enemies lets you know that you are a survivor. And if you have endured and survived all that has been thrown at you – just know you are on your way to the victor's circle. Yes, not only will you be victorious, but you will be more than a conqueror because of Christ in you the hope of glory.

No more sad faces. No more gloomy looks. No more hung down heads. Nothing but praise! Praise Him and let everybody know how good your God is! Praise Him before your enemies. Praise Him in and out of the sanctuary. Praise Him so the devil is terrified and runs. As long as you have breath, give God praise!

JANUARY 28

Nothing! Will Pull Me Away

ROMANS 8:35-39

Who shall separate us from the love of Christ? shall tribulation, or distress, or persecution, or famine, or nakedness, or peril, or sword? As it is written, For thy sake we are killed all the day long; we are accounted as sheep for the slaughter. Nay, in all these things we are more than conquerors through him that loved us. For I am persuaded, that neither death, nor life, nor angels, nor principalities, nor powers, nor things present, nor things to come, Nor height, nor depth, nor any other creature, shall be able to separate us from the love of God, which is in Christ Jesus our Lord. – King James Version

Do you think anyone is going to be able to drive a wedge between us and Christ's love for us? There is no way! Not trouble, not hard times, not hatred, not hunger, not homelessness, not bullying threats, not backstabbing, not even the worst sins listed in Scripture: They kill us in cold blood because they hate you. We're sitting ducks; they pick us off one by one. None of this fazes us because Jesus loves us. I'm absolutely convinced that nothing - nothing living or dead, angelic or demonic, today or tomorrow, high or low, thinkable or unthinkable - absolutely nothing can get between us and God's love because of the way that Jesus our Master has embraced us. – The Message Translation

Life is powerless when your mind is made up. Trials and tribulations may come, but you don't have to allow them to have control over your spirit and soul. Sickness and even death may

come, but they are not your masters. Take back your authority and power.

There is nothing that has the power to pull you away from the glorious grace of God. However, the enemy will attempt to bring situations and circumstances to the forefront of your mind. Remember, these are just distractions. The enemy will use any trick to attempt to pull you away from the love and security of your loving God. Hold on to God's hand for dear life.

Make your declaration today. Say it aloud so the devil knows you mean business. Shout it so that your family and friends know you are for real. And walk in your victory all day long. Enjoy the loving arms of your BIG DADDY God! He will make your joy full and complete. He will swap out your confusion and anxiety for peace. He will replace your sorrow with comfort. Nothing else matters. Nothing else or no one else has any power to do anything about it! Enjoy your God-filled life!

JANUARY 29
Stop Playing Games!
JAMES 2:14-17

14 What doth it profit, my brethren, though a man say he hath faith, and have not works? can faith save him? 15 If a brother or sister be naked, and destitute of daily food, 16 And one of you say unto them, Depart in peace, be ye warmed and filled; notwithstanding ye give them not those things which are needful to the body; what doth it profit? 17 Even so faith, if it hath not works, is dead, being alone. – King James Version

14 Dear friends, do you think you'll get anywhere in this if you learn all the right words but never do anything? Does merely talking about faith indicate that a person really has it? 15 For instance, you come upon an old friend dressed in rags and half-starved 16 and say, "Good morning, friend! Be clothed in Christ! Be filled with the Holy Spirit!" and walk off without providing so much as a coat or a cup of soup - where does that get you? 17 Isn't it obvious that God-talk without God-acts is outrageous nonsense? – The Message Translation

How often have you heard the phrase, "I'll be praying for you", in response to a need of an individual? Not to diminish the power or importance of prayer – because prayer is necessary and vital. But, do you believe that some people utilize the phrase simply as an excuse to not allow God to use them to meet the individual's need?

If someone comes to you and they tell you that they are hungry – what is the value of those words when their stomach is growling? And honestly, how spiritual is that when you have the resources to feed them? A friend tells you that their utility bill is $57. and it is about to get disconnected. Is it very spiritual that you have an extra $100 in your pocket but you tell them, "I'll be praying for you"?

Stop playing games! If God has blessed you and positioned you to be a blessing in the life of someone you should avail yourself. The real power of the gospel is not just in words on a page. But, the Gospel comes to life when it comes off the page and is demonstrated in your everyday life. It is so sad that often in the Christian community, the "Good Samaritan" (who is the most unlikely candidate to help) is the one who brings aid and assistance; while the priest and Levite find a way to cross over to the other side!

JANUARY 30

Be Real For HIM – Not Them!

COLOSSIANS 2:23

Which things have indeed a shew of wisdom in will worship, and humility, and neglecting of the body; not in any honour to the satisfying of the flesh. – King James Version

Such things sound impressive if said in a deep enough voice. They even give the illusion of being pious and humble and ascetic. But they're just another way of showing off, making yourselves look important. – The Message Translation

What really pleases God is a changed heart. Wonderful words and meaningless rituals do nothing to please God. However, words and rituals may get the attention of others. That is a dangerous way to exist. Your goal must be to please God and not man.

Be careful to avoid legalism and ritualism in your desire to serve God. There are certain acts which are spiritually correct and appropriate, but you cannot allow yourself to get lost in these acts and still miss God. It will make you "look saved" but still be lost. You may appear to "be holy" and still be unholy.

You don't need another conference or seminar – you just need to walk in His Word. You don't need another fast or consecration – you just need to obey Him. You don't need to make another faith confession – you need to just DO what you have been saying. You don't need to hear another Word – you need to follow what He has already spoken to you.

Don't get lost trying to find God. Allow His Spirit to lead and guide you and obey His voice. Do not look for approval from man – but trust God to show you His plan and then walk in it. Let God be your goal and not man!

JANUARY 31

God's Plan For Your Destiny!

PSALM 23:2

He maketh me to lie down in green pastures: He leadeth me beside the still waters. – King James Version

You have bedded me down in lush meadows, you find me quiet pools to drink from. – The Message Translation

God knows the plans and intents He has for your destiny. He knows the wealthy place that He desires to bring you to. He has a Father's heart towards you. Even though you have made mistakes and choices that did not please Him, He still loves you. And, He has not changed His mind regarding your future.

However, God has given you a free will. That means He allows you to make choices. It is dangerous sometimes to see what God has in store for you, but decide to take your own path or route to obtain it. The results can be catastrophic and deadly.

Imagine standing in the window of a skyscraper. As you look out the window, God shows you the blessing He has in store for you. Instead of waiting on God to bring the blessing to fruition, you ignorantly step out of the window to pursue it. Of course the end results are disastrous. You end up losing your life simply because you did not wait on God or seek directions from Him.

If you wait on God, He will direct you to the blessing He has prepared for you. Even if it means going down in order to get up, God knows best. If it means losing in order to gain, God still knows best. Trust God and follow God. He will lead you to the green pastures He has prepared and promised you.

FEBRUARY 1

Love Made Me Do It!

II CORINTHIANS 5:14

For the love of Christ constraineth us; because we thus judge, that if one died for all, then were all dead: - King James Version

Christ's love has moved me to such extremes. His love has the first and last word in everything we do. – The Message Translation

Love the unlovable. Go beyond the call of duty to reach the lost. Pray for your enemies. Forgive those who have offended you and done you wrong. Why? Because of the love of God!

When you truly experience the love of God in your life it is impossible for you not to embrace it and turn around and invest it in someone else's life. That is the power of God's grace and mercy. It multiplies and flows through your life into the lives of others.

It is not a natural thing but it is a spiritual thing. Your carnal nature would only operate in a selfish self-serving love that only loved those who had the capacity and reason to love you back. But the agape love of God takes you to a higher level. It goes beyond your comprehension and understanding.

So, remember the next time that you even surprise yourself by operating like God – just know that it was "love" that made you do it! God's love!

FEBRUARY 2

Keep Pressing And Pushing!

HEBREWS 10:36

You need to persevere so that when you have done the will of God, you will receive what he has promised. – New International Version

But you need to stick it out, staying with God's plan so you'll be there for the promised completion. – The Message Translation

God cannot and will not lie. Whatever He promised you, it will come to pass. Your responsibility is to not give up. You must keep pushing and pressing knowing that the promise is near. Your faith will bring you the victory.

Adversity comes in everyone's life. But, you must always understand that delay is never denial. Not now, does not mean not ever. Just learn how to wait on "Due Season". You want to make sure that God is your blessor. He will do it in due season. He will manifest what you need at the appropriate time.

Do not be discouraged if the journey seems long or the way seems hard. Keep your eyes and your mind on the prize. If you do exactly what God tells you to do, you are guaranteed to get exactly what God says you will get. Disobedience and slothfulness can cause setbacks. Learn to stay focused and keep doing the will of God. And you will see the blessing of God.

FEBRUARY 3
Can You Love Like That?
ROMANS 5:8

But God commendeth his love toward us, in that, while we were yet sinners, Christ died for us. – King James Version

But God put his love on the line for us by offering his Son in sacrificial death while we were of no use whatever to him. – The Message Translation

Are you judgmental when it comes to other people's lives? Do you categorize sin? Do you look at certain people and consider their sinful state better or worse than others?

Take into account that at one time you were also in need of a Saviour! You were lost and needed to be found. There was a debt of sin you owed that you did not have the ability to pay. The blessed part of God showing up in your life is that He did it when you did not deserve or even desire His presence and power.

While you were living an ungodly and sinful life, God was yet loving you and demonstrating it by sending His Son to die on Calvary's cross for your redemption. He did not wait for you to repent to die. He did not wait for you to be filled with remorse to die. He did not wait for you to say "I'm sorry" to die. But, he died when you were not even aware of what He had in store for you.

As a child of God, He expects you to demonstrate this same love toward others. That means you must love others no matter who, what, or where they are. You can love the sinner while hating the sin. Practice loving the same way God loves. Your love must be unconditional and without discrimination. You love simply because it is your nature to do so. Can you love like God loves?

FEBRUARY 4

Get Your Own Business!
II CORINTHIANS 5:18

For we hear that there are some which walk among you disorderly, working not at all, but are busybodies. – King James Version

And now we're getting reports that a bunch of lazy good-for-nothings are taking advantage of you. – The Message Translation

There is a dying world that needs to be evangelized. However, there are people content with simply spending their time spectating and commentating on everybody else's life. This is not God's will. It is God's will and desire that we be busy completing the task that He has assigned us.

First of all, the Word of God says that all have sinned. So, that means everyone is in the need of grace and mercy. Secondly, God sent His Son to redeem you from the curse. So, you are no longer your own – you have been bought with a price and you belong to Him. Thirdly, you must be mindful that judgment belongs to God. Be careful to refrain from the finger pointing ministry.

Your focus should first be directed to the mirror. Take care to minister to yourself first in order that you can learn to manifest compassion in the care of others. Afterwards, look for opportunities to further share the grace and mercy that has so abundantly been given in your own life. And finally, avoid people who treat you as trash can – always attempting to fill your ears and minds with other people's problems.

FEBRUARY 5

God Lives Through You!

II PETER 1:4

Whereby are given unto us exceeding great and precious promises: that by these ye might be partakers of the divine nature, having escaped the corruption that is in the world through lust. – King James Version

We were also given absolutely terrific promises to pass on to you - your tickets to participation in the life of God after you turned your back on a world corrupted by lust. – The Message Translation

God never changes His mind on the promises He makes to you! When you totally surrender your life to Him, He begins a transformation process in you. No longer are you just flesh and blood, but your spirit is now alive. The creative power of God begins to operate in your life.

Sick people will be healed as you exercise faith and lay your hands upon them. Demons will flee as you invoke the Name of Jesus and command them to depart. Miracles will abound in your life as you live in communion and fellowship with the Father. Doors will open and ways will be made as you align your life with the principles found in His Word.

Others will be blessed because of you and the connection you have developed with the True Vine. Continue to resist the devil, run from the appearance of evil, and forsake the desires of the flesh! God will show up and show out in your life in an awesome way that will bless you and amaze others around you. Your new testimony: "It's not me, It's the Jesus living on the inside of me"!

FEBRUARY 6

Get Ready For Greater!

HAGGAI 2:9

The glory of this latter house shall be greater than of the former, saith the LORD of hosts: and in this place will I give peace, saith the LORD of hosts. – King James Version

Receive this prophetic word into your life today. Stop talking about "the good old days". God has better days ahead for you! In the words of Donald Lawrence: *"You ain't seen nothing yet"*. Raise your level of expectation and watch God: The Exceeding and Abundantly God do greater things in your life.

Speak it and believe it. Decree it and declare it. Embrace it. By faith walk in the greater things that God has prepared for you. The only thing holding you back is your faith. God will honor your faith by surpassing your wildest dreams.

And not only is He going to make things better – He promises to cause peace to reign. Yes, He will bring you into greater and take away the worry, stress and strain. If you are ready for a season of peace, joy, and abundance – then praise God in advance and walk into it.

FEBRUARY 7
Peace In The Midst Of...
ISAIAH 54:10

"Though the mountains be shaken and the hills be removed, yet my unfailing love for you will not be shaken nor my covenant of peace be removed," says the Lord, who has compassion on you. – New International Version

God loves you so much that He allows you to exist in a safety zone. Isn't that wonderful? A safety zone in the midst of a war zone! Yes, trouble can be all around you – but because of His love for you and your faith in Him – peace will prevail in your life.

The perilous times that were prophesied of in the Bible are here. There are wars and rumors of wars and earthquakes in different places. You can turn on the news and hear of atrocities that cause you to wonder what is really going on in the minds of people. There are natural disasters. There are economic challenges that threaten the stability of families, communities and the nation at large. Sickness and disease are running rampart. Even the medicines that are available to treat certain infirmities have side effects that can sometimes be worse than the actual disease.

However, you serve a God that is very much alive. His love for you will prevail over every obstacle and challenge that may come against you. The promise of peace and protection that He spoke to you is still good. If you keep your mind on Him, He will keep you in perfect peace.

His love will not fail. So, hold your head up and embrace the peace of God that passes even your finite understanding. Yes, God will have mercy upon you and allow His glory to be made manifest and light up the darkness that may be surrounding you.

FEBRUARY 8
"Is" and "Can"!
HEBREWS 11:6

But without faith it is impossible to please him: for He that cometh to God must believe that He is, and that He is a rewarder of them that diligently seek Him. – King James Version

It's impossible to please God apart from faith. And why? Because anyone who wants to approach God must believe both that He exists and that He cares enough to respond to those who seek Him. – The Message Translation

Faith is a necessary ingredient for experiencing the presence and power of God in your life. On numerous occasions, Jesus encountered people and his reply to them was simply: "Your faith hath healed you". Wow! Look at what faith can do!

Your confidence must not be in the faith contact, but in the God who not only is willing but is able to do exceeding and abundantly above all that you ask or think. But, according to the writer in Ephesians 3:20, what He does is based upon the "power" or faith that you release.

So, don't get so fixated on the prayer cloth or the bottle of oil. You may call the preacher to come and pray for you, but what if he is busy or running late? Don't get lost in rituals or routines! All you need is the truth of God's Word. Have faith in God!

Believe that God IS God and beside Him there is none other. Believe that He IS your only answer and your only hope! After that, live knowing that He CAN do what you need most in your life. Not only CAN He supply your needs and grant your heart's desires, but know that He wants to! Know that He IS and that He CAN!

FEBRUARY 9

God Wants The Best For You

PSALM 35:27

Let them shout for joy, and be glad, that favour my righteous cause: yea, let them say continually, Let the LORD be, which hath pleasure in the prosperity of his servant. – King James Version

Let those who are happy when my name is cleared shout with joy and gladness. Let them always say, "May the LORD be honored. He is pleased when everything goes well with the one who serves him." – The New International Reader's Version

God desires good things for you! He wants you to prosper, be blessed, and be in good health. He is so concerned about your life that He orchestrates the events in your life (good and bad) to all work together for good for you. So, give Him praise!

Don't fall into the trap of gloom and depression when you are challenged. The enemy is simply doing his job: stealing, killing, and destroying. But, you have no need to fret because God is also doing His. But, you must continue to exercise faith to reap the benefits and rewards of a loving and caring Saviour who has come to give you life and that more abundantly.

It makes God happy when your needs are met. He loves you so much that His Word declares that he goes a step further and even gives you the desires of your heart as you delight yourself in Him. Don't listen to silly people telling you that it is okay to be broke!

God wants you blessed. For when you are blessed you are in a better position to be a blessing and make an impact for His glory in the earth realm. Get God's best!

FEBRUARY 10

Start On The Inside!

II CORINTHIANS 4:16

For which cause we faint not; but though our outward man perish, yet the inward man is renewed day by day. – King James Version

So we're not giving up. How could we! Even though on the outside it often looks like things are falling apart on us, on the inside, where God is making new life, not a day goes by without his unfolding grace. – The Message Translation

Often people allow what is happening on the outside to guide their thoughts and actions. Change your focus! Remember you are a spirit being created in the image of God your Father who is a spirit. The body is simply your earth suit that God has given you as you operate here in the earth realm. It is not eternal. It is not everlasting - Only your spirit is!

Don't allow aches and pains to consume your thoughts. Don't let physical challenges override what God has promised in the spirit. As you live a life of faith what you will find is that where your focus is - so also is the manifestation. In other words, if you allow negative thoughts to prevail you will find yourself depressed and filled with gloom. But, if you focus on the promises of God's word and by faith embrace those truths you will see them begin to manifest in your life.

God is renewing and strengthening your spirit man every day. Allow your heart to guide your life and watch your life change. Remember God's Word from III John 1:2, that as your soul (emotional man) prospers that also your physical body experiences health and prosperity. Look within for the blessing of the Lord and watch that blessing flow to every area of your life.

FEBRUARY 11
Be Selfish!
MATTHEW 7:3

And why beholdest thou the mote that is in thy brother's eye, but considerest not the beam that is in thine own eye? – King James Version

It's easy to see a smudge on your neighbor's face and be oblivious to the ugly sneer on your own. – The Message Translation

Take more energy and effort in taking care of the one in the mirror and life will be less complicated. It is senseless and useless to focus so much on other people and their issues. The Bible says that all have sinned and come short of the glory of God. All is all. That means that everyone has issues.

There is room for improvement in everyone. Focus your attention on applying God's Word to every area of your own life. It is spiritually immature to focus on the faults and failures of others when you have imperfections as well. Be selfish to the extent that you check your mirror, your closet, your business first before attempting to examine the condition of others.

Be careful not to classify sin. Sin is sin. There is no big sin or little sin. There is no white lie and black lie. Wrong is wrong. This is a trap that many people fall in. Instead of acknowledging self-error, the enemy encourages people to take a flashlight to shine upon the deeds of others.

Put the flashlight down. Turn on the spotlight and the flood light. Stand in the path of the light so that your own deeds (good and bad) may be exposed. Repent of sin in your life. And better position yourself to honestly help your brother or sister who has fallen and can't get up by being transparent with your own faults.

FEBRUARY 12

Faith! Controls Your Miracle

II KINGS 6:5-7

But as one was felling a beam, the axe head fell into the water: and he cried, and said, Alas, master! for it was borrowed. And the man of God said, Where fell it? And he shewed him the place. And he cut down a stick, and cast it in thither; and the iron did swim. Therefore said he, Take it up to thee. And he put out his hand, and took it.

God is still working miracles. He is Jehovah Shammah "The Lord Everpresent" and He is with you everyday at all times. When you release your faith He allows His power to be made manifest in ordinary everyday situations.

Remember these three things: 1) He is an everyday God, 2) He uses ordinary people to work miracles, and 3) He will bless you to recover even in the time of loss.

God is concerned about you and He uses ordinary people to work miracles in your life. You must always be careful not to worship the anointed individual – but worship only the God who made it possible. It is faith that moves the hand of God.

There will be times that you may suffer loss. Know that God is a restorer. Never stress over losing anything or anyone. God causes all things to work together for good for you. Learn to accept God's will and look for God to show up and show out!

FEBRUARY 13

Stop Making Noise!
I CORINTHIANS 13:1

Though I speak with the tongues of men and of angels, and have not charity, I am become as sounding brass, or a tinkling cymbal. – King James Version

If I speak with human eloquence and angelic ecstasy but don't love, I'm nothing but the creaking of a rusty gate. – The Message Translation

I may be able to speak the languages of human beings and even of angels, but if I have no love, my speech is no more than a noisy gong or a clanging bell. – Good News Translation

A renowned icon in the gospel radio industry, Irene Johnson Ware was famous for the adage: *"Love is - what love does."* That is such a true statement. Many people waste so much time making noise to attempt to prove their spirituality or their concern for others. But if you don't do anything, then you are actually wasting time. Love is an action verb and not just a state of being.

You may prophesy and know the mysteries of yesterday and tomorrow. However, if you cannot demonstrate the agape shown by Jesus Christ then you are wasting time with your knowledge. You may be able to sing, preach and pray until the congregation has goose bumps, but you are defeating the real purpose of your ministry if you don't exhibit love.

Focus today on demonstrating agape – unconditional love. Go out of your way to bless somebody. Forgive and receive someone without them even asking you or deserving your forgiveness. Practice empathy and sympathy. Produce the fruit of love in your daily walk. Show love in action in every relationship. Don't talk about love – just do it!

FEBRUARY 14
No Greater Love!
ROMANS 5:8

But God commendeth his love toward us, in that, while we were yet sinners, Christ died for us. – King James Version

But God put his love on the line for us by offering his Son in sacrificial death while we were of no use whatever to him. – The Message

On this day when many are celebrating love – never forget the greatest act of love ever expressed to humanity. The love of God in the sacrificial offering of His only begotten Son to save humanity from eternal death and damnation was the greatest expression of love possible.

God is love. His very essence is that of love. So, when God loves He is simply being Himself. You experience the manifested harvest of that in your life when He forgives, restores, reconciles, renews, protects, blesses, overshadows, and so on.

The awesomeness of His expression of love is that He did not wait for you to love Him back before expressing His love toward you. He did not wait until you stopped sinning. But, while you were cursing, fornicating, lying, backbiting, and living to please the desires of your flesh – He decided to love.

Yes, while you were yet in your sin – Jesus Christ died on Calvary for your sins. He who knew no sin, took on sin to pay the price for your sin. For this love you should be grateful. For this love you should be thankful. For this love you should give your all to please the One who loved you first and loved you best.

FEBRUARY 15

Love Is Greatest Thing!

I CORINTHIANS 13: 8,13

Love never dies. Inspired speech will be over some day; praying in tongues will end; understanding will reach its limit. But for right now, until that completeness, we have three things to do to lead us toward that consummation: Trust steadily in God, hope unswervingly, love extravagantly. And the best of the three is love. – The Message Translation

Learn to love with the agape love of God. That love is stronger, wiser, and better than anything! It is that type love that keeps relationships together and makes then stronger. It is that type love that mends broken hearts and broken lives. It is that type love that brings forgiveness and reconciliation.

Don't ever get lost in the superficial. But, learn to live life deep in the heart of things! Don't be afraid to love. Love strong! Love hard! God will guard your heart. Love with your heart, mind, soul, and body. But, always make sure that God is in your love.

Ignore people who are negative. Don't waste time with people who insist on living in hurt, despair, and depression. Free yourself from people who are not part of your destiny. No matter what you have experienced in life, the love of God is stronger! That love will last and never die. Everything and everybody else may change – but God's love will always remain the same.

FEBRUARY 16

Love Is Better!

PSALM 82:3

Hatred stirreth up strifes: but love covereth all sins. – King James Version

Hatred starts fights, but love pulls a quilt over the bickering. – The Message Translation

Life is short. Spend time being happy and not mad. It's so easy to allow your flesh to engage you in saying and doing mean things. This is not the will of God neither is it a good emotional outlet. Don't let the devil trick you or deceive you into going down that street.

Allow the true love of God to calm you down. Don't yell. Don't scream. Don't pout. Just smile and allow the compassion and forgiveness of your Heavenly Father to be made manifest in your life.

Yes, be just like God. No matter what the wrong that was done – look beyond the faults and see the need. The need is for you to treat them with the same understanding and patience you pray others would have for you. So, no more fussing – just love! Love is better!

FEBRUARY 17
Endure With A Smile!
II THESSALONIANS 1:4

So that we ourselves glory in you in the churches of God for your patience and faith in all your persecutions and tribulations that ye endure: - King James Version

We're so proud of you; you're so steady and determined in your faith despite all the hard times that have come down on you. We tell everyone we meet in the churches all about you. — The Message Translation

Your testimony is not just in words but it is moreso in your actions. Your ability to endure the storms of life and keep a smile on your face serves as a witness to others. It is so easy to throw tantrums and have a pity party when things go wrong. And then beckon for everyone to come and join your "woe is me" parade. But, God is not glorified in that! For none of that is of faith.

But, God is glorified when you allow your trust in God and your faith in Him to be evident through your walk of faith. Don't let the devil trick you into running away and hiding. Get up out of the bed and go about your regular responsibilities. Wash your face. Comb your hair. Dress for success. Fight the temptation of depression and isolation.

You already knew that *"Man that is born of a woman is of a few days, and those days full of trouble."* And you also read that *"Many are the afflictions of the righteous, but the Lord delivereth him out of them all."* So, keep pushing and pressing, knowing that victory already belongs to you. Your objective is to simply cross the finish line.

Let the world see you come out of the fire unharmed. You can make it if you simply determine within your heart and mind that you will! Victory is yours! Keep a smile on your face and endure to the end!

FEBRUARY 18
God's Got You!
ISAIAH 43:2-4

When thou passest through the waters, I will be with thee; and through the rivers, they shall not overflow thee: when thou walkest through the fire, thou shalt not be burned; neither shall the flame kindle upon thee. For I am the LORD thy God, the Holy One of Israel, thy Saviour: I gave Egypt for thy ransom, Ethiopia and Seba for thee. Since thou wast precious in my sight, thou hast been honourable, and I have loved thee: therefore will I give men for thee, and people for thy life. – King James Version

When you're in over your head, I'll be there with you. When you're in rough waters, you will not go down. When you're between a rock and a hard place, it won't be a dead end - Because I am God, your personal God, The Holy of Israel, your Savior. I paid a huge price for you: all of Egypt, with rich Cush and Seba thrown in! That's how much you mean to me! That's how much I love you! I'd sell off the whole world to get you back, trade the creation just for you – The Message Translation

It may look bad. It may feel bad. It may actually even be bad. But, you have no need to worry, fret, or fear because God is still in control. His love for you will not allow you to perish. No matter what the challenge is – the Greater One is on the inside of you and He will cause you to be victorious.

These are perilous times in which you live! Natural disasters, unexplained massive animal deaths, wars and rumors of wars, government distress, blighted communities with crime, and the list goes on. And because of these conditions many people are stressing out! But, as a believer you don't have to be unsettled because of all of the unrest! You can have peace that passes even your own understanding.

In the words of a good friend, "We have a superhero coming to the rescue!" Yes, God loves you with an everlasting love. His love for you will keep you from being destroyed. He is ever-present not only to keep you from being consumed because of His mercies. But, He empowers you to be a survivor, an overcomer, and more than conqueror: a testimony of His awesomeness in the earth realm.

FEBRUARY 19

Just Be A Blessing!

LUKE 6:34

And if ye lend to them of whom ye hope to receive, what thank have ye? for sinners also lend to sinners, to receive as much again. – King James Version

And if you lend to those from whom you expect repayment, what credit is that to you? Even 'sinners' lend to 'sinners,' expecting to be repaid in full. – New International Version

If you only give for what you hope to get out of it, do you think that's charity? The stingiest of pawnbrokers does that. – The Message Translation

When God has blessed you with time, talent and treasure – learn to be a blessing. Don't be stingy or a penny pincher. You hinder your own blessings in doing so. When your heart is right, simply be a blessing.

The Bibles says that it is more blessed to give than to receive. If you step out of the box and really look at the picture – the giver is awesomely blessed. All the receiver has is what was given. But, the giver has three things: 1) the balance of what was not given, 2) the joy of being a blessing, and 3) the promise of harvest for the seed sown.

Don't worry about what you do for others. Just do it out of the goodness of your heart and watch how God will bring increase, favor and blessings your way. Don't look at the person you blessed, God has a way of bringing your blessing back another way.

Practice this today: Find someone to be a blessing to. If someone you have blessed does not repay you, forgive them and move on. God will take care of you and will not allow you to experience lack. Look for open doors and windows as you are faithful in being a good steward of your time, talent and treasure!

FEBRUARY 20

You Gotta Love!

MATTHEW 22:39B

"...Thou shalt love thy neighbor as thyself."

The love that God wants you to demonstrate towards others can be found as you look in the mirror. There are no categories or departments to place others in. You are simply commanded to love them even as you love yourself. When you learn to operate in agape (the God kind of love), you will find it easy to love others.

How do you treat yourself? Would you intentionally place yourself in harm's way? Would you deliberately speak ill or negatively about yourself? Would you purposely bring injury to yourself? Of course not: not while in your right mind! No! The natural instinct and human action is to take all precautions and necessary measures to show care for and to one self.

This is the same attitude and disposition that God wants you to take regarding others. No matter whom they are or what they have done. Love them. Love the sinner, but hate the sin. Love the one who hurt you, and forgive the offense. Love those who are different. Love (and do not just pity) those who are less fortunate. Love even those who don't want to be loved. Love conquers all.

FEBRUARY 21
Every Action Is A Seed Sown
GALATIANS 6:7

Be not deceived; God is not mocked: for whatsoever a man soweth, that shall he also reap. – King James Version

Don't be misled: No one makes a fool of God. What a person plants, he will harvest. The person who plants selfishness, ignoring the needs of others - ignoring God! - The Message Translation

Everyone has desires and aspirations. People make plans and set agendas. But, understand no matter what you put on paper or even focus on in your mind will stand if you allow your actions to negate your intentions. Yes, what you do matters. Your actions dictate the "working" of your faith.

Some people waste time by living in spiritual denial land. They think that simply by going to church and quoting or learning a few scriptures – their future is secure. Some think that the paying of their tithes and singing in the choir or serving on the usher board is enough to guarantee good things to show up in their life. But, it takes much more than that.

Everything that you do in life is really a seed that is sown. So, be careful about being mean to people, or gossiping about people, or not being helpful to people. One day the seeds of your actions will manifest. Whatever you know that you will need in your future – sow it today!

Be merciful. Extend grace. Forgive people. Love everybody. Help all. Be kind and considerate. Promote others. Intercede and pray for everyone. For these are the fruit you need to flourish in your life!

FEBRUARY 22

Ministry or Misery?

I CORINTHIANS 15:33

Be not deceived: evil communications corrupt good manners.
— King James Version

Do not be misled: "Bad company corrupts good character."
New International Version

But don't fool yourselves. Don't let yourselves be poisoned by this anti-resurrection loose talk. "Bad company ruins good manners." — The Message Translation

Make certain that your "people connections" are for the right purpose and are beneficial and productive to your spiritual walk with God. There is a great difference between ministering to someone versus being part of their misery. There is an old adage: "Misery loves company." That is true and if you are not careful you can be pulled into other people's drama unaware and needlessly.

You do not have to treat people as if you are better than them. But, if they are not part of your destiny then you need to learn the ministry of disconnect. There are some people who your assignment is to minister to them. Ministering to them is not being their buddy and pal. Ministering to them means you have been placed in their life to help them change.

If you are not careful, what you thought was ministry will evolve into a mess. Instead of your light shining to help them out of darkness, your light will grow dim if you are not careful. Instead of you helping them to transform into the image of Christ, you will find yourself conforming to the ways of the world. Be careful and check every friendship and relationship and determine "what is your true purpose?"

FEBRUARY 23

Let Your Smile Welcome God!

PSALM 24:7

Lift up your heads, O ye gates; and be ye lift up, ye everlasting doors; and the King of glory shall come in. – King James Version

Wake up, you sleepyhead city! Wake up, you sleepyhead people! King-Glory is ready to enter. – The Message Translation

Faith pleases and moves God. Your faith is made evident through the change of your attitude. Expect the best. Seek the best. Believe the best. Things may be crazy at the moment, but you must make a conscience decision not to allow what you are going through determine your level of belief.

Against all odds – believe that God is yet able. Walk in what you believe. Your simple act of faith of trusting God is all that is needed for your miracle. God will respond to your faith just like He did with the woman with the issue of blood. Even the four men that brought their paralyzed friend to Jesus were met with a miracle because of the activation of their faith.

So, refuse depression. Decline discouragement. Reject all notions of abandonment and resignation. Put a smile on your face. Brighten your voice. And sing a happy song. Watch God show up and show out!

FEBRUARY 24
Run From The Players!
II TIMOTHY 3:5

Having a form of godliness, but denying the power thereof: from such turn away. – King James Version

They will appear to have a godly life, but they will not let its power change them. Stay away from such people. – God's Word Translation

They'll make a show of religion, but behind the scenes they're animals. Stay clear of these people. – The Message Translation

The Word exhorts you to put on your track shoes and run when you encounter people still playing games in the kingdom. Admittedly, no one is perfect but everyone should be striving for the mark for the prize of the high calling of God in Christ Jesus. That means every day you are crucifying your flesh. Your attitude must be in check. Your righteous living must be in check. Your lifestyle of praise into worship must be evident. Your prayer life must be active.

The time is over for book covers. You need the inside of the book to be made manifest. You don't need people who just sound right or look right. The world desperately needs people who can just be right. There is a need for people of true power in the kingdom. When they sing it must be anointed. Not just making you feel good, but lifting burdens and destroying yokes! When they preach it must be with power. Not just exciting you, but challenging and changing you.

So, no longer waste time hanging around people who refuse to "get it together"! Fellowship with like-minded people who are sincere in seeing God's Power made manifest in the earth realm. Congregate and hang with people who are doing all they can to be the church that God is calling for in these last and evil days.

FEBRUARY 25

A Demand On God's Word!
II CORINTHIANS 9:8

Bring your full tithe to the Temple treasury so there will be ample provisions in my Temple. Test me in this and see if I don't open up heaven itself to you and pour out blessings beyond your wildest dreams. – The Message Translation

God will not and cannot lie. It is impossible. And even if it was possible, because of His great love for you He would never do that! He guarantees His Word. But, He challenges you to place a demand on His Word through your actions.

The act or ministry of tithing is more about your obedience than just an amount. God is simply saying if you can follow this principle/law, He will respond by blessing you beyond measure. His blessings will be to such an extent that others connected to you will even be blessed.

The blessing of God because of your obedience is not limited just to your finances. God wants you to learn to put a demand on His Word. Test it. Try it. Prove it! And watch God respond. He hastens to fulfill His Word.

FEBRUARY 26

A Good Time To Praise!

PSALM 34:1

"I will bless the Lord at all times, His praise shall continually be in my mouth."

There are two times that you should praise God: when you feel like it and when you don't! Eventhough, praise is a by-product of your soul, your praise must not be based merely upon feelings, but your praise should be based upon who God is, what God has done, what He is presently doing, and how you expect His omnipotence and omnipresence to bless you in the future.

Because praise ushers in God's presence, it is relevant and important to always have *a praise* in your mouth. You need God to manifest in your life every day, every hour, every minute, every second, and every moment. Yet, you must do what it takes to bring forth the manifestation.

Remember when David commanded his soul (his emotional man) to *"Bless the Lord, Oh my soul and all that is within me."* in Psalm 103:1. How many times have you not "felt" like praising God? How many times have life's pressures weighed you so far down that you did not have the emotional stamina to do anything but cry, and be in pity. This is a great time to praise God!

There are times that you must put yourself in check. No matter what may be going on in the present and no matter how bleak or dismal the future looks, you must still reflect on what God has already done in your life. When you begin to reflect on what God has done, and how undeserving of His goodness you were, you would have no choice but to give Him praise. In the 103rd Psalm, David begins to reflect on the benefits that God afforded him. David, a man after God's own heart, is determined to bless God for who He is: the forgiver, the healer, the redeemer, the blessor, and the satisfier.

Stop whatever you are doing and give God a right here, right now praise. And every time you think about Him praise Him! Every time you hear somebody else mention Him, praise Him. Yes, all the time is the right time to give God praise.

FEBRUARY 27

Sacrificial Living For His Glory!
ROMANS 8:36

As it is written, For thy sake we are killed all the day long; we are accounted as sheep for the slaughter. – King James Version

They kill us in cold blood because they hate you. We're sitting ducks; they pick us off one by one. – The Message Translation

The enemy has his sights on you because of who you belong to. You have done nothing wrong to explain why you have been attacked as you have been. But, the devil is angry with God and because you belong to God you are his number one enemy.

But encouragement should fill your heart and mind as you cling to the truth of God's Word that declares, "Greater is He that is within you than he who is in the world." God is greater than any attack that the enemy can launch against you.

So, don't be so stressful over the devil's desire to steal, kill and destroy – just embrace God's promise of life and life more abundantly. Give God praise on good days and bad days. Celebrate God's awesomeness in happy times and sad times.

The more you willingly live a sacrificial and joyful life before the King, the more frustrated the enemy becomes. He wants you to give up and throw in the towel. Don't do it. Just keep on praising

God and in the words of the songwriter: "Be not dismayed whatever betides, GOD WILL TAKE CARE OF YOU"!

FEBRUARY 28
Treat Them Right!
ROMANS 12:17

Recompense to no man evil for evil. Provide things honest in the sight of all men. – King James Version

Don't pay people back with evil for the evil they do to you. Focus your thoughts on those things that are considered noble. – God's Word Translation

Don't hit back; discover beauty in everyone. – The Message Translation

"But you just don't know what they did to me!" That is a common expression that many people use to justify getting even with others. However, it is not God's Will for you to do wrong to a person simply because they did wrong to you. The Christian response to a wrong is to pray and forgive.

You never really get even. As soon as you operate in the flesh, then you are also caught up in sin. The Bible says even when you get angry, do not sin. You have to control your emotions and do not allow people to control your mind.

God has called you to a higher display of Christian virtue. You do not have to lower your standards to the actions of others around you. If they gossip, you simply close your ears. If they curse, you find a way to bless God. If they want to fight, you need to walk away.

God is watching your response. It is not the storm or crisis that you are enduring that speaks of your character. But, it is your response to the storm or crisis that speaks volumes.

FEBRUARY 29

God's Grace Manifest In You!
EPHESIANS 3:7

This is my life work: helping people understand and respond to this Message. It came as a sheer gift to me, a real surprise, God handling all the details. – The Message Translation

Whoever you are and whatever you become is not by your will alone, but because of the mighty working of God's power. This is not to say that you are mere robots or puppets. For God gets more glory out of your life when you make decisions based upon your heart's desire.

God deposits potential within you and it is up to you to either activate your faith (which all have been given) and allow His effectual working power to affect your ministry or you can live in doubt and disbelief. Living in doubt will only allow life to take control of you and hinder you them from walking in victory and being in charge of your life.

But because of the grace of God you are what you are. And it is God's will that you allow your life to be a living testimony unto others. Yes, let others see the good, the bad, and the ugly. And let God be glorified as you exhibit his love and compassion in your life. You are a product of His grace and His mercy.

MARCH 1
Be Straight With God!
PSALM 139:23

Search me, O God, and know my heart: try me, and know my thoughts: - King James Version

Investigate my life, O God, find out everything about me; Cross-examine and test me, get a clear picture of what I'm about; - The Message Translation

Living in denial is just like lying to God. There is a truth about yourself that you refuse to acknowledge and deal with. Yet, you cry out for the Lord to save and deliver you? It won't work. Not gonna happen! Until you become a person of integrity like David, you will always be held hostage by your imperfections and flaws.

David simply "manned" up and told God, "Look God it's me! I've done wrong and I need your help. Create within me a clean heart and give me the right spirit, so I will be of better use to You."

When you can walk in integrity and admit that you don't have it all together – you are in the best position to receive His grace and mercy for your life.

The slogan at Fellowship Church is "A Perfecting Place for imperfect people." Each week the saints come with a spirit of expectation that God will meet them and change them more and more into His glorious image. But, it takes being transparent and not being ashamed of your humanity to really tackle the "real issues" of your life. The divine is trying to shine forth out of the earthen vessels – but to help the light shine more brightly: "To thine self and God be true"! – Be straight with God!

MARCH 2
You Belong To God!
I CORINTHIANS 6:19-20

Or didn't you realize that your body is a sacred place, the place of the Holy Spirit? Don't you see that you can't live however you please, squandering what God paid such a high price for? The physical part of you is not some piece of property belonging to the spiritual part of you. God owns the whole works. So let people see God in and through your body.
– The Message Translation

You belong to God! Your spirit, soul and body all belong to God. No longer do you have to allow the directions of the enemy to control your life. You have been freed from the power of the wicked one. Now, you only have to submit and surrender to the will of your Heavenly Father.

The precious blood of Jesus that was shed on Calvary paid the price for your eternal salvation. His blood covers yesterday, today, and tomorrow. He gave His life so that you might live. You do not have to just live a regular, meaningless, dull life – but He wants you live an abundant, fulfilled, and blessed life.

Remember, you don't belong to you anymore. Stop living and making foolish choices and decisions. Be still and listen to the Spirit of God as He directs your life. Remind yourself that all of you belongs to all of Him! Seek His face for every move you make, every step you take.

MARCH 3
Let Mercy Abound!
II CORINTHIANS 4:1

Therefore seeing we have this ministry, as we have received mercy, we faint not; - The King James Version

Since God has so generously let us in on what he is doing, we're not about to throw up our hands and walk off the job just because we run into occasional hard times. – The Message Translation

God has so wonderfully set the pattern for all of your relationships. The same demonstration of mercy that He has deposited in your life, He expects you to share with others. As the Book of Lamentations reminds you, every morning you awaken to new mercies. Friends, family, co-workers and even strangers should experience that same ministry from you.

The next time you decide to allow the frustration of a moment to cause you to say or do something negative, remind yourself of God's mercy in your own life. God has blessed you even unearned and undeserved. God has held back judgment only to allow His grace and mercy to be magnified in your situation.

Follow the pattern and be a blessing in the lives of others. Let others rejoice and give God praise because of how you allow the goodness of God to shine through you. Don't be content with just allowing mercy to abide within you, but let it abound. Let your mercy be greater than any other action you decide to take.

MARCH 4

Confusion At The Altar!

COLOSSIANS 2:8

Beware lest any man spoil you through philosophy and vain deceit, after the tradition of men, after the rudiments of the world, and not after Christ. – King James Version

Watch out for people who try to dazzle you with big words and intellectual double-talk. They want to drag you off into endless arguments that never amount to anything. They spread their ideas through the empty traditions of human beings and the empty superstitions of spirit beings. But that's not the way of Christ. – The Message Translation

You cannot allow other people's experiences dictate how God will move in your life. God is a one-on-one God. He is as individual and specific to you as you are different from those around you. People can contaminate ministry and confuse young believers if care is not taken. Although, well-intentioned it is wise to not allow too many people to give directives when it comes to receiving ministry.

Just imagine a crowd of people with a young believer standing in the middle. What would you expect the believer to do or to receive after hearing the following commands? "Let go"! "Hold on"! "Call Jesus"! "Be Still"! "Stretch Out"! "Clap Your Hands"! "Leap For Joy"! "There It Is"! "It's On The Way"! "You Got It"!

Yes, that is truly a confusing scene. But, it is a scene that happens too often. People who are receiving ministry don't need cheerleaders or directors. They simply need to know God's Word, believe God's Word, and receive God's Word.

MARCH 5
Why The Wait?
EPHESIANS 5:16

Redeeming the time, because the days are evil. – King James Version

Make good use of every opportunity you have, because these are evil days. – Good News Translation

Make the most of every chance you get. These are desperate times! – The Message Translation

What are you waiting for? Why do you procrastinate? There is an old adage: Time waits for no one. You must realize that tomorrow is not promised to anyone. There is an assignment that God has given you. Don't waste time. There are people whose lives need to change. The testimony of your life needs to be made manifest unto them. Your praise can be the witness they need to come out of their depression and live the abundant life.

Take full advantage of the time God has blessed you with. Live each day to the fullest. Have no regrets in life. Do all you can while you can. Today, get out of the boat and walk on water. Today, open your mouth and prophecy to your atmosphere and situation. Today, bless and break what God has given you and watch Him multiply. Yes, keep asking and receive. Keep knocking and watch the doors open. Continue to seek and you will find. Today, give and see the promised increase.

These times of life are challenging. Evil is present on every hand. However, you have been given authority and power in the spirit realm and the earth realm. What are you going to do? You need to make a commitment to use every waking moment possible for good. Remember, it is God working in you both to will and to do of his good pleasure. (Philippians 2:13). The wait is over – walk into your destiny!

MARCH 6
How Big Is Your God?
PSALM 35:27

Let them shout for joy, and be glad, that favour my righteous cause: yea, let them say continually, Let the LORD be magnified, which hath pleasure in the prosperity of his servant. – King James Version

But those who want the best for me, Let them have the last word - a glad shout! - and say, over and over and over, "God is great - everything works together for good for his servant." – The Message Translation

Three things you must understand: God is constant. Man is not. Your faith is the key to receiving from God.

God is not like man. He does not change His mind. Whatever He promised yesterday is still good today and has no expiration date on it for tomorrow. So, God has been, still is and always will be the healer, the deliverer, the way maker, the keeper, and the list is endless.

Now, understand that man is ever-changing. The soulish part of man makes man so unpredictable. One day you are happy and the very next day you are sad. This lack of consistency is part of the hindrance from God's best.

However, when you exercise faith and simply trust God then you can experience the miraculous. Since God doesn't change – He is always bigger than big. The problem is your perception. Who is bigger? Your problem or your God?

When you learn to magnify Him through your prayer, your praise, your worship, and your faith you then will see God as He is – the victorious God who always blesses His children. God is great and yes He is greatly to be praised!

MARCH 7

Let The Error Go!

MATTHEW 18:33

Shouldest not thou also have had compassion on thy fellowservant, even as I had pity on thee? – King James Version

Shouldn't you be compelled to be merciful to your fellow servant who asked for mercy?' – The Message Translation

Be careful how you treat others! The actions you take each day are just like sowing seeds! A harvest is on the way. When dealing with forgiving, releasing, blessing, or helping others, always use your relationship with your Heavenly Father as your guideline. You never know when you might need that kind of harvest in your life.

Take into consideration the number of times that you have fallen short on your agreement with God. Think about the promises and commitments that you have not kept your word. What did God do? How did He respond? Did he throw you away? Did he talk about you to others?

Then if He is your Father and you are His child, allow His DNA to be made manifest in your character and reputation. Be a blesser, a forgiver, a restorer. Show mercy to those who may not even deserve it. If they owe you money and don't want to pay you, pray for them and let God work it out. If they brought emotional or physical damage to you, don't fight back – love them and move on.

Simply put – What would Jesus do? That is a relevant question for you to ask in handling the varied dynamics in your relationships with family, friends, co-workers, neighbors, and others! Learn to not hold onto negativity – release the error of others and embrace the love of God!

MARCH 8

God Is Fighting For You!
II CHRONICLES 32:8

With him is an arm of flesh; but with us is the LORD our God to help us, and to fight our battles. And the people rested themselves upon the words of Hezekiah king of Judah. – King James Version

He only has a bunch of mere men; we have our God to help us and fight for us!" Morale surged. Hezekiah's words put steel in their spines. – The Message Translation

Don't get overly concerned when you have adversaries. Everybody is not going to like you, support you, or embrace you. Sometimes the attack can become so overwhelming that you forget that you are not alone! You have to always remember and take into account that God is on your side.

Because you are living in the earth realm, flesh sometimes has a tendency to intimidate you. You may feel out-manned, out-numbered, and out-gunned. But, the flesh opposition is really just a distraction. The real war is in the spirit realm.

Stop wasting time fighting battles that aren't yours to fight. Learn to praise God in the midst of opposition and watch God fight on your behalf. Your enemies will begin to disappear before your very eyes. Be comforted and encouraged and know that God is your very present help. If you can rest on this assurance, your faith will work for you and not only please God but strengthen your heart and mind.

MARCH 9

Don't Get Distracted!
LUKE 8:14

And that which fell among thorns are they, which, when they have heard, go forth, and are choked with cares and riches and pleasures of this life, and bring no fruit to perfection. – King James Version

"And the seed that fell in the weeds - well, these are the ones who hear, but then the seed is crowded out and nothing comes of it as they go about their lives worrying about tomorrow, making money, and having fun. – The Message Translation

Going to church is right! Hearing the Word of God is a good thing! But until you can get the church and Word in you it is almost pointless. Many lives are unproductive because they are distracted from doing what it takes to bring the manifestation of the truth of God's Word to pass in their life.

Worrying, money, and fleshly pleasures are three adversaries to hinder your Christian walk. You must learn to utilize these for your good. Tomorrow should be viewed in the light that even though you cannot tell the future – you know that God is always in control. It is not wrong to envision and dream. But, always submit your ideas to God and then trust Him and not flesh to bring them to pass.

Money itself is not evil. It is the love or idolization of it that puts you in trouble. God in His Word declares that He gives you power to get wealth. So, evidently God wants you to have money. The more money you have the better opportunity you have to be a blessing in someone's life. And, God wants you to enjoy this life – He wants it to be abundant. However, you must learn the parameters and draw the line. Stop operating in gray areas, and just do things God's way.

No more distractions. Hold on tight to the Word that you hear and allow it to be active in your everyday life – and see how God blesses you.

MARCH 10

Following Jesus!
MATTHEW 4:22

And they immediately left the ship and their father, and followed him. – King James Version

and they were just as quick to follow, abandoning boat and father. – The Message Translation

How important is God to you?

True discipleship requires forfeiture of everything that you consider dear and precious. God does not require that you don't have family, friends, possessions or earthly things. He wants you to have your life in divine order. Positioning is everything. God must be first. This means that other things and not God must be put on the back burner.

Are you committed to following Him?

The truth in the seriousness of your relationship is determined by the sacrifices that you make. Simply going to church is not the answer. Many people go to church every week but have no real relationship with Christ. They have simply adapted the church into their schedule of events. God demands more. But, it must come from your heart.

You must willingly forsake all to follow Him.

MARCH 11
The Awesome Potential Within You!

I JOHN 3:2

Beloved, now are we the sons of God, and it doth not yet appear what we shall be: but we know that, when he shall appear, we shall be like him; for we shall see him as He is. – King James Version

But friends, that's exactly who we are: children of God. And that's only the beginning. Who knows how we'll end up! What we know is that when Christ is openly revealed, we'll see him - and in seeing him, become like him. – The Message Translation

Care must be taken in judging books by their covers. You really never know what is contained in a book until you open it and read it. The same is with the lives of people. Often people are judged and categorized by their exteriors. That is dangerous. The Word of God exhorts us to know no man by the flesh, but by the Spirit.

Your exterior can be misleading: it can be dressed up, but it does not change what is on the inside. It can be plain and boring, but it does not alter what is within. This is why people of the world do not understand the spiritual and emotional stamina of Christians. You endure because of the investment that God has made on the inside of you.

Your potential (greatness) is hidden. It is good that you grew up in the projects. It is good that you went through that sickness. It is good that you suffered hell in that relationship. These were distractions that the enemy (and other folk) thought would discourage and deny you. But, you heard the Word of the Lord in Jeremiah 29:11: *"For I know the thoughts that I think toward you, saith the Lord, thoughts of peace, and not of evil, to give you an expected end."*

You are victorious because of the hidden potential within you!

MARCH 12

You Can Be Better!

III JOHN 1:2

Beloved, I wish above all things that thou mayest prosper and be in health, even as thy soul prospereth. – King James Version

We're the best of friends, and I pray for good fortune in everything you do, and for your good health - that your everyday affairs prosper, as well as your soul! – The Message Translation

Your soul is the seat of your emotions, will, desire, and mind. Your mind dictates to your body the actions it takes. You can change your season and your environment by adjusting your soul. When you learn to have a positive attitude you draw positive energy to yourself. Good things begin to happen because of the power of your tongue and the faith you release.

However, when you allow negativity to cloud your mind, your actions correspond. If you allow doubt and fear to grip your mind you will live that kind of life. You will always find yourself looking for things to go wrong. You will always see how and why things won't work out for you.

Today, decree and declare that better is on the way! Cause your soul to flourish and prosper. Not only will you feel better but better things will begin manifesting in your life. You will sow good seeds of faith and a positive harvest of plenty will show up in your life. You can control your future and destiny by simply believing and applying God's Word.

MARCH 13
Have Strong Faith!
ROMANS 4:20

He staggered not at the promise of God through unbelief; but was strong in faith, giving glory to God; - King James Version

He didn't tiptoe around God's promise asking cautiously skeptical questions. He plunged into the promise and came up strong, ready for God, - The Message Translation

What seems to be impossible and unimaginable is in the scope of things possible and probable with God. He has a wonderful track record of taking nothing and making something. He turns lives completely around. But, faith is the material that He uses!

Countless instances in the Word of God where people have been healed and delivered, the Bible declares that it is because of their faith. Your salvation and new relationship with God is based upon your faith in His grace and mercy. Whatever you need in your life today, is made available to you by your faith.

So, don't allow the enemy to confuse you with statistics, generational curses, gossip, rumors or lies. Ignore the nouns (people, places, things and ideas) that don't line up with what God's Word declares. Instead, strengthen and increase your faith by simply believing God. Walk in what you decree and declare. Thank Him and praise Him as though it were already made manifest. And look at the results in your life as the promises come to pass!

MARCH 14

See The Good – Experience The Glory!

II CHRONICLES 20:17

You won't have to lift a hand in this battle; just stand firm, Judah and Jerusalem, and watch God's saving work for you take shape. Don't be afraid, don't waver. March out boldly tomorrow - God is with you." – The Message Translation

Stop allowing what is before you to defeat you! The fear of possibility has crippled the lives of so many people! Learn to trust God and remember that He will always get the glory out of your life. You have to encourage yourself and keep decreeing that "all things work together for my good".

Change your perception about difficult things in life. When you are traveling this road of life and find rocks in the road, stop seeing them as stumbling blocks. Acknowledge that they are blessed stepping stones to take you closer to fulfilling your destiny. What appears to be a setback is really a set up. Yes, God is taking you to greater.

And sometimes in life – things are subtracted in order to add to. And sometimes things are divided in order to multiply. Spiritual mathematics can never be understood by the carnal mind. But, when you are spiritual God will reveal His plan and purpose to you by His Spirit. So, until His will is clear – stand still and praise Him! It's all good!

MARCH 15

Today – See His Goodness

PSALM 27:13

I had fainted, unless I had believed to see the goodness of the LORD in the land of the living. – King James Version

I am still confident of this: I will see the goodness of the LORD in the land of the living. – New International Version

Here is something I am still sure of. I will see the Lord's goodness while I'm still alive. – New International Reader's Version

"Something good is going to happen to you, this very day..." were the lyrics of the theme song of Oral Roberts' television program for years. These words are a powerful confession. It is a declaration of trust in an all-powerful and loving God. Regardless of what else is happening around, victory is still the end result.

Challenges do come every day. But, Christians have learned that this is simply a part of life. God promised you an abundant life – however, you have an adversary that desires to steal, to kill and to destroy. Learn to ignore the devil's temptation for you to give up or lose heart. Stay focused and remain prayerful.

Good things are happening in your life. Yes, God awakened you this morning. But, He has even more wonderful and great miracles to bring into manifestation in your life today. Look for God. Be a God chaser today. Pursue Him in your praise. Woo Him in your worship. Embrace him in your prayers and study of His Word. He is bringing good things to light for you today!

MARCH 16
Get Up And Get Busy!
PROVERBS 12:27

The slothful man roasteth not that which he took in hunting: but the substance of a diligent man is precious. – King James Version

A lazy life is an empty life, but "early to rise" gets the job done. – The Message Translation

Abundance does not determine success. Just as, a long life does not equate to a productive life! If you have possessions but do nothing with them, then you devalue your possessions. Your life is just like the man who only had received one talent and buried it instead of investing it and getting a return.

Stop planning and start pursuing! Stop dreaming: wake up and start doing! Stop wondering and hoping! It's time to get busy and utilize your faith to propel you to destiny. Don't talk about it. Be about it! Just do it!

Slothfulness has no reward. But diligence and patience will always pay off. Whatever God has placed in your hands – whether it be little or much – do something with it. Trust God and watch God bless you.

MARCH 17
Stop Focusing On Your Weakness!
II CORINTHIANS 12:9

And he said unto me, My grace is sufficient for thee: for my strength is made perfect in weakness. Most gladly therefore will I rather glory in my infirmities, that the power of Christ may rest upon me. – King James Version

and then he told me, My grace is enough; it's all you need. My strength comes into its own in your weakness. Once I heard that, I was glad to let it happen. I quit focusing on the handicap and began appreciating the gift. It was a case of Christ's strength moving in on my weakness." My grace is enough for you, my strength is made perfect in weakness" – The Message Translation

Many people across the globe celebrate St. Patrick on this date.

The reality of St. Patrick as revealed in the "Confession" shows someone in whom the grace of God was powerfully active. The Lord habitually uses weak and fragile people to accomplish his will, to build up his kingdom. Weak though he was, Patrick's success laid in his recognition of the Gospel's power to transform, transfigure and uplift, and this is as true for us in the 21st century as it was for him in the fifth. (Clabaigh, 2010, Crosswalk)

It is not God's will that you allow imperfections to hinder His grace in your life. Whatever your issue, fault or problem – you must allow God's Word to minister to that area of your life and embrace the grace and mercy extended to you by God. Whatever the thorn that may be in your flesh, recognize it for what it is and where it is. First, it is a thorn and thus a distraction. Second, it is in your flesh and not in your spirit.

Stop wasting time living your life being focused on distractions. If there are shortcomings in your life continue to pray about them, repent (turn) from them, and walk by faith in God's Word toward your deliverance. However, do not live a life of guilt and unforgiveness toward yourself. Rise up and move on. You are a spirit being created in God's image. Learn to walk in the spirit and not after the flesh. Focus on your spiritual assignment and not a flesh distraction. God's grace is greater.

MARCH 18

Sing A Song For Your Enemy

II CHRONICLES 20:22

As soon as they started shouting and praising, God set ambushes against the men of Ammon, Moab, and Mount Seir as they were attacking Judah, and they all ended up dead. – The Message Translation

Stop being so moved by the threat of the enemy. God will move on your behalf when you release your faith! Your praise is not just a weapon but it is the manifestation of your faith. It takes faith to say that you have victory when all you can see is defeat all around you.

Open your mouth and begin to sing praises unto God. Decree out of your mouth who He is, what He has done, and what you expect Him to do! Exalt His Name! Magnify His Name in your mouth. This will bring confusion and insult to the devil. He expects you to give up and be frustrated. But, you have the Greater One inside of you and have the promise of God to be victorious.

Sing! Sing! Sing! And while you are singing get so excited and add a little shouting and dancing to your singing! Your praise will distract and disgust the enemy to such an extent that not only will it thrust you to victory, but it will also destroy the intent and plan of your adversary.

MARCH 19

Keep Meeting Together!
HEBREWS 10:25

Not forsaking the assembling of ourselves together, as the manner of some is; but exhorting one another: and so much the more, as ye see the day approaching. – King James Version

not avoiding worshiping together as some do but spurring each other on, especially as we see the big Day approaching. – The Message Translation

Church is not just the building, but it is the actual gathering of like-minded believers together. God's Word encourages you to continue to meet on a consistent basis to experience spiritual growth and development. God promised that He would return for "the church" – your job is to be ready for His return.

The "assembling" together is more than just having worship services consisting of singing, praying, reading scriptures, preaching and teaching, etc. But, it also gives the understanding of allowing relationships to develop believers. The real need is to foster Christian relationships inside and outside of the church building.

There will be challenge relationships, encouraging relationships, and even grooming relationships. Challenge relationships help you to develop more Godly traits as you learn to love the unlovable and get along with those who make it challenging to embrace. Encouraging relationships help you to endure times of storm, tests, and trials as God will place people in your life with the sole purpose of strengthening you. Grooming relationships help you to grow into a more rooted and grounded believer.

Remember, in your Christian walk with God – He will cause all things to work together for good for you. So, take every advantage to identify with a local assembly to be "assembled" into the disciple that God desires you to be. Don't get stuck in that once a week meeting ritual. Take advantage every day!

MARCH 20

Success Is Yours!

JOSHUA 1:8

"This book of the law shall not depart out of thy mouth; but thou shalt meditate therein day and night, that thou mayest observe to do according to all that is written therein: for then thou shalt make thy way prosperous, and then thou shalt have good success." – King James Version

"Never stop reciting these teachings. You must think about them night and day so that you will faithfully do everything written in them. Only then will you prosper and succeed." – God's Word Translation

God has ordained success for your life. The only hindrance to your success is your willingness and obedience to walk into it. Yes, God wants you to prosper (break forth) in every area of your life: your health, your finances, your relationships, your walk with Him, even the desires of your heart. It is God's will that you be blessed.

However, obstacles are a part of the package deal in life. Stop stressing over obstacles, and learn to make lemonade with the lemons of life. The righteous were foretold of many afflictions, but they were also promised deliverance from each one of them. God is your very present help in trouble. God is your rock, your sword and your shield. He is your all in all. Trust Him to be God in every area of your life.

Don't be your own worst enemy. Don't fight yourself. No longer speak or think negative thoughts. Remind yourself of what God desires for you. And always remember, you cannot do it on your own. You need Him.

Your success is not based upon your strength. Your success is not based upon your resources. But, your success is based upon your faith in God and His Word. What He has promised – even when you don't see it – walk by faith and not by sight in it. Change your thoughts. Refocus your perception. Adjust your attitude. If you learn to take it, you can surely make it.

MARCH 21
The Lord's House
PSALM 122:1

"I was glad when they said unto me, Let us go into the house of the Lord." – King James Version

When an invitation is extended for you to go to a place that you really want to go – you are naturally excited and glad. You begin thinking about what you are going to wear, how you are going to fix your hair (ladies), if you are going alone or "who" will you take with you. For that moment, your excitement can be so strong that it puts everything else on pause.

This is the type excitement that should come when an invitation is extended for you to share at the Lord's house. You should be exceedingly glad! You are going to your Father's house.

The blessing of the house of the Lord is the manifested presence of the Lord in the place. Eventhough, God is all places at all times – He has the unique way of showing up all over again. And, when this experience takes place transformation occurs in your life. Hurt yields to healing. Depression gives way to joy. Confusion moves and allows peace to enter. Anger steps back and allows love to come to the forefront.

This type of activity is enough to make anybody glad. Run to the Lord's house. And open the door with a "Thank You" on your lips. Wave and clap your hands with a thunderous praise. With this type excitement – He will meet you there and allow you to bask in a worship experience that will bless your day and your life.

MARCH 22
God Has A Job Opening For You!
MATTHEW 4:19

And he saith unto them, Follow me, and I will make you fishers of men. – King James Version

Jesus said to them, "Come with me. I'll make a new kind of fisherman out of you. I'll show you how to catch men and women instead of perch and bass." – The Message Translation

If you pay close attention, the people that Jesus approached to utilize in the kingdom were already active and busy. It did not matter whether their profession was morally correct or if there was some shadiness about their business. He used people who had a mind to be productive. Matthew was a tax collector, Paul was a tentmaker, Luke was a physician, and James, John, Simon, and Andrew were fishermen.

When Jesus becomes the Lord and Saviour of your life, He changes you into a productive vessel for the kingdom of God. You may have skills you acquired in the world, but He will show you how to use those same parts of your body for God's glory. If you have a past that you are not extremely proud of – that's okay. God already knows about it. But, evidently He saw something in you to still cause Him to make plans to utilize you in His service.

There is work for you to do in the earth realm. He already has your assignment "job duties and details" prepared for you. He is the one who qualifies you and certifies you. Stop allowing flesh (people) to attempt to validate you. Man cannot stamp an approval (or voice a dis-approval) on what God has already declared and decreed. Stop with the excuses and get busy for God!

MARCH 23
"I Can I-Tis" A Good Condition
PHILIPPIANS 4:13

I can do all things through Christ which strengtheneth me. —
King James Version

Today, develop a condition of "Icanitis". Pronounced "*I can eye tis*". Yes, stop allowing the enemy and people under the control of the enemy to hold you back and hinder you. Believe God's Word and walk by faith into what God said you CAN DO! You will experience such a joy and fulfillment that will be contagious to others around you. Yes, your condition will not only be a witness tool but it will encourage you and thrust you into a season of blessing and favour.

"*I have come into the world as light, so that no one who believes in me should stay in darkness." John 12:46* — You do not have to live in or walk in darkness. Jesus is the light of the world. When you have Him in your heart, you have a light that no man can put out. You have a light that causes others to see His glory manifest in you.

I have told you these things, so that in me you may have peace. In this world you will have trouble. But take heart! I have overcome the world! " John 16:33 — You do not have to live in confusion or fear. Jesus came to bring you a higher level of peace. His peace will surpass your own understanding. You will find yourself going through storms and situations, yet not being troubled or stressed out by their impact.

"I have told you this so that my joy may be in you and your joy maybe complete" John 15:11 – You can defeat depression and gloom. Joy is not the absence of sorrow, but it is the presence of God. As you worship God you will find a new sense of excitement and wonder at the miraculous power of God to cause your inner man to leap and jump because of God's goodness to you. Your outer man also responds and tears of joy replace sobs of sorrow.

"When you pass through the waters, I will be with you; and when you pass through the rivers, they will not sweep over you. When you walk through the fire, you will not be burned; the flames will not set you ablaze." Isaiah 43:1,2 – You are protected. You can have confidence of divine protection no matter what you go through. Life's circumstances and situations may look bad, feel bad, or even be bad. Bu you have a promise from God that whatever you go through will not destroy you, but will define and develop your character. You will be protected and made better by everything that you go through.

Today – Testify! I CAN walk in the light. I CAN have the peace of God. I CAN have joy unspeakable. I CAN walk in divine favour and protection. I CAN DO ALL THINGS THROUGH CHRIST WHICH STRENGTHENETH ME!

MARCH 24

From Bitter To Better!

RUTH 1:20

And she said unto them, "Call me not Naomi [that is, Pleasant]. Call me Mara [that is, Bitter], for the Almighty hath dealt very bitterly with me. – Third Millennium Bible Translation

Sometimes life has a way of making you emotionally bankrupt. After you have done all that you know to do and it seems as if instead of getting better, things get worse – you are faced with the challenge of pressing on. God has a way of still showing up and showing out to bless you. That is the beauty of covenant, favor and just being blessed.

God keeps His word with His people. He will not change His mind on His promises to you. His love for you will cause favor to come and bless your life. Even at times when it seems as though failure has been served for your dinner, you can trust that God's faithfulness will show up at the same dinner table.

Encourage yourself through praise and worship and draw nearer to God. Don't get stuck in the trap of past problems or current challenges. There is a fantastic future that has your name on it. Keep making lemonade from your lemons. There is nothing that can happen in your life that God is not able to cause to still work in your favor. Remember, all things will still work together for your good.

MARCH 25

No Other Choice – But To Wait!

ISAIAH 40:31

But they that wait upon the LORD shall renew their strength; they shall mount up with wings as eagles; they shall run, and not be weary; and they shall walk, and not faint. – King James Version

But those who wait upon God get fresh strength. They spread their wings and soar like eagles, They run and don't get tired, they walk and don't lag behind. – The Message Translation

As a true believer, you have no other option but to wait on God. Your waiting should be done in patience and with joy. You must learn to have full confidence that not only is God going to show up, but He will show out!

When you give up you are saying that the devil is right. You cannot feed into the lies and negativity of the enemy. Whatever he speaks, learn to believe just the opposite. Also, giving up says that your faith is weak. Remember, it is your faith that is on trial. You must keep the faith! And finally, when you give up your actions are saying that God was wrong! Of course this is impossible because it is impossible for God to lie or fail.

As a true believer you must learn to wait in patience. Luke 21:19 encourages you, *"In your patience possess your souls."* Yes, when you learn to hang in there until God manifests the promise it gives you time to get your mind together. Also, you must keep an expectancy in your spirit. That confidence is what will reward you. And finally, wait for God with a thankful and grateful heart. Thank Him in advance for coming through just for you. The end result will be an awesome blessing with renewed strength and success!

MARCH 26

He Is A Right Now God!
PSALM 46:1

God is our refuge and strength, a very present help in trouble.
– King James Version

God is a safe place to hide, ready to help when we need him. –
The Message Translation

There is no storm, trial or tragedy in life that is greater than God. He will come to your rescue and bring you the peace, comfort, and safety that you need. He loves you enough to weather storms with you. He allows His Spirit to comfort and strengthen you in the midst of the challenge. You are never alone, He is always there.

Some question, if He loves me so much why would He allow such horrible things to take place? The answer is that He not only loves you, but He trusts you enough to keep your hand in His hand and come out of the test with a testimony. Remember the spiritual forecast. His Word has already told you that there would be storms, trials and afflictions in the lives of believers. But, He also promised that you would be victorious and overcomers in the midst of all these things.

Have a positive outlook on life. Let your faith kick in! When trouble comes; simply rest in Him and trust in His Word. He will hide you. He will help you. He will strengthen you. He will keep you. He's doing it even now!

MARCH 27
Peace Is God's Blessing
I CORINTHIANS 14:33

When we worship the right way, God doesn't stir us up into confusion; he brings us into harmony. This goes for all the churches - no exceptions. – The Message Translation

There is no mistake about it - confusion is a work of the flesh and not the Spirit. When people are not on the same page it is because someone has decided to walk in disobedience. God is a God of order. When He gives directions they are detailed and specific. He won't lead you blindly. But, you must trust Him. When your mind does not understand - it is because He is communicating with your spirit.

Every time someone jumps up and declares that "God said" does not mean that God said anything. The scriptures say that the prophets are subject to the prophets. You need to pray for a spirit of discernment. Don't judge the person but consider the message. Confusion comes because people get connected to flesh and not spirit. Everything that sounds like "God" may not necessarily be God. And be careful, not to discount people who you feel God can't use or speak through.

God chooses the foolish to confound the wise. Perfect peace is brought to those who stay connected to the God of peace. Even when things happen around you that you don't always understand, God will give you peace that passeth even your own understanding. God will bless peace to prevail in your mind, in your relationships, and most importantly in your walk with Him!

MARCH 28

God Is Waiting For You!
HEBREWS 4:15-16

For we have not an high priest which cannot be touched with the feeling of our infirmities; but was in all points tempted like as we are, yet without sin. Let us therefore come boldly unto the throne of grace, that we may obtain mercy, and find grace to help in time of need.

There is a reason that you can run to the throne of God and find mercy. Jesus Christ, your elder brother and your high priest, is making intercession for you. He knows and feels everything that you go through. He understands the challenges in your flesh.

He wants you to utilize the access that has been granted unto you. Don't allow the enemy to make you run and hide in some dark room. Don't waste time beating yourself up over a fault or failure. But, learn to repent daily and petition God for strength to walk in victory.

As you humbly come to the throne, God will have compassion upon you. He will forgive you of your sins. He will create a clean heart and renew the right spirit within you. He will fill your life with mercy and allow an abundance of grace to consume your life.

MARCH 29
Relatives Can't Relate
MATTHEW 10:36

And a man's foes shall be they of his own household. – King James Version

Well-meaning family members can be your worst enemies. – The Message Translation

Those who are closest to you in blood would seem to be the ones closest to you in love. However, that is not always true. The scriptures even declare that a *"brother is born for adversity, but a friend loveth at all times."* (Proverbs 17:17) So you would ask yourself why would my own flesh and blood be what is worst for me?

The expression that love is blind is true. Sometimes, the love people have for those close to them hinder them from being cognizant of the real need in that person's life. This is one of the dangers of people who suffer from an addiction. Family members often live in denial. This pretention that there is no problem or refusal to acknowledge the severity of the actual problem can be devastating for the one with the issue.

Also, those related to you have what is also called "soul ties" and sometimes have difficulty in adjusting to change. When you have been born again or God has directed you to operate differently from your past, it can sometimes be met with indifference, hostility or non-approval. It is at this time, you have to understand that you much choose to pursue your true destiny or remain stuck in your past.

When those related to you cannot relate to you, it does not mean that they don't love you. But, it does mean that they may not be what is best for you. You have to make a choice of how to live your life before God when you are faced with living an extraordinary life with God versus living an ordinary life with folk.

MARCH 30
Embrace The Fire!
DANIEL 3:17-18

If it be so, our God whom we serve is able to deliver us from the burning fiery furnace, and he will deliver us out of thine hand, O king. But if not, be it known unto thee, O king, that we will not serve thy gods, nor worship the golden image which thou hast set up. – King James Version

If you throw us in the fire, the God we serve can rescue us from your roaring furnace and anything else you might cook up, O king. But even if he doesn't, it wouldn't make a bit of difference, O king. We still wouldn't serve your gods or worship the gold statue you set up." – The Message Translation

Often, people look at adversity as the forfeiture of your destiny or the negating of a promise that has been made unto you. But, actually quite the contrary is the truth. These are awesome opportunities for God's glory to shine even brighter than ever before.

Learn to embrace whatever the Lord allows and permits in your life. God loves you enough, that even when you are targeted by the enemy – He has a way to cause good and bad to work out for your good. Stop trying to avoid the fire!

Staying in the fire requires: Faith, Integrity, Reality and Endurance. Your faith is made evident by what you do and not just what you say. Your actions prove what you really believe. Being integral with God and yourself is the key to walking in true liberty and deliverance. Always conduct reality checks on yourself throughout life. Be real enough with yourself to acknowledge life's unplanned and sometimes undesired events. And finally, you will need endurance which is the ability to "stick-it-out" until it is over.

Don't try to avoid the fire. Embrace whatever comes along in life reminding yourself that God has promised to never leave you alone. Not only will He go through the fire WITH you but He will bring you out with an awesome testimony.

MARCH 31

The Same Folk!

LUKE 23:21

But they cried, saying, Crucify him, crucify him. – King James Version

But they kept shouting back, "Crucify! Crucify him!" – The Message Translation

Don't get excited when people celebrate you and seemingly like you or approve of you. That can be dangerous or disastrous. You may find yourself left out in the cold – all alone! You should only seek approval from two people: GOD and yourself. Seek to please God first! And learn how to make yourself happy in life.

The same people that celebrate you one day may be the same people who will attempt to destroy you the next day. Don't allow your heart and soul to be a puppet to other people's whims! Learn to simply stay in God's will.

When people change their minds about you – do what Jesus did: Forgive them. Learn to love everybody. Learn to forgive everybody. Understand that often people do not operate in the spirit but in their soulish nature. They may be fickle and change their minds simply based upon how they feel. You must take care to live above that type of scrutiny. Live for God. Live for you!

APRIL 1
Don't Be Fooled!
EPHESIANS 4:14

Then we will no longer be infants, tossed back and forth by the waves, and blown here and there by every wind of teaching and by the cunning and craftiness of men in their deceitful scheming. – New International Version

Then we will no longer be babies. We will not be tossed about like a ship that the waves carry one way and then another. We will not be influenced by every new teaching we hear from people who are trying to fool us. They make plans and try any kind of trick to fool people into following the wrong path. – New Century Version

There is an adage: "You are what you eat"! If there is any truth to this statement: You must be careful about your spiritual diet. When you hear a message preached, taught, or even sung you must be certain that it is being "rightly divided" and not misinterpreted. You must also be careful that what you hear is actually God's Word and not man's invention.

As you grow spiritually, you must mature to the extent that you understand how to discern when people are speaking. You need to be wise enough to know when God has spoken through them. Also, you must be able to tell when they are being used of the devil or if they are just operating out of their own fleshy desires or thoughts.

Remember that every good thing is not a God thing. Pray and ask God to send the right people to speak into your life. Find people who are connected to the Father and will feed you with truth and not just fables and emotional hoopla. Don't just go to the church of your choice. But, go to the church of God's choice. Make certain to find yourself in a place where God's word is taught with clarity and you have an understanding in all your getting.

APRIL 2

Giving Up = Telling Lies

HEBREWS 10:35

So don't throw it all away now. You were sure of yourselves then. It's still a sure thing! – The Message Translation

You cannot give up! That is not even an option. When a child of God tries to give up, in essence you are telling three lies: 1) The devil was right, 2) Your faith is weak, and 3) God was wrong. All three of these are untruths!

The devil is a liar. He is the father of lies. He never was right and never will be. You must have this understanding whenever he encourages you to throw in the towel and quit.

Your faith is not weak because it is a gift of God. Your responsibility is to activate it and utilize it. That is why the enemy hates you and attacks you. He realizes that this is your connection to God and one of the ways that you please God.

God is God. He does not and cannot lie. He makes no mistakes and cannot err. When He speaks it is settled. He has promised to never leave you nor forsake you. So, even when life seems to be rough, He is there with you to bring you out victorious.

So, don't give up. Just know that better days are ahead. Decree and declare that God is in charge, the devil is defeated and that your faith is taking you somewhere.

APRIL 3
Keep It Real With God!
MATTHEW 15:8

This people draweth nigh unto me with their mouth, and honoureth me with their lips; but their heart is far from me.

Don't go through the motions with God. Always keep it real! Since God is omniscient, He knows everything already anyway. He knows your yesterday, today and even your tomorrow. But, He wants you to make the relationship with Him real. He wants you to love Him enough to simply trust Him.

So, when you are having a Psalm 51 Day (You have sinned and need to repent), He is there ready to create a clean heart and renew the right spirit within you. He loves you so much. He knows when you are right and He understands when you are wrong. He does not condone error, but He forgives.

From this day forward, make a commitment to always keep the lines of communication open and real with God. Say what you mean and mean what you say. Do not simply give Him lip service. Tell Him the truth and then come to Him broken and repentant so that He can renew and restore.

APRIL 4
Lucky or Blessed?
JEREMIAH 29:11

For I know the thoughts that I think toward you, saith the LORD, thoughts of peace, and not of evil, to give you an expected end. – King James Version

I know what I'm doing. I have it all planned out - plans to take care of you, not abandon you, plans to give you the future you hope for. – The Message Translation

Luck is defined as a combination of circumstances, events, etc., operating by chance to bring good or ill to a person. There are many individuals who believe that the things that happen in their life are haphazard and coincidental. However, believers need to reconsider that thought and understand that your life is in divine order as you follow the leading of God's Spirit.

When you make bad choices and decisions the end results are negative. That has nothing to do with luck. It has everything to do with operating outside of God's will and plan. However, when you allow His Spirit to lead, guide and direct you the results are positive. Even when you follow God's plan and it seems as if things are not going well, you have to remember His Word. God promised that all things would work together for good to those who love Him and are called unto His purpose.

Favor is not fair! It is not earned or deserved. The blessing of the Lord upon someone's life is because of God's sovereignty. He can bless whomever, whenever – simply because He is God. It is not by chance but it is an act of love. The grace and mercy that God extends is not by chance – but an act of love. No longer consider luck as having any control in your life. Always know that your times are in His hands.

APRIL 5
The Blood Of Jesus
HEBREWS 9:12

Neither by the blood of goats and calves, but by His own blood He entered in once into the holy place, having obtained eternal redemption for us. – King James Version

He also bypassed the sacrifices consisting of goat and calf blood, instead using his own blood as the price to set us free once and for all. – The Message Translation

The Word of God declares that ALL have sinned and come short of God's glory. That means that everyone has a payment due. Romans 6:23 says that, "the wages of sin is death..." That is a price none can afford to pay. However, the second part of that same verse declares, "...but the gift of God is eternal life." This should cause you to rejoice to know that God loved you enough to provide a way for you to not only have eternal life, but abundant life as well.

Jesus' death on Calvary was the ultimate sacrifice for your sins. Yes, what He did on Calvary covered yesterday, today, as well as tomorrow. There is nothing that you can do – that Calvary cannot cover. His blood will never lose its power. It is strong enough to save even the worst of all sinners.

His blood that was shed on Calvary bought us back. You needed to be redeemed and His blood did that. His blood brought reconciliation. There was separation between earth and heaven. But the cross provided the access from earth to glory. His blood secured your spiritual adoption into the royal family. Not only was there a legal transaction made to bring you into right relationship with God, but as you accept the work on Calvary a blood transfusion takes places in the spirit. You truly become the sons of God. And His blood also cleanses you from all sin. No penalty and no more passion. His blood is powerful enough to take away not only the guilt of sin, but even the desire to return.

Thank God for the blood of Jesus!

APRIL 6

Your Blessings Have Your Address!

DEUTERONOMY 28:2

And all these blessings shall come on thee, and overtake thee, if thou shalt hearken unto the voice of the LORD thy God. – King James Version

All these blessings will come down on you and spread out beyond you because you have responded to the Voice of God, your God: - The Message Translation

You don't have to run looking for blessings. You don't have to get in a prayer line to get your blessings. You don't have to stay up all night long weeping and wailing, hoping that God will hear your voice and pity your groan to get your blessings. The key to your blessings is found in the title of an old hymn of the church: "Trust and Obey".

The way to see your blessings manifest is through your obedience. Obey the Word of God. Hear the voice of God and do what you hear. Follow the leading of the Spirit of God. I Samuel 15:22 reveals God's desire: obedience not sacrifice. Stop allowing flesh to dominate your life, and be spirit-filled and spirit-led.

When you are in covenant relationship with God, He orders your steps. That means that when He is ready to bless you, He knows where to find you! Just keep doing what God called, anointed, and blessed you to do. When you do this, your blessings will overtake you and fill your life. If you do it right, God will bless it right!

APRIL 7
You Will Survive!
ACTS 27:4

And the rest, some on boards, and some on broken pieces of the ship. And so it came to pass, that they escaped all safe to land. – King James Version

Life can be challenging sometimes. Storms of life will rage and it may seem like everything around you is falling apart. However, that is not a reason to stress out. What you have to remember are the promises found in God's Word. You are already victorious. You are an overcomer. Be like Paul in II Corinthians 4:8-9, *"We are troubled on every side, yet not distressed; we are perplexed, but not in despair; Persecuted, but not forsaken; cast down, but not destroyed"*. Keep your attitude in check and know that you will survive.

The fact that you are reading this devotional proves that you are a survivor. Yes, you have endured many things in life – and it was God that brought you through "that" and it is the same God that will bring you through what may be facing you even now. Your assignment is to hold on to God's Word and not let go!

If nothing that is around you or connected to you lasts, your faith in God's Word will bring you safely through. Making it safely to land is the manifestation of God answering your prayers regarding your healing, your relationships, your finances. You may suffer loss of things that you thought would sustain you but God will reveal to you what you really need to survive. Don't worry about the storm or the ship – for you are protected and kept by the Master of the storm.

APRIL 8
How Deep Did You Dig?
LUKE 6:47-49

47 Whosoever cometh to me, and heareth my sayings, and doeth them, I will shew you to whom he is like: 48 He is like a man which built an house, and digged deep, and laid the foundation on a rock: and when the flood arose, the stream beat vehemently upon that house, and could not shake it: for it was founded upon a rock. 49 But he that heareth, and doeth not, is like a man that without a foundation built an house upon the earth; against which the stream did beat vehemently, and immediately it fell; and the ruin of that house was great.

Building a foundation is a process! It does not just happen! It does not happen overnight. It does not always come easy. It does not occur without challenges. But, the depth that you dig will determine your ability to withstand challenges in the future.

Storms will come in every life. Regardless of whether you are a sinner or a saint, a true Christian or just a habitual church attendant – spiritual, emotional, financial and physical storms will come. The strength of your foundation will determine how you weather the storms.

You must be rooted and grounded in the Word of God to have a solid foundation. Simply knowing scriptures is not enough. The devil knows scriptures. Going to church on Sundays and participating in the choir or usher board is not enough. Social clubs do the same type ritual.

In building a spiritual foundation you must hear the Word, believe the Word and obey the Word. Live by the Word on a daily basis. You will be surprised at the results in your life when you have God's Word as your support system. Dig deep into God's Word and you will weather every storm.

APRIL 9
Sanctified Satisfaction!
PHILIPPIANS 4:12

I know both how to be abased, and I know how to abound: every where and in all things I am instructed both to be full and to be hungry, both to abound and to suffer need. – King James Version

I'm just as happy with little as with much, with much as with little. I've found the recipe for being happy whether full or hungry, hands full or hands empty. – The Message Translation

As you grow spiritually and become more mature, you learn to give up the child attitude of having to have everything you want! You learn how not to throw spiritual and emotional fits and tantrums when things don't go your way.

With the knowledge that God is your Shepherd, every need in your life is supplied. And in the words of the songwriter: "I'd rather have Jesus than silver and gold". You can learn how to live a life of simply trusting God every day. He has an awesome track record. He won't ever leave you alone. He will never fail you. He will always love you.

When you are at your lowest, He will manifest His presence in your situation. This gives you the confidence and the testimony that nobody but God could have done this. When the odds are against you, stand with quiet resolve and "let God work".

Being content is really just having the knowledge that your steps are ordered by Him, and wherever you are – it is for His glory and for His praise. Being content is being fully persuaded that all things are working for your good and giving the joyful resolve to simply wait for God's victory to be made manifest!

APRIL 10

Keep On Keeping On!

LUKE 18:1

And He spake a parable unto them to this end, that men ought always to pray, and not to faint; - King James Version

Jesus told them a story showing that it was necessary for them to pray consistently and never quit. – The Message Translation

Have you ever felt that you were at the end of your rope and did not have the strength or desire to tie a knot and hold on? Have you ever felt like you had exhausted all of your energy and resources? Have you ever felt like the battle was too long and too fierce, and you wanted to just wave your white flag of surrender?

Giving up is NOT an option for a believer! You have to remind yourself that the God you serve will manifest your victory at the right time and place. Your responsibility is to simply pray and praise. Keep your head up and be confident that you will come out on the winning side.

You must be persistent like the woman before the unjust judge. She was going to keep crying out until he ruled in her favor. You have to be like Jacob who wrestled all night long with the angel. He was determined not to let go until he was blessed.

You need that same stamina and persistence in your daily life. Quitting is not an option. Giving up is not part of the plan. But, you must endure and hang in there! In the words of the little old lady, "You gotta' keep on keeping on".

APRIL 11
Lose Yourself In Him!
PHILIPPIANS 3:9

And be found in Him, not having mine own righteousness, which is of the law, but that which is through the faith of Christ, the righteousness which is of God by faith: - King James Version

and be embraced by him. I didn't want some petty, inferior brand of righteousness that comes from keeping a list of rules when I could get the robust kind that comes from trusting Christ - God's righteousness. – The Message Translation

Have you ALWAYS crossed all of your "t's" and dotted all of your "i's"? Of course the answer is not! Because of this flesh suit, even at your best the Word of God tells the truth: that your righteousness alone is still as filthy rags.

But, now you can rejoice that your righteousness is not found in you but in Him. When you learn to lose yourself in Him you will experience a new walk with God that you could never have imagined. Yes, your lifestyle of prayer, praise and worship will take you to another dimension of holy and righteous living that you never even dreamed was possible.

Just flip the script of your life. Stop trying to find a bunch of rules and regulations to keep, that your flesh already intends on breaking. Instead, focus on loving Him. Yes, your complete love and adoration for Him will cause your life to be led and driven by His Spirit. You will find yourself walking in true holiness and righteousness that is not yours but His. Lose yourself in Him and find peace, joy and righteousness in the Holy Ghost!

APRIL 12

Robeless Ministry!

II CORINTHIANS 5:18

And all things are of God, who hath reconciled us to Himself by Jesus Christ, and hath given to us the ministry of reconciliation; - King James Version

All this comes from the God who settled the relationship between us and him, and then called us to settle our relationships with each other. – The Message Translation

There is a calling on your life! Yes, God wants you operating in ministry. You don't need a robe. You don't have to wear a clergy collar. You don't need a degree from the seminary. All you need to do is to learn how to give to others what God has given to you.

Sin separated you from God. It was because of the love of God made manifest through the sacrificial work of Jesus Christ on Calvary that brought you back into fellowship with the Father. God loved you while you were still in your mess! And His love was what caused your relationship to be mended.

There are countless people that you encounter every day. Some of them are complete strangers. Others work with you, go to school with you, live in the community with you and some actually live under your own roof. It is your job to share the love of God with them.

There is no time to be critical or judgmental. You have to love them the same way God loved you. Look beyond their faults and see their true needs! Take off the robe and roll up your sleeves. It's time to do real work in the kingdom. Win someone to Christ today!

APRIL 13

You Can Have What You Say!

JOB 22:28

Thou shalt also decree a thing, and it shall be established unto thee: and the light shall shine upon thy ways. – King James Version

You'll decide what you want and it will happen; your life will be bathed in light. – The Message Translation

It is your time to move to the next glory of God's awesomeness in your life. You have received blessings because of the goodness and mercy of God. But, God wants to take you to the dimension of decreeing and declaring a blessing. Yes, you can open your mouth and use the creative power of God to be a blessing in your life and the lives of others.

God's Word is sure and steadfast. He has already settled it in the heavens and the earth. But, you must align yourself with it and release your faith to see the manifestation of it in your life. Remember, you were created in His image and likeness. That means that it is normal and natural for you to operate just like Him.

"And God said..." and then He saw it and saw that it was good. You have to use your tongue for your benefit by speaking blessings. Stop agreeing with the enemy by being afraid to say what you cannot see. If you could see it, then there would be no need to have faith for it. But, because you cannot see it – that places it in the "But God Can" category!

Today – decree and declare what God has said about you. Let your words fill the atmosphere. Command that the blessing of the Lord be made manifest and that it continually abides with you. Say it loud and believe what you are saying! And watch God work!

APRIL 14

Not Better—Just Different

II CORINTHIANS 6:17

Wherefore come out from among them, and be ye separate, saith the Lord, and touch not the unclean thing; and I will receive you, - King James Version

So leave the corruption and compromise; leave it for good," *says God. "Don't link up with those who will pollute you. I want you all for myself.* – The Message Translation

God's command for separation does not mean existence, but it refers to fellowship. As a Christian, you must still exist in the world, but God commands that you be different. You should not pattern your ways after unbelievers. There must be a separation.

Whatever God has delivered you from is now for the history books. You must reckon or consider yourself dead to your old ways. And if your old ways are dead then they no longer influence your present life.

You must never have the attitude or demeanor that you are better than others who may still be in the struggle. Don't forget, you used to have the same address. But, you must learn to express love and compassion for them without doing what they are doing!

God's call for your life is to live healed, whole, and delivered. Be an example of the grace and mercy that is available to others. Your hand changes from fellowship to ministry. Your connection is no longer as a comrade but as a deliverer and an ambassador for God.

APRIL 15
God Will Make A Way!
GENESIS 22:5

And Abraham said unto his young men, Abide ye here with the ass; and I and the lad will go yonder and worship, and come again to you. – King James Version

Abraham told his two young servants, "Stay here with the donkey. The boy and I are going over there to worship; then we'll come back to you." – The Message Translation

Sometimes the challenges of life will encourage you to stop trusting God. But, always remember that God does not change His mind on His promises. Whatever He has spoken will come to pass. You must continue to live a life of trusting and obeying. They go hand in hand. You cannot honestly trust without obeying.

As you operate in faith and do what God directs you to do – never change your confession. Even when it looks like destruction is all around, keep the promise of God in your mouth.

In the midst of sickness, declare that you shall live and not die. In the midst of financial challenges decree that you prosper. In the midst of confusion and trouble, keep your mind on Him and receive perfect peace. When relationships seem to be on the rocks, open your mouth and confess that what God has joined together will stay together. Learn to call those things that may be not as though they were.

God will always make a way out of no way. Yes, He will provide a "ram in the bush" for your miracle. Your job is simple: trust God and obey God. Do not doubt that what He promised will be performed. God can and God will!

APRIL 16

Perception Is Powerful!

NUMBER 13:33

And there we saw the giants, the sons of Anak, which come of the giants: and we were in our own sight as grasshoppers, and so we were in their sight. – King James Version

Thoughts and words are powerful! Whatever you speak out of your mouth is a seed that produces fruit after its own kind. Your thoughts precede the actions you take which basically determine your level of faith. Faith is not just what you think but it is what you do!

When you look in the mirror what do you see? How do you feel? You cannot allow the influence of others to determine your vision. You cannot allow your situation or circumstance to define you. But, you have to look through spiritual eyes and see yourself as God sees you.

When you allow your natural eyes to determine who you are, you limit your potential. You cannot expect others to believe for you what you cannot believe for yourself. When you determine your limitation – you actually begin to live within the parameters that you have determined. People of faith believe that the sky is the limit. Children of God believe they can do all things through Christ which strengthens them. Saints believe that with God all things are possible! What do you believe?

APRIL 17

Just Obey!

DEUTERONOMY 28:1-2

And it shall come to pass, if thou shalt hearken diligently unto the voice of the LORD thy God, to observe and to do all His commandments which I command thee this day, that the LORD thy God will set thee on high above all nations of the earth: And all these blessings shall come on thee, and overtake thee, if thou shalt hearken unto the voice of the LORD thy God.

There is a blessing in obeying God. He is not so interested in outward expressions of religion as He is in true service and devotion from the heart. Remember the phrase: *"Obedience is better than sacrifice."* (I Samuel 15:22) Don't draw near to Him with your lips if your heart is not walking in the same direction. (Isaiah 29:13)

God promises to cause His blessings to find you. You don't have to look for them. You don't have to beg for them. You don't have to bargain with God for them. Simply obey. He promises that if you are willing and obedient you will eat the good of the land.

Just imagine yourself going about your daily activities and all of a sudden out of nowhere blessings come. This is God's intent for your life. Your part – obey! His part – He will bless! Your household will be blessed. Your job will be blessed. Your finances will be blessed. Your physical body will be blessed. Your relationships will be blessed. Everything that you set your hand to, will be blessed. Just obey!

APRIL 18

Fasting For Victory!
MATTHEW 4:2

"And when He had fasted forty days and forty nights, He was afterward an hungred." – King James Version

"Jesus prepared for the Test by fasting forty days and forty nights. That left him, of course, in a state of extreme hunger," - The Message Translation

Fasting is a spiritual act that brings a believer to a closer walk with God. Fasting should not just be the act of forsaking your body of food, but should be accompanied by intense prayer to strengthen the spirit and soul. The heart of one fasting is especially sensitive to the things of God during a period of fasting.

Even though, during a period of fasting the inner man is being strengthened the outer man is weakened and susceptible to severe challenges. It is at this time that true believers remember which part of their three-part being should be in charge. Yes, you must allow your spirit to be in control. Your soul and body are being tested and if you allow them to rule your life you place yourself in danger of sin.

Pass the test! Physically you might be hungry. Emotionally you might be challenged. But, spiritually you are being made stronger. You are being prepared for an encounter with the enemy. Let your spirit man push you to victory! Life will be sweeter as you defeat the enemy! Victory will be the new normal for your life.

APRIL 19

What Is Your Decision?

MATTHEW 4:22

And they immediately left the ship and their father, and followed Him. – King James Version

They immediately followed him, leaving the boat and their father behind. – New Living Translation

Where is your level of commitment? How strong is your faith? Who is leading your life today?

Following Jesus requires forsaking all! Forsaking in these terms does not mean not to have care for, but dictates a priority and order that did not exist before. God expects to be first! You cannot have anything or "anybody" before Him. You must prefer Him first.

Your allegiance to Him is displayed not just by you "confessing" to be a Christian. But, your allegiance and devotion is shown through your actions. The Bible says they immediately left and followed Him.

Your prayer life, your praise life, your service life, and your worship life must take the place of your carnal and everyday life. Your actions must correspond to the principles of God's Word. Your giving, your attitude, your sacrifice must all line up with God's will.

Have you left "all"? Are you following Jesus? Are you looking back? Have you totally surrendered and submitted your life to Him? He wants to be your Lord and not just your Saviour!

APRIL 20
It's Your Turn Now!
ROMANS 6:5-11

5 Each of us is raised into a light-filled world by our Father so that we can see where we're going in our new grace-sovereign country. 6 Could it be any clearer? Our old way of life was nailed to the Cross with Christ, a decisive end to that sin-miserable life - no longer at sin's every beck and call! What we believe is this: 7 8 If we get included in Christ's sin-conquering death, we also get included in his life-saving resurrection. 9 We know that when Jesus was raised from the dead it was a signal of the end of death-as-the-end. Never again will death have the last word. 10 When Jesus died, he took sin down with him, but alive he brings God down to us. 11 From now on, think of it this way: Sin speaks a dead language that means nothing to you; God speaks your mother tongue, and you hang on every word. You are dead to sin and alive to God. That's what Jesus did. – The Message Translation

Okay! He got up! He arose! Now, you follow suit!

Yes, it is your turn. Follow the example of your elder brother Jesus Christ. The resurrection has taken place, so you do not have to live bound any longer. You can walk in the newness of life and live life abundantly.

The sin that had you captivated has been defeated. The ways of your old nature no longer have power over you. Do not listen to them calling your name. Those ways are the cries of deception that lead to destruction. Get up from the grave of sin, guilt and shame. Rise to holiness, favour and blessings!

You have the power! God gave you the authority and ability to walk after the Spirit. Live a blessed and bountiful life without condemnation. No more fear. No more worry. No more stress. The sin that had you consumed with grief has been carried away.

The words of Wilbur Chapman seem most appropriate... *"Living, He loved me. Dying, He saved me. Buried, He carried my sins far away. Rising, He justified freely forever. Someday He's coming, oh, glorious day!"*

APRIL 21
You Might As Well Smile
PROVERBS 15:30

The light of the eyes rejoiceth the heart: and a good report maketh the bones fat. – King James Version

A twinkle in the eye means joy in the heart, and good news makes you feel fit as a fiddle. – The Message Translation

Watching the news on the television, reading the newspaper, and listening to the desperation and complaints of society can make you depressed. But, in the midst of all of the negativity around you – your faith can make you strong. Don't be captivated by bad news!

There's still good news! God is still God and He will never change. Sick people are being healed. Broke people are being financially blessed. Relationships are being restored. Lost people are being saved. This is happening right now, today! In your city, In your town, on your street, and in your home! God is doing great things! See the manifestation of His glory.

Change your focus. The enemy only wants you to see the half-empty glass. But, your faith will show you the same glass half-full. The scriptures say that the pure in heart shall see God. Yes, in every situation God will reveal Himself to His people. You will see His goodness, His mercy, His love shine through like the sun even on a cloudy day or at midnight. Smile!

APRIL 22
Holler Louder!
MARK 10:48

And many charged him that he should hold his peace : but he cried the more a great deal, Thou Son of David, have mercy on me. – King James Version

Many tried to hush him up, but he yelled all the louder, "Son of David! Mercy, have mercy on me!" – The Message Translation

Don't be silent when your help is near! That is a trick of the enemy – to shut you up and sit you down. Don't play into his devices! When help is near – do all you can to get the deliverance that you need.

There will be family and friends who may try to discourage you because of your past. They want to highlight your limitations. There are church folk who will tell you "It don't take all of that"! They want to control what you do and how you walk out your relationship with God. You must learn to put those people on IGNORE! That's right! Pay little or no attention to them and their opinion.

Praise God in advance for what you need Him to do and what you are expecting. Praise Him however you want to. Yell! Scream! Run! Dance! Shout! Clap! Stomp! Shake! Whatever you feel led to do to show God that you are excited about who He is and what He is doing – just do it!

He will not only hear your cry – but He will answer and bless you. Your healing, your deliverance, your peace, your prosperity, your needs, and even your desires are en route to you! Just keep giving God praise and thanking Him in advance! Your praise not only gets His attention but it welcomes Him into your situation. And when He shows up – it's a done deal!

APRIL 23

True Giving!
II CORINTHIANS 8:2

How that in a great trial of affliction the abundance of their joy and their deep poverty abounded unto the riches of their liberality. – King James Version

They have been severely tested by the troubles they went through; but their joy was so great that they were extremely generous in their giving, even though they are very poor. – Good News Translation

Fierce troubles came down on the people of those churches, pushing them to the very limit. The trial exposed their true colors: They were incredibly happy, though desperately poor. The pressure triggered something totally unexpected: an outpouring of pure and generous gifts. – The Message Translation

Your giving is not determined by your check book alone, but by your heart. You cannot allow even the symptoms of lack or poverty to contaminate your attitude when it comes to giving. God will bless you for being a blessing especially when you may not be financially in position to do it. God does not measure your giving just by what you give, but He monitors what is left. That is what determines how sacrificial your giving really is.

Your zeal and excitement for giving should be genuine. You should look for good ground to sow seed and places to make spiritual investments for the glory of God. If you have little, dedicate the little you have to God. Trust Him in your giving and watch Him multiply even your seed sown. That is true giving! Giving that comes from the heart and not just the hand!

APRIL 24

"Dunamis" In Your Life!

ACTS 1:8

But ye shall receive power, after that the Holy Ghost is come upon you: and ye shall be witnesses unto me both in Jerusalem, and in all Judaea, and in Samaria, and unto the uttermost part of the earth. – King James Version

What you'll get is the Holy Spirit. And when the Holy Spirit comes on you, you will be able to be my witnesses in Jerusalem, all over Judea and Samaria, even to the ends of the world." – The Message Translation

The fullness of the Holy Spirit in your life empowers you to be a more effective witness in the earth realm. Just imagine, with a bicycle you can ride across town in a half hour time span. But, that same distance can be traveled in a car in possibly 10 or 15 minutes. Use that analogy to see the difference the Holy Spirit in your life. You are equipped with a supernatural force that can help you to accomplish more for the kingdom of God. You can go further, you can last longer, and you can accomplish more all for God's glory.

The Spirit of God makes you a more effective witness. That was the promise made in Acts 1:8. When you are endued with power from on high: look for change at home, in your neighborhood, on your job, at the church, in the city, and all across the nation where you travel. You will be able to reach people regardless of racial, ethnic, social, or sexual orientation or background. God will make you a powerhouse witness tool in the earth realm.

Your life will change. You will experience overcoming power like never before. Even when challenges come in your life, the power of the Holy Ghost will cause you to rise up and still walk in victory. Weapons may form, but they won't prosper. Floods may come, but you won't drown. The manifested presence of God's Spirit in your life will give you a new way to handle life! His dynamite power "*dunamis*" will make you an explosive force to be reckoned with.

APRIL 25
Hold On To Your Faith!
I PETER 1:7

That the trial of your faith, being much more precious than of gold that perisheth, though it be tried with fire, might be found unto praise and honour and glory at the appearing of Jesus Christ: - King James Version

Pure gold put in the fire comes out of it proved pure; genuine faith put through this suffering comes out proved genuine. When Jesus wraps this all up, it's your faith, not your gold, that God will have on display as evidence of his victory. – The Message Translation

Your faith is comparative to gold that endures the test of the fire. Pure gold does not perish but endures. Pure faith is not destroyed but survives. This is your testimony and this is God's glory: your faith.

The mere fact that you have had trials and tribulations is not all that important. For the Bible declares that the rain and sun come to both sinner and saint alike. So, what you go through is not what defines you as an overcomer. But, HOW you go through and HOW you come out is what characterizes you.

No matter what it looks like or feels like – keep standing on God's Word. No matter what you hear or see - keep trusting in God's Word. No matter what others do or where they may go – stay rooted and grounded in God's Word. It is this type faith that will catapult you to the place for God's greatest glory and your greatest victory.

APRIL 26
All For One!
I CORINTHIANS 12:25

That there should be no schism in the body; but that the members should have the same care one for another. – King James Version

The way God designed our bodies is a model for understanding our lives together as a church: every part dependent on every other part, the parts we mention and the parts we don't, - The Message Translation

It's not all about you! The world does not revolve around you. There is no "I" in team. No man is an island. All of these are very familiar phrases that have been used countless times. However, the application of them in practical daily living is sometimes lacking.

The members of the Body of Christ must learn to demonstrate agape and phileo love within their own ranks. The church must learn to build itself up by encouraging and preferring one another. When one hurts, others should run to the rescue of the one hurting and help! When one has a reason to rejoice, all should celebrate by planning and throwing a party.

The same way that your physical body parts work together for the completion of tasks – so should the church. There is no room for competition in church. There is one goal and purpose. Use your individualized gifts for the perfection of the work of the Body as a whole.

APRIL 27

God Is Great And Greatly To Be Praised

EXODUS 15:2

The LORD is my strength and song, and He is become my salvation: He is my God, and I will prepare him an habitation; my father's God, and I will exalt Him. – King James Version

God is my strength, God is my song, and, yes! God is my salvation. This is the kind of God I have and I'm telling the world! This is the God of my father - I'm spreading the news far and wide! – The Message Translation

God is an awesome God. He is faithful to His promises. He always fulfills His Word. He blesses even the undeserving. His love never fails. He protects. He defends. He sustains.

Practice His presence today. Sing songs of praise. Utter testimonies of His goodness. Boast and brag about His awesomeness. Engage in prayer and meditation. Welcome Him into every area of your life today. Allow His glory to fill your atmosphere and environment.

Refuse to be distracted. Don't let trivial nouns (people, places, things or ideas) cloud your revelation of WHO God is to you! Be an intentional praiser. Worship on purpose.

Be an advertisement for GOD today! Everywhere you go, let others know who you serve, who you love, and who you adore.

Make His Name great in the earth realm. Let others see His glory made manifest in your life and encourage them to praise HIM with you! He is worthy!

APRIL 28
Holding On – Is Your Only Option!
ACTS 27:44

And the rest, some on boards, and some on broken pieces of the ship. And so it came to pass, that they escaped all safe to land. – King James Version

Then he ordered the rest to follow on planks or some other pieces [of wood] from the ship. In this way everyone got to shore safely. – God's Word Translation

There is a blessing in obedience and connection. Too often people allow storms to blow them off course. You cannot be discouraged or dismayed to the extent that you give up or lose hope. You have to be assured in your heart that the Word of the Lord will stand forever. Whatever God told you on yesterday is still good today and will continue to be true on tomorrow.

God places safety zones in your life. His Word is a safety zone. Worship is a safety zone. Wise counsel from godly people is a safety zone. And, the church is a safety zone. You have to be careful to never forsake a safety zone. It is the only protection you have from your challenges and the adversary.

When all hell breaks loose in your life, hold on. When the challenges that you face seem to be more than you can handle, hold on even tighter. You may be battered and wearied by the storm, but if you refuse to "let go" you will come out victorious in the end. And, you will have a testimony of how it was the Lord that kept you when you did not know how you would make it. Just hold on!

APRIL 29

Reposition Your Tongue!

EPHESIANS 4:29

Let no corrupt communication proceed out of your mouth, but that which is good to the use of edifying, that it may minister grace unto the hearers. - King James Version

Don't say anything that would hurt [another person]. Instead, speak only what is good so that you can give help wherever it is needed. That way, what you say will help those who hear you. – God's Word Translation

Words are such a powerful tool. Guard your lips and think before you speak. If what you are about to say does not edify, build up, and strengthen – consider being silent. Even when you have been offended, practice the art of forgiveness. Don't lash out or retaliate with evil words.

When you have allowed harsh and unkind words to flow from your lips, it is just like hammering nails in a fence. Even if later in the day you decided to remove the nails, the holes are still there. It is the same when you say hurtful and damaging words.

Treat your words as seeds. Only plant what you want to grow. Speak positive and up-building things about people and to people. Speak uplifting and encouraging words even to yourself. Remember, faith comes by hearing. Allow your ears to only hear the good, and position your heart and mind to believe and expect the same.

APRIL 30
What Did Jesus Say?
LUKE 8:22

Now it came to pass on a certain day, that He went into a ship with his disciples: and He said unto them, Let us go over unto the other side of the lake. And they launched forth. – King James Version

One day he and his disciples got in a boat. "Let's cross the lake," he said. And off they went. – The Message Translation

It is good to hear the voice and commands of the Lord. But, it is even more important to obey His voice and remain faithful regardless of the circumstances. If the Lord invites you to journey to your destiny, be confident that you will arrive safely. Stop allowing the distractions and roadblocks on the journey to dismay you.

In life, there will be many attacks by the adversary. Everything may not work out just as you had hoped or planned. But, there are two spiritual truths you must embrace during your life journey. First, God promised that all things (good and bad) would work together for your good. Secondly, He promised never to leave you nor forsake you.

So, step back and allow Him to be God and be in charge. Stop attempting to make Him your co-pilot. Adopt the attitude of the hymn writer: "Jesus, Saviour, Pilot Me". Follow His lead and you will never go astray. Even when things seem to unravel and fall apart in life, that does not negate His promise to take you to your promised destiny.

MAY 1

Favor Is On The Way!

PROVERBS 3:4

So shalt thou find favour and good understanding in the sight of God and man. – King James Version

If you do this, both God and people will be pleased with you. – Good News Translation

Set yourself up for future blessings by the choices you make today! Life is a harvest and each day you awaken to the fruit of the seeds you have sown yesterday. The blessing and the favor of God are not hard to come by.

God's Word is the most important thing in your life. Read it. Study it. Memorize it! Meditate on it! Share it! And most importantly, Obey it! The blessings that come from allowing God's Word to be alive and reign in you will make you happy and surprise others.

Embrace mercy and truth in every relationship. Sow seeds of graciousness with others and watch the bountiful harvest that God returns unto you! People who don't know you and even some who don't like you will be a blessing to you and they won't even understand why or how. That is how favor works! God conditions and turns hearts.

MAY 2
His Power In Your Life!
ACTS 1:8

But ye shall receive power, after that the Holy Ghost is come upon you: and ye shall be witnesses unto me both in Jerusalem, and in all Judaea, and in Samaria, and unto the uttermost part of the earth. – King James Version

What you'll get is the Holy Spirit. And when the Holy Spirit comes on you, you will be able to be my witnesses in Jerusalem, all over Judea and Samaria, even to the ends of the world. – The Message Translation

It is sad that some have minimized the work of the Holy Spirit to physical and emotional manifestations in a worship service. It seems that some are confident with just coming to church and "getting happy." But, this is not the intent of God in a true believer's life.

God wants to make an impact in the earth realm. He wants to use men, women, boys and girls to be vessels of honor for His glory. God wants non-believers to be encouraged and edified by believers. The true purpose of the power is to be a more effective witness in the earth realm.

Signs and wonders will accompany the lives of true believers. And, the Holy Spirit will not only make you "feel" good, but He will show you how to "be" good. He will lead, guide, direct, teach and comfort you. Being filled with the Spirit is to be under His influence and control.

If you were pulled over today, would you be guilty of a D.U.I. "Driving under the Influence"? You should be LIVING under the influence every day to allow His power to make the maximum impact in the earth realm.

MAY 3
That's Not Faith!
JAMES 2:17-20

Even so faith, if it hath not works, is dead, being alone. Yea, a man may say, Thou hast faith, and I have works: shew me thy faith without thy works, and I will shew thee my faith by my works. Thou believest that there is one God; thou doest well: the devils also believe, and tremble. But wilt thou know, O vain man, that faith without works is dead? – King James Version

Isn't it obvious that God-talk without God-acts is outrageous nonsense? I can already hear one of you agreeing by saying, "Sounds good. You take care of the faith department, I'll handle the works department." Not so fast. You can no more show me your works apart from your faith than I can show you my faith apart from my works. Faith and works, works and faith, fit together hand in glove. Do I hear you professing to believe in the one and only God, but then observe you complacently sitting back as if you had done something wonderful? That's just great. Demons do that, but what good does it do them? Use your heads! Do you suppose for a minute that you can cut faith and works in two and not end up with a corpse on your hands? – The Message Translation

Don't fool yourself! Quoting scriptures and making "confessions of faith" or faith statements is not faith. Decreeing and declaring: "But, I believe..." is not faith either. The Bible says that demons believe as well. (Smile). You don't want to be in that category. Your faith must be more than mere verbal assertions. Faith is much more than just what you say, think or feel.

It is when your actions align themselves with what you are saying is when faith is made manifest. You must "do" what you are saying! Even if what you are believing for, trusting in, or hoping for is not manifest you must change your operation. Walk in it! Embrace it! Live it!

Peter had faith for real. He did not just sit in the boat and wait for Jesus to get there. But, he got out of the boat and walked on the water to where Jesus was. Even though, in the midst of that walk he began to sink – he still had the testimony and example of true faith because of what he did.

Today, tell yourself: "Talk is cheap"! Put actions with your words! Go and embrace and pursue what you are believing God for. God honors real faith. And that is what it takes to please God. No more whining and complaining, action is your objective for today! Do what you are saying and see it come to pass!

MAY 4

Learn And Do Your Part

EPHESIANS 4:16

From Him the whole body, joined and held together by every supporting ligament, grows and builds itself up in love, as each part does its work. – New International Version

Under His control all the different parts of the body fit together, and the whole body is held together by every joint with which it is provided. So when each separate part works as it should, the whole body grows and builds itself up through love. – Good News Translation

When God created you, He gave you purpose and destiny. It is your responsibility to learn the specific calling upon your life and obey His Word in order to be used in the earth realm for His glory. Every person is important in the kingdom. There is a gifting in you that benefits the Body of Christ as a whole.

The Body of Christ is strengthened and made better when each part functions as it was designed to. Don't get lost trying to "do your own thing". But, pray and ask God to reveal unto you exactly how you are to function. The Body suffers when people operate outside of their calling.

Many churches, and organizations within churches, end up with "drama" because people want to do what they want to do. Learn your ministry. Understand your anointing. Realize your purpose. Walk in your calling. You will be renewed and refreshed for being in God's will and others will be blessed because of you doing your part!

MAY 5

Go Through And Come Out
ISAIAH 43:2

When thou passest through the waters, I will be with thee; and through the rivers, they shall not overflow thee: when thou walkest through the fire, thou shalt not be burned; neither shall the flame kindle upon thee. – King James Version

When you're in over your head, I'll be there with you. When you're in rough waters, you will not go down. When you're between a rock and a hard place, it won't be a dead end – The Message Translation

Stay encouraged because you are not alone and you will survive. Yes, there will be challenges in life. But just know that they have no power over your destiny. Your responsibility is to not quit or give up. God will do His part and be your deliverer.

When situations and circumstances evolve accept them for what they are. Do not give them emotional or spiritual power over you. Ask God to reveal the purpose for the challenge. Learn all you can about the reason for the attack. Pray to God and release your faith in Him for Him to simply demonstrate His power and awesomeness.

You are not alone! And when God delivers you, there will be a testimony in your mouth of what He did for you. What you are going through cannot and will not destroy you! You won't drown. You won't burn. But, you will survive!

MAY 6
Obedience Brings Deliverance!
JOHN 9:7

And said unto him, Go, wash in the pool of Siloam, (which is by interpretation, Sent.) He went his way therefore, and washed, and came seeing. – King James Version

and said, "Go, wash at the Pool of Siloam" (Siloam means "Sent"). The man went and washed - and saw. – The Message Translation

God often chooses things that make little to no sense, to intervene and bless you. Your response must be simple obedience. Taking time to think about or consider the directions usually results in doubt, fear, and confusion. The enemy will do anything he can to hinder your obedience.

Don't play into the whims of the enemy. You are not smarter than God. You are not wiser than God. And, until He brings revelation you don't know the mind of God. But, His Spirit will speak to you and share with you God's plan for your life.

Making sense is not a prerequisite for deliverance. Obeying God may seemingly take you out of the way or disturb your comfort zone – but just do it. There is a blessing in doing the unexpected to receive the unimaginable. Give God a try.

MAY 7

Don't Let People Shut You Up!

MARK 10:48

And many charged him that he should hold his peace: but he cried the more a great deal, Thou Son of David, have mercy on me. – King James Version

Many tried to hush him up, but he yelled all the louder, "Son of David! Mercy, have mercy on me!" – The Message Translation

Don't let people control or dictate your relationship with God. People have their own agendas and motives. Some are happy with knowing that you are in a position of need. Some people desire to take advantage of being able to manipulate and control your life because of your dependency upon them. Also, there are others who live with flashlights. As long as they can find something negative about you to shine the light on, it keeps the light (or attention) away from them.

God's response to prayer and praise is to show up and of course "show out." He inhabits the praises of His people. He hears and answers the prayers that are made unto Him. You must learn to be fervent and consistent. Giving up or slowing down is not an option!

Learn what it takes "for you" to get God's attention. It should be based upon His Word and your personal walk (experience) with Him. Stop allowing yourself to try and pattern your relationship with God based upon what others do or have done. God wants you to be unique and simply be yourself. He will ignore those around you, just like you should do!

Your emotions may get His attention, but your faith will move His hand!

MAY 8
Relationship Matters!
RUTH 1:16

But Ruth said, "Don't force me to leave you; don't make me go home. Where you go, I go; and where you live, I'll live. Your people are my people, your God is my god; - The Message Translation

The beauty of the relationship between Ruth and Naomi is that they were in-laws but treated each other like blood relatives or even moreso as friends. The impact of their relationship prompted Ruth to not leave her mother-in-law even after her own husband had died. This action spoke volumes into what had been established down through the years.

As a believer, God wants you to learn to be committed to others no matter what storms, tests, or trials may arise. In order for this to take place you have to make certain that you are connected to people who are part of your destiny. Too often time and energy is wasted on attempting to make people who were only designed to be temporary, permanent in your life.

When you are divinely connected, you will share like passions, desires and goals. Nothing, including time and turmoil, can pull you apart. You will undergird each other and enhance each other's lives. Yes, life will be even better blessed when the right connections are formed and maintained. God positioned you in the body to matter to corresponding parts. Who matters in your life?

MAY 9

Go Get Yours!
II KINGS 7:3

And there were four leprous men at the entering in of the gate: and they said one to another, Why sit we here until we die? – King James Version

Four men who were suffering from a dreaded skin disease were outside the gates of Samaria, and they said to each other, "Why should we wait here until we die? – Good News Translation

Change can be wonderful. If you find yourself in a place of stagnancy, there is no reason to just sit there and complain. There is a better place that God has prepared for you if you simply trust Him and walk towards your blessing.

The four leprous men mentioned in the text refused to sit any longer and simply perish. They made a choice to change. They made a decision to move. And when they moved by faith, even into the enemy's camp, God blessed them. God blessed them to such an extent that He caused fear to rise in their enemies. They ran away without even taking their possessions. When the lepers arrived to the camp it took them four days to gather all of the spoil of the enemy.

If you dare yourself to do something that you have never done, you will definitely see and receive something that you never have had. Yes, change your existence. No more wishful thinking. Just get up and walk in the promise. Wake up from your dream and chase the reality of favor and blessings belonging to you.

MAY 10
Time To Celebrate
ESTHER 9:22

As the days wherein the Jews rested from their enemies, and the month which was turned unto them from sorrow to joy, and from mourning into a good day: that they should make them days of feasting and joy, and of sending portions one to another, and gifts to the poor. – King James Version

As days on which the Jews had rest from their haters, and the month which for them was turned from sorrow to joy, and from weeping to a good day: and that they were to keep them as days of feasting and joy, of sending offerings to one another and good things to the poor. – Basic Bible In English Translation

When God has been good to you and has caused your enemies to be defeated, it is time to celebrate. When you can look at how God has turned bad things around in your favor, it is time to celebrate. When your life has been spared and your struggle is over, it is time to celebrate.

The Jews had been condemned to die because of the wicked plot of Haman. However, God intervened and through the works of Esther, Mordecai and the king all that had been planned for the Jews had now been turned around and done to their enemies. Their sorrow had been turned to joy and they declared a time of feasting and joy.

Today, consider the goodness of God in your life. Reflect on the victories that God has given you. Think about the negative that could have been, but how God has brought you out. Muse upon the favor and blessings God has poured upon you. Consider the grace and mercy that has been made manifest in your life. God has prepared a table before you – even in the presence of your enemies!

Now, do as the Jews and celebrate. Take this opportunity to bless somebody. Even go and be a blessing in the lives of those less fortunate. Share what God has blessed you with into the lives of others. Watch and see how God blesses you even more and how your joy increases because of your acts of kindness. That is true celebration – Be so happy that you are a blessing!

MAY 11

Great Things Are Still Coming!

HEBREWS 10:35

Cast not away therefore your confidence, which hath great recompence of reward. – King James Version

So don't throw it all away now. You were sure of yourselves then. It's still a sure thing! – The Message Translation

Difficult days may come. Perilous times may be present. Persecution may arise. Distress and dismay may show up. But, none of these things should change your first hope.

Often people allow what they are going through to hinder their progress for where they are going to. But, it is God's will that you learn to wipe your eyes and keep fighting, keep marching, keep hoping, and keep trusting. Keep the same excitement that you had at the beginning of the journey!

Your prophetic word for the day is: "It's still gonna happen"! What? The promise that God made! The prophecy that was spoken! The word that excited you and stirred hope in you! Keep your faith working for you and endure until the manifestation arrives. God won't let you down. Great things are on the way.

MAY 12
Help Is Everpresent
HEBREWS 2:18

For in that He himself hath suffered being tempted, He is able to succour them that are tempted. – King James Version

He would have already experienced it all himself - all the pain, all the testing - and would be able to help where help was needed. – The Message Translation

Even when you feel like your back is against the wall – be encouraged for you are not alone. Not only is God ever present as "Jehovah Shammah" to help you, but He has a point of reference. Yes, every test or trial that could come against you, He has experienced it so He knows exactly how you feel.

He is less than a call away. You can call His Name or just think about Him and He will show up and show out. So, in the midst of your challenge begin to praise and worship Him. Change your attitude and focus. Don't allow the enemy to make you feel hopeless. Keep hope alive by trusting in God.

Yes, He is there! Where? Right there - where you are! On the mountain or in the valley – be confident and know that He is there. You do not have to go through the test alone. He has already passed the test. If you follow His lead, you will come out victorious. He knows, He cares and He shares.

MAY 13
The Spirit Of A True Mother
JUDGES 5:7

The inhabitants of the villages ceased, they ceased in Israel, until that I Deborah arose, that I arose a mother in Israel. – King James Version

Warriors became fat and sloppy, no fight left in them. Then you, Deborah, rose up; you got up, a mother in Israel. – The Message Translation

Giving birth to a child is a wonderful and awesome experience. But, being a mother also involves the molding and shaping of that child. Motherhood encompasses the sorrows and joys of praying, correcting, celebrating, chastising, and so much more.

A real mother will fuss and tell you that she is not doing anything else. And then, she will be the first one to show up to help. Real mothers have faith. They believe against all odds. They have real faith because they "work" their faith by continuously intervening and encouraging.

In the scripture passage above, Deborah brought back life. She was the catalyst to encourage the people to fulfill their destiny. That is the role that many mothers take today. They are encouragers. They are cheerleaders. They are personal trainers. A real mother refuses to accept failure or defeat. She always believes in her child. She rallies behind them until success is made manifest.

MAY 14

Get Busy For Others!

GALATIANS 6:10

As we have therefore opportunity, let us do good unto all men, especially unto them who are of the household of faith.
— King James Version

Right now, therefore, every time we get the chance, let us work for the benefit of all, starting with the people closest to us in the community of faith. — The Message Translation

God has been good to you. Now it is time for you to reciprocate that goodness to others. You are in need of a blessing from God. Now it is time for you to sow into the lives of others and watch God bring the same harvest into yours. Today is the day to take and make time to be a blessing!

Sometimes life's hustle and bustle gets the best of you. You get up running and go all throughout the day only to get to the end of the day and ask yourself, "Where did time go?" But, it is God's will and His plan for you to slow down long enough to look around you. Find someone that has a deficit where you have abundance and begin to share.

Share your joy. Share your happiness. Share your resources. Share your talent. Start with fellow believers and continue into the world by allowing your light to shine before all men. This is God's desire in your life – that you would allow your hands to be His, your feet to be His, your mouth to be His. Be a vessel of honor and let God bless others through you!

MAY 15

Kingdom Blessings!

LUKE 5:7

And they beckoned unto their partners, which were in the other ship, that they should come and help them. And they came, and filled both the ships, so that they began to sink. – King James Version

They waved to their partners in the other boat to come help them. They filled both boats, nearly swamping them with the catch. – The Message Translation

There is no competition in the kingdom! The mentality of trying to do better than others is worldly and fleshly. The Word of God encourages you to place others' good even before your own.

When your motive is purely to glorify God, it does not matter who gets the credit. All that matters is that someone gets helped and blessed. When people are saved and delivered, everyone should rejoice. When churches grow and do great exploits, all should rejoice along with them. When Christian businesses are booming and expanding, everyone should rejoice and continue to support them.

In the kingdom you are connected. You are all blessed together. When one succeeds, all succeed. When one triumphs, all win. Stay kingdom minded and work together for the up-building of the kingdom! Let the King be glorified and praised!

MAY 16
Talk To Your Body!
I THESSALONIANS 4:4

That every one of you should know how to possess his vessel in sanctification and honour; - King James Version

He wants all of you to learn to control your own bodies. You must live in a way that is holy. You must live with honor. – New International Reader's Version

Learn to appreciate and give dignity to your body, - The Message Translation

Your body is the temple of the Holy Ghost. Each day you should strive to honor that temple and remind yourself that God lives in you. Your thoughts, beliefs and attitudes must line up with God's Word. These are the things within that control the things without. The words that you say and the actions that you take should be representative of the One who resides within you.

When your soulish man (your mind, will, intellect and emotions) attempt to derail your spirit man's attempt to walk in holiness – open your mouth. Begin to make affirmations and declarations of who you are in Christ Jesus. Command your lips to only praise. Command your tongue to speak only truth. Command your feet to go only where God leads you. Command your hands to be instruments for God's use.

Talk to your body. Remind your body that you are holy and sanctified! Yesterday is gone and this is a brand new day. Love to live for Jesus!

MAY 17
Conforming To The Christ!
ROMANS 12:2

And be not conformed to this world: but be ye transformed by the renewing of your mind, that ye may prove what is that good, and acceptable, and perfect, will of God. – King James Version

Don't become so well-adjusted to your culture that you fit into it without even thinking. Instead, fix your attention on God. You'll be changed from the inside out. Readily recognize what he wants from you, and quickly respond to it. Unlike the culture around you, always dragging you down to its level of immaturity, God brings the best out of you, develops well-formed maturity in you. - The Message Translation

Sometimes people get caught up in trying to please others to make them happy. Sometimes it happens in homes, or on jobs, or even in the church! But, you have to be careful that you don't lose yourself in pleasing flesh and then you miss pleasing God.

God's Word is your blueprint. Jesus Christ is your example. The Holy Spirit is your guide. God wanted to make certain that you did not go astray, so He revealed Himself in His fullness to make certain that every part of you (spirit, soul and body) knew that He had a plan for your life.

Now, make a conscious decision to live only for Him. When others attempt to get you to do it their way – immediately check with God and find out if it is His way! You devalue and cheapen yourself when you become carbon copies of other people. But, you become an invaluable treasure when you simply pattern your life after the divine purpose and plan of God and become the awesome original He designed you to be.

MAY 18
A Simple Act Of Obedience
JOHN 2:1-5

1 And the third day there was a marriage in Cana of Galilee; and the mother of Jesus was there: 2 And both Jesus was called, and his disciples, to the marriage. 3 And when they wanted wine, the mother of Jesus saith unto him, They have no wine. 4 Jesus saith unto her, Woman, what have I to do with thee? mine hour is not yet come. 5 His mother saith unto the servants, Whatsoever he saith unto you, do it.

God places opportunities for you to be a blessing to others everyday. You must disregard your own agenda and simply obey. Jesus' mother intervened in a natural situation in search of a supernatural solution. And a simple act of obedience turned into a blessing for all involved.

Sometimes you do not see the overall impact of fulfilling a simple request. But, learn to live with humility and operate in obedience. If you are asked to sing a song, simply sing it without making a lot of excuses. You never know who will be encouraged by your song ministry. If you are asked to participate on a program, do it without fanfare. Your participation may actually serve to strengthen and help someone else.

Prepare yourself to be used of God. He will reveal to others the anointing and power that He has placed within you. And when someone makes a request for you to be helpful – just do it! It is a simple act of obedience that often has a domino effect of blessing others all around you.

MAY 19

Keep On Keeping On!
LUKE 18:1

And he spake a parable unto them to this end, that men ought always to pray, and not to faint; - King James Version

Jesus told them a story showing that it was necessary for them to pray consistently and never quit. – The Message Translation

Have you ever felt that you were at the end of your rope and did not have the strength or desire to tie a knot and hold on? Have you ever felt like you had exhausted all of your energy and resources? Have you ever felt like the battle was too long and too fierce, and you wanted to just wave your white flag of surrender?

Giving up is NOT an option for a believer! You have to remind yourself that the God you serve will manifest your victory at the right time and place. Your responsibility is to simply pray and praise. Keep your head up and be confident that you will come out on the winning side.

You must be persistent like the woman before the unjust judge. She was going to keep crying out until he ruled in her favor. You have to be like Jacob who wrestled all night long with the angel. He was determined not to let go until he was blessed.

You need that same stamina and persistence in your daily life. Quitting is not an option. Giving up is not part of the plan. But, you must endure and hang in there! In the words of the little old lady, "You gotta' keep on keeping on".

MAY 20

Get Dressed For Victory

EPHESIANS 6:10-18

10 Finally, be strong in the Lord and in his mighty power. 11 Put on the full armor of God so that you can take your stand against the devil's schemes. 12 For our struggle is not against flesh and blood, but against the rulers, against the authorities, against the powers of this dark world and against the spiritual forces of evil in the heavenly realms. 13 Therefore put on the full armor of God, so that when the day of evil comes, you may be able to stand your ground, and after you have done everything, to stand. 14 Stand firm then, with the belt of truth buckled around your waist, with the breastplate of righteousness in place, 15 and with your feet fitted with the readiness that comes from the gospel of peace. 16 In addition to all this, take up the shield of faith, with which you can extinguish all the flaming arrows of the evil one. 17 Take the helmet of salvation and the sword of the Spirit, which is the word of God. 18 And pray in the Spirit on all occasions with all kinds of prayers and requests. With this in mind, be alert and always keep on praying for all the saints.

Have you ever lost a battle? Have you ever suffered defeat? It surely is not a good feeling. When you know that you are a child of God, you feel as though victory should always be on your side. But, be honest and ask yourself, "Do I have in my possession what I need for victory?"

Take off doubt, put on hope. Take off fear, put on courage. Take off shame, put on confidence. Take off bad language and put on praises. Take off negative words and thoughts, put on the Word of God.

Today, dress yourself for victory. When you are under attack or suffer a setback, run to God's Word. For God's Word makes several promises to you. God's Word will be your shield and buckler. His Word will be your weapon of mass destruction. God's Word will be your sword of the Spirit. God's Word will sustain and keep you. God's Word will preserve and strengthen you.

Even though, weapons may form against you – they cannot prosper. Remember, God has equipped you with a spiritual arsenal that will keep you on the winning side. Keep God's Word in your heart. Let it always be on your lips. Keep it at the forefront of your mind. And you will see victory again and again.

MAY 21

The Perfect Prayer Partner
ROMANS 8:26

Likewise the Spirit also helpeth our infirmities: for we know not what we should pray for as we ought: but the Spirit itself maketh intercession for us with groanings which cannot be uttered. – King James Version

Meanwhile, the moment we get tired in the waiting, God's Spirit is right alongside helping us along. If we don't know how or what to pray, it doesn't matter. He does our praying in and for us, making prayer out of our wordless sighs, our aching groans. – The Message Translation

Prayer is so vitally important to the life of the believer. The old folk used to sing, "Prayer changes things". Well, prayer can change things, people, anything and everything. But, for the prayer to be effective it must be in accordance with God's will. When prayer is made based upon God's plan, you can be assured that it is already a done deal.

Because your mind is finite, there are times when praying completely on your own is inadequate. You honestly cannot think of everything or even remember everything that you should be praying about. God has sent His Holy Spirit to live within you. According to the Word of God, "the Spirit searcheth all things, even the deep things of God". Now, just think about how awesome it is to have the Spirit of God come alongside you to help you pray.

You can be assured that what the Spirit speaks is God's will and will come to pass. You could not find a better prayer partner. Open your mouth today and allow the rivers of living water to flow out of your belly (your innermost being). God has some things to say that will bless you and others all around you.

MAY 22
God Expects More!
GENESIS 9:7

And you, be ye fruitful, and multiply; bring forth abundantly in the earth, and multiply therein. – King James Version

You're here to bear fruit, reproduce, lavish life on the Earth, live bountifully!" – The Message Translation

God has blessed you and empowered you with an awesome tool called "Faith". With faith you have creative power, increasing power, overcoming power, and much more. But until you exercise your faith nothing will happen. That's right – get up and do something!

God has created and designed you to do great things and make a great impact in the earth realm. His desire is that you take what He has invested in you and operate in His principle of "sowing and reaping, seedtime and harvest". He wants you to be blessed to be a blessing. This only happens when you take the first step of sowing.

Learn to sow your time, talent and treasure in things of the kingdom and watch God bring an awesome harvest to the works of your hands. But, remember to be a successful farmer – even after sowing you must take care of the ground in which you have sown. You must fertilize and care for the plants that are produced. When you are faithful to your part, God who is always faithful will bless you even more.

MAY 23
God Honors Faith!
MATTHEW 21:32

For John came unto you in the way of righteousness, and ye believed him not: but the publicans and the harlots believed him: and ye, when ye had seen it, repented not afterward, that ye might believe him. – King James Version

John came to you showing you the right road. You turned up your noses at him, but the crooks and whores believed him. Even when you saw their changed lives, you didn't care enough to change and believe him. – The Message Translation

What will it take for some to believe? Why do some get upset when God honors the faith of others?

God is no respector of persons. What He makes available for one, He makes available for others. He is an equal opportunity God. Caution must be taken not to allow doubt or faithlessness in your spirit. Care must be taken not to look upon others with disdain who have the blessings of God manifesting in their life.

Heaven will be heavily populated with many people who others wrote off. And on the opposite end of the spectrum, there are many who have made reservations for hell and don't even realize that they are going. Why? Unbelief.

To experience the glory of God – have a childlike faith and believe God regardless of what you see, hear or experience. Salvation is available for all who believe. Prosperity belongs to those who will sow. Healing will be obtained by those who walk by faith. Deliverance will be maintained by those who embrace it.

If you miss out on any of the wonderful things that God is offering – don't be upset with others. Grab a mirror and minister to yourself and encourage yourself. Believe and receive!

MAY 24

How Much Do You Have In The Bank?
II KINGS 20:2-5

Hezekiah turned from Isaiah and faced God, praying: Remember, O God, who I am, what I've done! I've lived an honest life before you, My heart's been true and steady, I've lived to please you; lived for your approval. And then the tears flowed. Hezekiah wept. Isaiah, leaving, was not halfway across the courtyard when the word of God stopped him: "Go back and tell Hezekiah, prince of my people, 'God's word, Hezekiah! From the God of your ancestor David: I've listened to your prayer and I've observed your tears. I'm going to heal you. In three days you will walk on your own legs into The Temple of God. – The Message Translation

Have you ever been in such an emotional state that you could hardly function? You tried to sing but the melody would not come. You tried to pray but could not find the words to say. You tried to read God's Word but could not focus. It is a lonely and defeated feeling.

However, if you take the example of Hezekiah today – you will find a merciful and favorable God yet reaching out to you in the midst of your calamity. In the midst of your trial, He will deliver.

When you had the opportunity, how much did you pray? When nothing was wrong, how intense was your praise? When your money was good, how faithful were you in your tithes and offering? When your health was fine, how intense was your worship?

When you make regular deposits in your spiritual bank, you will have sufficient funds to make a withdrawal in your time of need. When you are overwhelmed and don't know what to do – simply turn your face to God and He will hear your cry, see your tears, and pity your groans. He will remember what you have done and He will bless you over and over again.

MAY 25

Be Filled With The Holy Ghost
JOHN 7:38

He that believeth on me, as the scripture hath said, out of his belly shall flow rivers of living water. – King James Version

Rivers of living water will brim and spill out of the depths of anyone who believes in me this way, just as the Scripture says." – The Message Translation

Visualize a man sitting next to a river. The man is thirsty so he leans over and drinks water from the river. Is he "filled"? Technically speaking, no! Even if he drinks a great amount, he is still not "filled". Yet, the river from which he drank is now a part of him. Take this same man and place him in the river. No, not waist deep. Place him on the bottom of the river. How much water do you suppose would he consume (or would consume him)?

That same picture is what God wants to do with you. Do not be satisfied with simply coming unto Jesus, meeting Him and then leaving going on your way without allowing Him to bring to maturity all that He desires to do within us. God wants the rivers of the Holy Ghost to consume every area of your spirit, soul, and your body. Just like the man at the bottom the river, God wants you to die to sin, the flesh, and self, and then learn to live unto Him.

The Baptism in the Holy Ghost is an integral part of every powerful believer's life. For this experience is the same experience that occurred in the disciples' and others' lives all through the Book of Acts. If you think you have the power now, accept the challenge to allow the rivers to flow in your life. If you think you're a great prayer warrior, teacher of the Word, witness or child of God — you would be pleasantly surprised after experiencing the Baptism in the Holy Ghost.

MAY 26

Duty and Sacrificial Love
I JOHN 3:16

Hereby perceive we the love of God, because He laid down His life for us: and we ought to lay down our lives for the brethren. – King James Version

This is how we've come to understand and experience love: Christ sacrificed his life for us. This is why we ought to live sacrificially for our fellow believers, and not just be out for ourselves. – The Message Translation

Real mothers will go without eating just so their child will not starve. That happens because of love. True friends will take away from their own bill money just to keep the lights on at someone else's house. That happens because of love. Committed and dedicated men and women volunteer to go to war to ensure liberty and justice for all. That happens because of love.

Jesus Christ demonstrated the true love of God by sacrificing His life for all. It did not matter what condition you were in, His love superseded your sin. The scriptures declare, *"But God commendeth his love toward us, in that, while we were yet sinners, Christ died for us."* (Romans 5:8). That happened because of love.

This is the same demonstration of duty and love many soldiers down through the ages have exemplified. They have given their lives even for some who did not even care that they were in harm's way. But, their love for their country and the principles for which it stands compelled them to live sacrificial lives.

Take time today to thank and praise God first for Jesus who set the example of sacrificial living. Then take time and reflect upon the memories of those fallen soldiers who gave their lives for the cause of others. And finally, find some who are still on the battlefield and tell them "Thank you for all that you do" and pray God's blessing upon their life.

MAY 27
Live By The Word!
EPHESIANS 5:15

See then that ye walk circumspectly, not as fools, but as wise,
- King James Version

So then, be very careful how you live. Don't live like foolish people but like wise people. – God's Word Translation

Decisions and choices that you make govern the actions that you take. Those actions become the seeds that are sown which determine your future and your harvest. You must learn to live your life by the Word of God. Don't allow feelings or emotions to get in the way. Do not allow the opinions of others to cloud your decision-making.

Learn to pray about everything! Seek God's face on everything you do. When you read, study, and obey His Word you position yourself to operate in the wisdom of God and thus receive the manifested blessings of God.

God will give wisdom to those who ask. God's wisdom will cause you to operate in a way that will breathe new life into your relationships, your finances, your career, your physical body, your mental state, and into every other area of your life. Stop allowing the enemy, people, and your own emotions to hinder your walk. But, walk carefully always keeping the Word of God first!

MAY 28
God Wants To Use You!
II CORINTHIANS 4:7

But we have this treasure in earthen vessels, that the excellency of the power may be of God, and not of us. – King James Version

If you only look at us, you might well miss the brightness. We carry this precious Message around in the unadorned clay pots of our ordinary lives. That's to prevent anyone from confusing God's incomparable power with us. – The Message Translation

God is so awesome. He is so wonderful. He loved you so much that He made a spiritual investment in you. Eventhough, He knew all about you. Yes, with all of your flaws and imperfections – God invested His power in you in order to make an impact in the earth realm. He has entrusted you with the glorious testimony and message of the Gospel of Jesus Christ.

Never forget that you are still human. Yes, created in the image and likeness of God – but still human. You are trapped in an earth suit while in the earth realm. The problem with an earth suit is that it is susceptible to faults and failures. This is why each day you are still "working out" your salvation with fear and trembling. You must always focus on asking God to be your strength even in weakness. The earth suit helps you not to get the big head and think more highly of yourself than you ought to.

Because of the warfare in the flesh, some people discount God's Spirit. But, you must understand that God uses ordinary people –

people with issues, people with problems, people with conditions – to do His work. There are a long list of imperfect people that God used to bring "perfection" or spiritual maturity and deliverance to the earth realm.

Abraham lied. Moses murdered. David committed adultery. Peter cursed. Paul persecuted. And the list goes on. Yet, these were great men of God "in earthen vessels". God used them to do great things. Abraham was the Father of Faith. Moses led the Children of Israel out of Egypt. David was a man after God's own heart. Peter had the revelation of who Jesus is and preached and thousands were added to the church. Paul wrote over half of the New Testament.

Whoever you are – remember God wants to use you. Pray every day for God's Spirit to help you to overcome your earth suit and stay in position to be used of God. Keep your attitude in check. Monitor your relationships with others. Strive to live holy and walk upright everyday. But, even moreso never forget that God has entrusted you with an awesome gift to be shared in the earth realm – don't allow "you" to get in the way of the move of God.

MAY 29
Tell The Children
I CORINTHIANS 14:33

We will not hide them from their children; we will tell the next generation the praiseworthy deeds of the LORD, His power, and the wonders He has done. – New International Version

We're not keeping this to ourselves, we're passing it along to the next generation - God's fame and fortune, the marvelous things he has done. – The Message Translation

You have a spiritual and moral responsibility to help your children! They need to know who God is and what He has done and what He can do! With this knowledge of God – they will be able to excel and do great things in the kingdom. You will be proud, God will be glorified, and they will be edified.

They need to hear you praying, see you praising, and watch you living sanctified lives to God's glory and praise. Share with them your struggles and your pain. Let them know if it had not been for God on your side, you would not even be able to be with them today. They should learn how to strengthen their relationship with God as they hear your testimony and watch your lifestyle.

You don't have to be perfect – just be real. They can appreciate that! Share with them the good and bad and have no secrets! The kingdom of God will be made stronger because of the investment you make in the lives of the children!

MAY 30
His Glory In Your Life!
ROMANS 6:4

Therefore we are buried with him by baptism into death: that like as Christ was raised up from the dead by the glory of the Father, even so we also should walk in newness of life.

Jesus is your example of how to live the new life God has made available for you. Do not pattern your life after flesh, but look unto Jesus the author and finisher of your faith. As you identify with what Jesus did you will see God at work in your life.

Jesus took your sins and carried them far away. As He died and arose by the glory of the Father, He gave you the opportunity to do the same. You can die to sin and live a new holy and sanctified life by the glory of the Father. Allow your old nature to die. Do not resuscitate or resurrect your old man. But, allow God to bring a glorified new man into existence.

God is willing to show you how to live the new life. He sends His Word! His written Word. His preached Word. His revealed Word. His manifested Word. His Word allows His glory to be made manifest in your life. Yes, from glory to glory you will be changed. You will be transformed.

It is a marvelous miracle. God's glory made manifest in your life. Yes, when you are born again it is God being glorified in the fact that what was once lost is now found. It is the glory of God that saves. It is the glory of God that renews. Let His glory show forth in your life!

MAY 31
Do You Really Believe?
MATTHEW 9:28

And when He was come into the house, the blind men came to Him: and Jesus saith unto them, Believe ye that I am able to do this? They said unto him, Yea, Lord. – King James Version

When Jesus got home, the blind men went in with him. Jesus said to them, "Do you really believe I can do this?" They said, "Why, yes, Master!" – The Message Translation

Sometimes the odds you face may seem incredible. Obstacles and challenges that come your way appear to be more than you can bear. Be careful not to get lost in the problem, when the solution is always before you. Simply believe.

You don't have to know "how" God is going to do it. "When" He is going to do it should not even be a concern. Your faith must kick in and simply rest in the assurance that He will do for you what you cannot do for yourself.

His Word never changes! His promises never fail. He is the healer. He is the deliverer. He is the way maker. He is the keeper.

Just know that you do not serve a past-tense God. He is ever-present! Always showing up and showing out in your life! Just believe!

JUNE 1
Why Are You Not Hungry?
MATTHEW 5:6

Blessed are they which do hunger and thirst after righteousness: for they shall be filled. – King James Version

"You're blessed when you've worked up a good appetite for God. He's food and drink in the best meal you'll ever eat. – The Message Translation

FOOD is a basic need for the human body! When God created you – He made you dependent upon food in order for your body to function properly. Hunger is a normal, natural instinct to address a basic need for the human body. When a person does not experience hunger – that is a true tell sign that something is wrong or malfunctioning on the inside. The malfunction could be physiological or psychological!

Consider Your Appetite
1. If you are not eating – something is wrong
2. If you are not getting a balanced diet – something will be wrong
3. If you are not getting fluids – you will dehydrate

The same principles in the natural also apply to the spiritual! When you don't have a desire for the Word of God – something is wrong within you. When you don't get a balanced feeding of God's Word – you are setting yourself up for imbalance and potential disaster.

Your spiritual food is God's Word! You need God's Word to survive! You must read it, study it, hear it, meditate upon it, and most important apply it and live it! Some people are spiritually sick because of a lack of God's Word!

God promised that those who hunger and thirst would be empowered to prosper and be filled. Some people are not equipped to do work in the kingdom because they have no desire to get what it takes to effectively operate in the Kingdom. Develop a hunger for God's Word.

JUNE 2

Who Is Praying For You?

I SAMUEL 7:8

They said to Samuel, "Do not stop crying out to the LORD our God for us, that He may rescue us from the hand of the Philistines." – New International Version

They pleaded with Samuel, "Pray with all your might! And don't let up! Pray to God, our God, that he'll save us from the boot of the Philistines." – The Message Translation

Intercession is standing in the gap for another. It is a powerful and effective tool in the prayer ministry. Learn to connect with people who are connected to God. Having others to pray on your behalf does not imply that you don't know how to pray for yourself. But, a spiritual principle of "touching and agreeing" is activated.

God promised that if you connected with someone that He would honor the faith of that union. Whatever you bind on earth, He would bind in the heavens. And whatever you loose on earth, He will also loose in the spirit realm. What you are going through is not just a natural encounter.

Life is a spiritual battle. The enemy is scheming and plotting to defeat you at any cost. When you employ the spiritual strength of others, you engage in offensive and defensive spiritual maneuvers that bring victory to your situation. Just make certain to get someone on your side who will cry out on your behalf with spiritual fervency and effectiveness.

JUNE 3
Bring Somebody Back!
II CORINTHIANS 5:18

And all things are of God, who hath reconciled us to Himself by Jesus Christ, and hath given to us the ministry of reconciliation; - King James Version

All this comes from the God who settled the relationship between us and him, and then called us to settle our relationships with each other. – The Message Translation

You have a Christian duty to the same thing for others that God did for you! God brought you back into fellowship with Himself through the shed blood of His Son Jesus on the cross of Calvary. He did not hold you accountable for all the wrong you had done. But, instead He allowed His Only Begotten Son to pay the cost for your sins. He forgave you and gave you a new opportunity to live an abundant life through Him.

The "finger pointing" ministry that some people embrace is not the way God treated you. He loved you in spite of. He loved you instead of. He loved you because of. Do you have the "love of God" manifest in your life?

Find someone who is lost and tell them how much God loves them. God's love, evident through your actions, will change lives. Love them to repentance. Love them to confession. Love them to sanctification. Love them to holiness. The love of God is greater than anything!

JUNE 4
When The Heat Is Turned Up!
DANIEL 3:17-18

If it be so, our God whom we serve is able to deliver us from the burning fiery furnace, and He will deliver us out of thine hand, O king. But if not, be it known unto thee, O king, that we will not serve thy gods, nor worship the golden image which thou hast set up.

How many go willingly into a fire? If anything, people run, hide, and pray not to go through anything. Prayers get longer and praise gets louder! "Lord, please help me!" "Oh, Jesus!" Somehow, they hope that they can get God to change His mind regarding certain tests, storms, and trials. Scripture teaches that it is not just emotions that move God. But, it is your faith that moves the hand and the heart of God. Learn that going through makes you stronger. You should be made better and not bitter because of your trials.

If your steps are ordered by the Lord, you must learn that just as there are mountaintops, there are also valleys that must be trod. If the Lord is truly ordering your steps, why would you "rebuke" the Lord? Sometimes, you must learn to accept your plight in life and know that God is yet able to bring forth the deliverance that you need. You must have faith as the Hebrew boys. You must walk with your chests pushed out and your head held up high, with the testimony in your mouth, "Our God is able to deliver us! And, if He does not deliver us, it does not mean that He can't!"

You must walk in victory even in the midst of what you are going through, knowing that you are not walking alone. You must ignore whatever is going on around you and trust the God who said, "He would never leave you nor forsake you." Walter Hawkins recorded a song many years ago that had great truth to it: "Don't Wait Till The Battle's Over – Shout Now"! That is so true. Because you do know in the end you are going to win. You must believe that you are already a winner.

JUNE 5

Disappointments Come

I SAMUEL 30:6

David was in great danger; for the people spoke of stoning him, because all the people were bitter in spirit for their sons and daughters. But David strengthened himself in the Lord his God. – New Revised Standard

There will be days when it seems that nothing is working out in your favor. There will be times when everything that can go wrong, seems to go wrong. You begin to feel powerless and useless. Doubt comes to blur your vision. Insecurity comes to cloud your confidence.

These are the days and times that you have to be still and listen for that still, small voice deep within urging you to "go on", "fight on", and "hold on". Do not wait for your neighbor or friend to stop by and speak wonderful words of encouragement to you. You do not have time to wait for the prophet or preacher to show up and speak life into your situation.

Get up from your misery. Wipe your eyes of dismay. And begin to remind yourself of all that God has promised you. Take your mirror (the Word of God – James 1:25) and remind yourself of who and what God said you are. Pat yourself on the back and tell yourself that "it's already alright". And then stand still and trust that God has your back and that this is one of those "all things work together for good days".

JUNE 6
God Ain't Sharing His Glory!
ISAIAH 42:8

I am the LORD: that is My name: and My glory will I not give to another, neither My praise to graven images. – King James Version

I am God. That's my name. I don't franchise my glory, don't endorse the no-god idols. – The Message Translation

Praise God for your anointing and your gifting – but never get it twisted. It is not yours. It is God's! Whatever good there is within you and whatever good flows from you is only because God put it there and allowed it to be so.

It is dangerous not to give credit to God for who He is and what He has done! First and foremost, never take credit for what you could not do alone without Him. Always be mindful to acknowledge that all of your accomplishments are because of God and God alone.

Secondly, be careful not to put men and women on pedestals. No matter how anointed they are they are still only vessels. Be careful not to begin to glorify them and forget the God who blessed them who should be receiving all the glory, honor and praise. In society today, people have a tendency to get flesh-oriented and begin to celebrate and worship flesh. This is not God's will or plan.

It is good to compliment people on a job well done. It is right to thank people for their work in the kingdom. But care and caution must be taken to never cross the line of giving high praise and honor to them when it belongs to God.

JUNE 7
Spirit-Filled Day!
EPHESIANS 5:18

And be not drunk with wine, wherein is excess; but be filled with the Spirit; – King James Version

Don't get drunk on wine, which leads to wild living. Instead, be filled with the Spirit – God's Word Translation

Don't get drunk with wine, because it makes you lose control. Instead, keep on being filled with the Spirit – Complete Jewish Bible

An excess of wine can alter your perception and control your actions. Have you ever heard the expression, "That's that wine talking!" – in response to someone who was drunk? Alcoholic beverages are also called "spirits". Drinking alcohol can cause people to act in a variety of odd ways. The writer makes a comparison between wine and the spirit of God.

Your challenge today is to be filled with the Spirit of God. When you talk, let others say "That's the Spirit of God talking". When people see how you respond and react, let there be no doubt in their mind that you are under the influence of the Holy Spirit. Allow God's Spirit to control every part of your life.

He is the Comforter. He has been called to lead, guide, and direct you. He speaks to you. He seals you. He teaches you. He reminds you of what God's Word says. He intercedes for you. He searches your heart.

Your challenge today: Pray without ceasing. Pray until the Spirit of God takes over your prayer language. Praise into worship. Praise God until you reach that place where the Spirit of God takes you into sweet fellowship with God. Read the Word. Allow God's Word to consume you to the extent that joy and peace prevail regardless of any challenges that you go through.

JUNE 8
Blessed With Power – Twice!
ROMANS 8:14-17

"For as many as are led by the Spirit of God, they are the sons of God. For ye have not received the spirit of bondage again to fear; but ye have received the Spirit of adoption, whereby we cry Abba, Father. The Spirit Itself beareth witness with our spirit, that we are the children of God: And if children, then heirs..."

Your inheritance in the Lord affords you certain rights and privileges. Just because of who you are (and whose you are) there is authority that has been given to you. You are doubly blessed with both exousia and dunamis. Both are power gifts from God.

Exousia is the authority, or right or privilege that has been afforded to believers. Exousia is good, but God knew that you would need more than just the "legal right" in order to effect your victory in the earth realm. He knew that you would not only need power that "says something", but you also would need power that "does something".

The other word – dunamis – means special miraculous power. Think of it as the very power of God, because God is the only one who can work a miracle. In the Book of Acts, Chapter 1 and verse 8 the Word of God declares, *"But ye shall receive power..."* This power is not just referring to the right or authority to be effective, but the very ability to accomplish what needs to take place.

So God had blessed you not only with power that says who you are and what your rights are, but He has blessed you with power that the devil has to flee, mountains have to come down, valleys have to come up and crooked places are made straight.

JUNE 9
Use The Throne – Not The Phone!

JEREMIAH 33:3

Call unto me, and I will answer thee, and shew thee great and mighty things, which thou knowest not. – King James Version

'Call to me and I will answer you. I'll tell you marvelous and wondrous things that you could never figure out on your own.' – The Message Translation

Regardless if it is a 911 call or a 411 call, know that God is waiting to hearing from you. He wants to be there for you in time of crisis and even when nothing is wrong. He is the best source for information and revelation.

Stop wasting time trying to get information from people who don't have the complete answer. Even at their best, they can only give you partial information. For, the Scriptures say that we "prophesy in part". That means if God doesn't reveal it, you cannot have the knowledge.

You don't have to rely on second-hand information when you have a Heavenly Father who longs to talk with you. Yes, He does use people to share things with you. However, the ultimate is the personal relationship with you that none other can compare. Be careful in putting more confidence in man than God. Man is limited, God is limitless.

Don't put your faith and trust in flesh. Seek God for the answers to your questions. If you need advice, He is the Mighty Counselor. He has given you access. It is up to you to be spiritual and not carnal. Keep the Sunday School hymn ringing in your heart: "And He walks with me and He talks with me, and He tells me I am His own…"

Others don't have your answer! What you need won't come through the telephone. But, run to the throne of God and He will answer you!

JUNE 10
Who Is Really In Charge?
EPHESIANS 5:18

And be not drunk with wine, wherein is excess; but be filled with the Spirit; - King James Version

Don't drink too much wine. That cheapens your life. Drink the Spirit of God, huge draughts of him. – The Message Translation

How many times have you heard someone make the expression? "The devil made me do it!" If that statement is true, that is a sad state of affairs for a Christian. The Scriptures declare that the body of a believer is the temple of the Holy Ghost. That means that the actions of a Christian should be consistent with the directives of the Spirit of God.

Your spirit man must be governed by the Spirit of God. You should not allow other NOUNS – people, places, things or ideas – to influence your thoughts or your actions. Being drunk does not relate only to wine. But anytime you allow anything on the outside to come and take control over your inside – you are out of order!

Have you ever heard the expression, "That's that wine talking!" Usually, this is in response to the actions of someone who is drunk. After drinking an excessive amount of alcohol they lose their inhibitions and begin to speak and act differently from the norm. The Bible says that this should never exist in Christians. There should never be an exterior force allowed to enter you to change who or what you are except the Holy Ghost.

The Spirit of God should be the only force that leads, guides and directs you. When you are continuously filled with the Spirit, your actions correspond to what really pleases God. Pray to the Father that the infilling of the Holy Ghost would not just be an event or one-time experience. But, welcome the Holy Ghost to indwell your life and empower you to live a victorious and God-filled life everyday!

JUNE 11
And It Fell Not!
MATTHEW 7:25

And the rain descended, and the floods came, and the winds blew, and beat upon that house; and it fell not: for it was founded upon a rock. – King James Version

Stop worrying and stop fretting about your victory. It has already been promised, decreed and declared. God is not going to change His mind. You have gone through storms, but understand more are on the way. Yes, you will be subjected to challenges, trials, temptations and so much more. However, the mere fact that you are reading these words dictate that you are already a winner.

Your foundation your substance and your durability are what keep you from falling. Your foundation is the Word of God. Everything around you may crumble, but God's Word is sure and steadfast. Your hope must be built on nothing else than Jesus' blood and His righteousness. Stand on the Word of God.

You must remember that you are your Father's child. Yes, your spiritual DNA causes you to be an overcomer and more than a conqueror because it is in your blood. Also, you are what you eat! Every experience and indoctrination with the Word has made you what you are today. You are stronger, wiser, and better because of the knowledge you have gained from God's Word.

Finally, you have been through storms before and whatever you are going through even now will also pass. You have God's Word within you and the foundation of your life is laid in Christ Jesus – You have no choice but to survive and prosper. You are the church – and the gates of hell shall not prevail! Bask in His glory and enjoy your victory!

JUNE 12
Your Life Will Not Perish
GALATIANS 3:14

But there's no need to dwell on that now. From now on, things are looking up! I can assure you that there'll not be a single drowning among us, although I can't say as much for the ship - the ship itself is doomed. – The Message Translation

Sometimes too much value is placed on temporal things that will eventually perish. Don't be distracted from the deliverance that God intends for you by trying to hold onto things that are not a part of your destiny.

You may be experiencing a storm in your life right now. Have confidence that God will bring you through the storm. However, when He does it may not be as you thought or planned. Don't focus so much on flesh, but be spiritual and simply trust God. Ride out the storm and watch God bless. Your life will be spared and made better.

Today, foreclosures, repossessions, and unemployment are all on the rise. But, just know that in the midst of all of these challenges God is still God! He is your source and your security. You may lose a house, a car, a job, or other possessions. But, when your faith is secure in God, you can lose all these things and God will spare you to receive double for your trouble!

Decree and declare that, "It's already alright"! Things are getting better. Whatever may be lost is not important. What God saves is most important! He will bring you out alright!

JUNE 13
The Holy Spirit: Your Personal Teacher!

I JOHN 2:27

But the anointing which ye have received of him abideth in you, and ye need not that any man teach you: but as the same anointing teacheth you of all things, and is truth, and is no lie, and even as it hath taught you, ye shall abide in Him. – King James Version

But they're no match for what is embedded deeply within you - Christ's anointing, no less! You don't need any of their so-called teaching. Christ's anointing teaches you the truth on everything you need to know about yourself and him, uncontaminated by a single lie. Live deeply in what you were taught. – The Message Translation

God has blessed the Body of Christ with so many gifts: apostles, prophets, evangelists, pastors and teachers! These all serve the purpose to perfect you, mature you, strengthen you and develop you. But, even higher and more equipped than all of them together is God Himself!

When you experience the fullness of the Spirit of God in your life, He gives direction to you. No longer do you need a rule book (or people) to regulate and guide your life. He (the Spirit of God) will direct you in what to say and what not to say. He will tell you where you should and should not go. He will reveal to you the people that you should connect with and He will also show you the people with whom you need to experience the ministry of "disconnect". He will help you to pray. He will tell you how to dress and carry yourself in a way that pleases Him.

The presence of the Voice of the Spirit of God does not mean you don't still need preachers and teachers. But, you must grow to the place of realizing that there will be times that God will by-pass flesh and speak directly to you. Remember, you have a personal relationship with Him. He values that. So should you!

JUNE 14
Do You Have A "YES" For God?
MATTHEW 9:28

And when Hhe was come into the house, the blind men came to him: and Jesus saith unto them, Believe ye that I am able to do this? They said unto him, Yea, Lord. – King James Version

When Jesus got home, the blind men went in with him. Jesus said to them, "Do you really believe I can do this?" They said, "Why, yes, Master!" – The Message Translation

God wants to know: "Do you believe that He is able"? Choirs sing about. Deacons pray about it. Ministers preach about it. Everybody talks about it. But, how many people can "be" about it? Against all odds, can you believe that He is able?

Erase the doubt. Ignore the conversation of the enemy. Disconnect yourself from the negative family and friends who keep telling you how it won't work out. Stop looking at the pictures the devil paints to show you doom and gloom. Refuse to allow the mistakes of your past to bring guilt and condemnation.

It does not matter what the arena of your challenge is: finances, relationships, employment, or even your mind or body – God is able! He just needs a yes from you. His Word promises that He is able to do exceeding abundantly above all that you can ask or think, but it is according to the power that you release. (Ephesians 3:20) It's all about your faith level.

More than you have ever done before: just trust God. Live the faith life and know that He is able. Tell Him YES! Yes, He is your healer. Yes, He is your deliverer. Yes, He is your way maker. Yes, He is you all in all. Just tell Him "Yes, you know that He is able"!

JUNE 15
Somebody Needs You!
PSALM 82:3

Defend the poor and fatherless: do justice to the afflicted and needy. – King James Version

You're here to defend the defenseless, to make sure that underdogs get a fair break; - The Message Translation

Waste no more time complaining about your own sorrows and woes. There is always someone in worse shape than you. Focus your energy and effort in being a blessing to them. God has a way of recompensing back to you much more than you sow.

Yes! Sacrifice your time, talent and treasure in the lives of others. There are people who are your assignment. Your passion is the fulfillment of their promise. Yes, God has promised to bless them, to help them, to strengthen them – and you are the answer to their prayers.

Look within yourself and identify two things. Locate your strengths and discover your passion. The people who you are supposed to help will fall in the "Need Category" in those areas. Your strength addresses their weakness and your passion bring cure to their pain.

You can do it! Find someone today and be a blessing! Watch what God does in return in your life.

JUNE 16
Reposition For Reward!
II KINGS 7:3

And there were four leprous men at the entering in of the gate: and they said one to another, Why sit we here until we die? – King James Version

It happened that four lepers were sitting just outside the city gate. They said to one another, "What are we doing sitting here at death's door? – The Message Translation

Sitting idly by waiting for life to happen is not profitable. You have to make up your mind to simply trust God and dare to go into the unknown. If you are in covenant relationship with God, then you already know that He orders your steps. So, in your prayer time as you hear God speak and give you directions don't be afraid to go!

Your condition is irrelevant. Don't allow your condition to place you in a pity party. Don't let people sit up and feel sorry for you. Learn to encourage yourself.

Get up from doing nothing and do something! As the saints of old used to sing, "Let Jesus lead you." As you release your faith and get up and trust God, awesome blessings await you. Reposition yourself for the greatest reward of your life. Being in the right place at the right time can change everything. Grab life by the horns and go for it! Victory already belongs to you!

JUNE 17
The Pursuit Of Peace!
PSALM 34:14

Depart from evil, and do good; seek peace, and pursue it. – King James Version

Turn your back on sin; do something good. Embrace peace - don't let it get away! – The Message Translation

Peace is not automatic. It must be sought after and obtained. Your peace is impacted by how you feel about yourself, how you allow your feelings about what others say or do affect you and your relationship/position with God. Peace is defined as a state of tranquility. It is rest from worry or concern. Peace may also be characterized by harmonious fellowship.

God's peace is awesome. According to Philippians 4:7, (*And God's peace, which is far beyond human understanding, will keep your hearts and minds safe in union with Christ Jesus.* – Good News Translation) God's peace supercedes human intellect and understanding. You can have storms raging in your life, you can be troubled on every side – yet, if God's peace fills your heart – you will walk around as though you did not have a care in the world.

Real peace begins within one's self. You must focus on spiritual things. Stop allowing pronouns (people, places, things or ideas) to hinder your peace. The absence of peace is the presence of a carnal mind. And, a carnal mind is the breeding ground for worry and unhealthy stress – which can kill you!

Peace with others is not dependent upon others. Stop waiting on others to initiate resolution. You must focus on being a peacemaker. Always look for a way to build people up. Practice the art of forgiveness and reconciliation. Your peace and holiness should go hand-in-hand. Look to God as your example of how you are to maintain peace even in challenging times.

Remember that God's Word is the source of your peace. He has already told you in His Word that tribulation and tests would come. But, He also promised to give you peace unlike the peace that the world offers. His peace is everlasting and always enduring. His peace will make you walk around like a rich man and your bank account may be in the negative. God's peace will make you walk by faith in your healing in the midst of negative reports from the doctors. God's peace will keep you all day, all night, wherever you may be! Find peace in God's Word and never let it go!

JUNE 18
My Soul Is Anchored!
I PETER 4:19

Wherefore let them that suffer according to the will of God commit the keeping of their souls to Him in well doing, as unto a faithful Creator. – King James Version

So then, those who suffer because it is God's will for them, should by their good actions trust themselves completely to their Creator, who always keeps his promise. – Good News Translation

So if you find life difficult because you're doing what God said, take it in stride. Trust him. He knows what he's doing, and he'll keep on doing it. – The Message Translation

One of the founding fathers of America, Thomas Paine, wrote: "These are the times that try men's souls." The quote was accurate then in the 1700s and even so much more now in the 21st century. People's souls (mind, will, intellect, emotions) are being challenged everyday. However, the believer must learn to trust the Creator who created the soul to also keep the soul.

Do not be discouraged by what you may be facing or enduring. Continue to look unto the author and finisher of your faith. God is a comforter and a keeper. Your responsibility is to simply "Do the Word". God has your back when you live a life of obedience to His Word. He will always come to your rescue at the appropriate time – "Due season".

Your life does not have to be an emotional rollercoaster! Learn to trust God with your emotions. When you surrender completely to Him, situations and circumstances will lose their power over your soulish man. Things that used to "push your button", make you cry, bring on depression will all of a sudden lose their ability to illicit negative emotions from you. Follow the exhortation of the hymn writer, Joseph M. Scriven, and "take everything to God in prayer."

JUNE 19
God: The Pattern For Fatherhood
GENESIS 1:27

So God created man in his Own image, in the image of God created He him; male and female created He them. – King James Version

God created human beings; He created them godlike, Reflecting God's nature. He created them male and female. – The Message Translation

When a seamstress prepares to sew a garment she will often use a pattern. When a cook prepares a dish, he often will use a recipe. A successful father preparing to be a good dad will use the best role model: GOD Himself.

God provides fathers with the tools required to be successful in parenting. Simply operate in the principles of God and you will not go wrong. Know God and then you will have a better knowledge and understanding not only of your purpose, but your function as well.

God designed you to be a giver. He empowered you to the extent that the blessing on your life would be so full that other lives would be impacted. God has instilled within you the capacity to be a forgiver. His pattern of grace and mercy replicated in your life becomes the source of compassion and understanding for others. God's care and concern for your well-being extends even through the omnipresence of His Spirit. Good fathers will make the sacrifice to be ever-present in the lives of their children.

The simple solution: Do it like God. Be like God in all you actions, attitudes, and attributes. He is your pattern – now follow the pattern and see a blessed life!

JUNE 20

Heh God! "Happy Father's Day"

MATTHEW 7:11

If ye then, being evil, know how to give good gifts unto your children, how much more shall your Father which is in heaven give good things to them that ask Him? – King James Version

As bad as you are, you wouldn't think of such a thing. You're at least decent to your own children. So don't you think the God who conceived you in love will be even better? – The Message Translation

God is good all the time! And every day He keeps on blessing you! You should thank Him and praise Him every opportunity you get. But, it is also good to set aside special times to go over and beyond the ordinary in your expression of appreciation.

Natural (earthly) fathers deserve appreciation for being fathers. Natural fathers, who practice being like "the Heavenly Father", have characteristics that make you appreciate them even more! They correct you when you are in error. They have compassion on you when you need it. They comfort and console you when you are down. And they challenge you to achieve success and be blessed.

As you honor earthly fathers, grandfathers, and godfathers – don't forget to stop and give a special "Happy Father's Day" Praise to your Heavenly Father! He is a great Father, full of love and mercy! Honor Him!

JUNE 21
You Are In His Image!
GENESIS 3:4-5

And the serpent said unto the woman, Ye shall not surely die: For God doth know that in the day ye eat thereof, then your eyes shall be opened, and ye shall be as gods, knowing good and evil. - King James Version

The serpent told the Woman, "You won't die. God knows that the moment you eat from that tree, you'll see what's really going on. You'll be just like God, knowing everything, ranging all the way from good to evil." - The Message Translation

Be careful to not fall for the deceit and trickery of the devil. Don't allow lust or covetousness to take you out of God's will. Know who you already are in God and don't be deceived by allowing the enemy to send you on a wild goose chase.

The serpent encouraged Eve to step out of the will of God by tempting her with the ability to "be just like God". The biggest problem is that Eve evidently forgot who she was. When God created man, He made man in His own image after His own likeness. Eve was already like God! Not only did God make man in His own image, but He also gave man dominion.

Don't get caught up trying to get something that you already have! Within you is an awesome treasure and gift of God. His Word declared that He has given you all things that pertain to life and godliness. So, you don't have to waste time looking outside for what God has already invested inside.

Look within! Learn the purpose and calling that God has already declared concerning you. Search within and discover the awesome wonder that God has done. He has great expectations for you. Even before you were formed in your mother's womb, God made an awesome deposit in you.

JUNE 22
Who Will You Bless Today?
I PETER 4:10

As every man hath received the gift, even so minister the same one to another, as good stewards of the manifold grace of God. – King James Version

Be generous with the different things God gave you, passing them around so all get in on it: - The Message Translation

God has given you – TIME, TALENT, AND TREASURE. What you do with these three gifts determine if you are a faithful steward or not.

Time is a gift from God. You are a faithful steward of time when you honor and respect it as a gift from God. That means you show up on time. You start on time. You operate in a timely fashion. And you do not waste time by losing focus or being frivolous.

God has blessed you with talent. Whether you sing in the choir, preach in the pulpit, greet people at the door, or sweep and clean the bathrooms – they are all giftings from God. Learn to sow your talent into the kingdom of God. When God has blessed you to be able to perform a certain task – learn how to bless others with that gift. If you are good with numbers – bless someone by doing their taxes for free. If you are good with children – volunteer to keep someone else's children and give them a break. If you are a good steward of your talent – you will not always try and get paid for everything you do. The Bible says that if you give to the poor, it is just like lending to the Lord. You can set yourself up to be blessed by God, when you learn to bless others.

And of course, God is watching your stewardship with your treasure. As good Christians – you should pay tithes because it is right. You should give liberal offerings with a cheerful heart. You should sow financial seeds to be a blessing and live expectantly of the return that God has promised you. When you are a good steward with your treasure, it is not always the amount you give – but God often looks to see what is left. Do you give sacrificially? God did. He gave His only begotten son. The widow did. She gave all that she had. God is not asking you to give everything you have, but He does want you to give in proportion to how He has prospered you. This shows you being a good steward with your treasure.

Today, look within and ask yourself – Is God please with my stewardship? My talent, my time and my treasure.

JUNE 23
Blessed And Unmovable!
PSALM 1:3

And he shall be like a tree planted by the rivers of water, that bringeth forth his fruit in his season; his leaf also shall not wither; and whatsoever he doeth shall prosper. – King James Version

Be blessed. Stay blessed. Don't allow NOUNS (people, places, things, or ideas) to move you!

Don't take the suggestions of people who don't have Godly advice or Word-based solutions. Don't allow your actions in life to be patterned after those who are not living a holy and sanctified life. Don't allow your emotions to be governed by success or failure, but simply remain confident in the power of your God.

Get in the Word of God and keep it in your heart and mind. All day long and even at night, rehearse His Word to allow your ears to hear and bring faith into manifestation. His Word will bring healing. His Word will cause the enemy to flee. His Word will keep, sustain and bless you.

Nothing that occurs in life will get the best of you. You may experience temporary seasons of challenge. Just patiently await your appointed time and know that in due season you will manifest His glory.

JUNE 24
Let Go And Let God!
LUKE 12:29

And seek not ye what ye shall eat, or what ye shall drink, neither be ye of doubtful mind. – King James Version

"What I'm trying to do here is get you to relax, not be so preoccupied with getting so you can respond to God's giving. – The Message Translation

Stop worrying and stop stressing over the basic needs of your life. God loves you and has promised to provide for you. God has a way of making provisions in strange and odd ways to mankind. But, He has a track record of always coming through in time and on time.

When you feel there is not enough food, stop for a moment and consider is this a time that you should be fasting and praying. Sometimes, people get so preoccupied with what they feel that they forfeit God's opportunity for the greater blessing.

Your steps are ordered by God. Your life is in His hand. He promised to supply your needs. So, the next time you feel as if something is missing – realize that it must not be a need. If it was truly a need God would have already made provisions for it. He won't fail you. And, He will never let you down. Just let go, and let God!

JUNE 25
Make Sure It Counts!
MATTHEW 7:23

And then will I profess unto them, I never knew you: depart from Me, ye that work iniquity. – King James Version

And do you know what I am going to say? 'You missed the boat. All you did was use me to make yourselves important. You don't impress me one bit. You're out of here.' – The Message Translation

Can you recall growing up in school and your teacher gave you an assignment that really had no point or purpose. It was called busy work. Just something to keep you occupied for a set time or season. That was frustrating wasn't it?

Or have you ever been on a job where upper level management required excessive amounts of paperwork that both you and management knew would never be viewed or checked. Again, that is busy work. Did it make you frustrated and have a negative attitude?

Well, sometimes people find their own busy work and it still yields the same results – it doesn't count. Do not deceive yourself in overindulging in a great deal of what you deem as "church work", but in the eyes of God it is busy work and it does not count.

If you are on the praise team or in the choir, make certain that God assigned you there. If you are working on the usher board, make sure that is your calling. If you decide to feed people who are hungry or clothe people who are naked, make certain your motives are right. And if you part your lips to tell somebody that "The Lord said", make sure He said it!

You must be careful to be sensitive to the voice of the Spirit to complete the assignment or task that God has assigned. You cannot just do what you want to do and think you will be rewarded. You must be led by God to do His work. Remember, only what you do for Christ will last!

JUNE 26
Let Your "Yesterday" Help Somebody Else's Today!
EPHESIANS 2:3

Among whom also we all had our conversation in times past in the lusts of our flesh, fulfilling the desires of the flesh and of the mind; and were by nature the children of wrath, even as others. – King James Version

We all did it, all of us doing what we felt like doing, when we felt like doing it, all of us in the same boat. It's a wonder God didn't lose his temper and do away with the whole lot of us. - The Message Translation

You are not in a position to look at others who may be still lost in sin with an eye of disgust and contempt. Don't forget, you have a yesterday! That's right, you have a past. And, you were doing some of the same (maybe even worse) things that others are doing. But, it was God's grace and mercy that kept you and did not allow you to die in your sins. He gave you the opportunity to accept Him and live a new life in Christ.

There is no need in focusing on your past deeds. But, don't ever forget where you come from. Somebody needs your testimony to strengthen their walk. Always be willing to share your story of how God delivered you and brought you out. And, you need the remembrance to remind you to stay dependent upon God. You didn't get it together on your own, and for sure you can't keep it together by yourself. You need God everyday!

Now get busy helping somebody. You already know their excuses. You already know the "game" they will try to play on you. You already know their language. Remember, that used to be you! But, praise God – you are a new creature and old things have passed away. Let your past be a blessing to somebody else's present. Let your "yesterday" help somebody else's today so they can be delivered and celebrate and also have a "yesterday".

JUNE 27
Act Like Your Daddy!
ROMANS 12:21

Be not overcome of evil, but overcome evil with good. – King James Version

Don't let evil get the best of you; get the best of evil by doing good. – The Message Translation

Two wrongs do not make a right. Many have heard that expression for years, now put it into practice. You will always win by allowing the Spirit of God inside of you to dictate your attitude and actions. Getting back at someone or getting even with someone is not the godly way to handle things.

God has called you to forgiveness. Yes, no matter what the aught or the fault, treat others the same way God has treated you. He forgave you. Now you forgive others.

When you are challenged to respond in a negative fashion to someone else, shock the devil and even surprise yourself by doing good. Yes, bless them and do not curse them. Help them and do not hinder or hurt them. Pray for them and express agape love (the unconditional love of God) towards them.

God will bless you for walking in his Word. They may even be won to the kingdom because of your demonstration of grace and mercy. And, you will feel much better by living in love and obeying God's Word.

JUNE 28
The Battle Is His – The Victory Is Yours!
II CHRONICLES 20:22

And when they began to sing and to praise, the LORD set ambushments against the children of Ammon, Moab, and mount Seir, which were come against Judah; and they were smitten. – King James Version

God has already designed your victory. Believe God. Trust His Word. Hear His prophets. Obey His voice. Stop fretting and struggling over things that you cannot handle on your own. Realize that the God you serve is bigger than anything that can come against you. Open your mouth and offer praise unto your God and watch Him show up and bring victory in your situation.

The inhabitants of Judah and Jerusalem were stressed because of the enemies that had gathered against them. However, the man of God Jahaziel told them that the battle was the Lord's and not theirs. It did not matter how big their enemy was, all they had to do was stand still and they would see the salvation of the Lord.

Today, trust that God has your back. Do not be afraid. Do not be discouraged. Go forward and face your challenges knowing that God is going to handle your battle. Walk forward with a praise on your lips. Push forward with a shout of victory in your voice. March forward with a dance of praise in your step. Press forward with a confident declaration of your God as the Omnipotent One.

Yes, victory is already yours. Change your attitude. Adjust your expectation. Realize that your God is bigger, badder, and better than anything you are facing. Your God is so awesome that when you praise Him – whatever was coming against you will self-destruct and have no power over you. Go ahead and praise Him right now!

JUNE 29
The Issue In Your Life!
MARK 5:25-34

"A woman who had suffered a condition of hemorrhaging for twelve years - a long succession of physicians had treated her, and treated her badly, taking all her money and leaving her worse off than before - had heard about Jesus. She slipped in from behind and touched his robe. She was thinking to herself, "If I can put a finger on his robe, I can get well." The moment she did it, the flow of blood dried up. She could feel the change and knew her plague was over and done with. At the same moment, Jesus felt energy discharging from him. He turned around to the crowd and asked, "Who touched my robe?" His disciples said, "What are you talking about? With this crowd pushing and jostling you, you're asking, 'Who touched me?' Dozens have touched you!" But he went on asking, looking around to see who had done it. The woman, knowing what had happened, knowing she was the one, stepped up in fear and trembling, knelt before him, and gave him the whole story. Jesus said to her, "Daughter, you took a risk of faith, and now you're healed and whole. Live well, live blessed! Be healed of your plague." – The Message Translation

An issue can be a consuming crisis, a persistent problem, a continuing challenge or even an enduring event. Making a parallel from the background scripture passage to life today, an issue is not a welcomed condition. Issues can bring on isolation, even though they are common to everyone. Yes, everybody has issues. Issues can be short-lived or they may last a long time. Issues can leave you bankrupt – financially, emotionally, and even spiritually.

One of the tricks of the enemy is to encourage denial. Until you even acknowledge that an issue exists there can be no relief from it. Once you acknowledge that there is an issue you must become dissatisfied enough to demand change. If not, change will never come.

Recognize that you do not have the power to deliver yourself. No, flesh cannot bring deliverance to what is spiritual. Not only can you not help yourself, but often people can be a hindrance. Some people will be a discouragement by telling you the reason why you should just accept life the way it is. Others will help delay your deliverance by enabling you and causing you to keep using them as a crutch.

Be cautious of people. Other people can make your issues worse. Jesus is the only answer for your issue. You have to see Jesus for yourself – not based on religion but relationship. Your issue can be resolved when you trust and obey.

You need to experience a personal spiritual awakening. It takes different things for different people to receive God's manifestation. Your spirit must be sensitive to know what God is saying YOU need to do. Don't pattern your deliverance after other people's lives. But read, study and walk in God's Word for yourself.

True deliverance will occur when you release your faith. If you can believe then you have positioned yourself to receive. Real change comes when you get sick and tried of things as they are. There is an answer for your issue. In the words of Andrae Crouch, a famous songwriter, decades ago, "Jesus is the answer for the world today…"

JUNE 30
Follow The Spirit!
JOHN 16:13

Howbeit when He, the Spirit of truth, is come, He will guide you into all truth: for He shall not speak of Himself; but whatsoever He shall hear, that shall He speak: and He will shew you things to come. – King James Version

But when the Friend comes, the Spirit of the Truth, he will take you by the hand and guide you into all the truth there is. He won't draw attention to himself, but will make sense out of what is about to happen and, indeed, out of all that I have done and said. – The Message Translation

No crystal ball. No tarot cards. No horoscope. No secret incantation in a candle-lit room. You do not need to run to people with familiar spirits to get information. The answers to the questions that have plagued your mind are available through the Spirit of God.

Whatever you need to know you can receive it directly from God. The Word of God says in I Corinthians 2:10 that *"the Spirit searcheth all things, yea the deep things of God."* The things that your eyes have not seen, nor your ears heard – God will reveal them to you by His Spirit.

God does not want you living in the dark. He wants you to walk in the light. Live in the light. He wants you to have knowledge of His will, His purpose and His plan. He wants you to use His Spirit for the intent given: to lead and guide you into all truth.

JULY 1
Go Over And Beyond!
MATTHEW 26:7

The real believers are the ones the Spirit of God leads to work away at this ministry, filling the air with Christ's praise as we do it. We couldn't carry this off by our own efforts, and we know it. – The Message Translation

What a wonderful feeling and knowledge to know who you are in Christ Jesus. When you realize the awesome sacrifice that God made for you through His only Son, it will change your life forever. No longer will you find yourself lost in meaningless rituals and practicing patterns that accomplish little. Your spirit has been made alive in Christ!

By yourself – you are nothing. But, with Him not only can you do all things, but you are an awesome vessel of honor to His glory and praise. You can worship God in spirit and in truth. You can enter that secret and special place of communion and fellowship with Him. The Sunday School song takes on new meaning as you experience Him "walking with you, and talking with you, and telling you that you are His own".

Your flesh may get tired, but you will always have a YES in your spirit. When you are a true believer, a special part of you will always cry out to God and hunger and thirst for more of Him. Bask in true worship. Long for His presence! Worship Him like never before!

JULY 2

Signs That You Are Ready To Be Free!

LUKE 19:3-4

He wanted desperately to see Jesus, but the crowd was in his way - he was a short man and couldn't see over the crowd. So he ran on ahead and climbed up in a sycamore tree so he could see Jesus when he came by. – The Message Translation

When a person is really ready to be free, they will do more than just talk about it. Don't waste time listening to people complain about how bad things are in their life. When they get sick and tired of being sick and tired – they will make a change.

When your heart is ready for a change you will not allow anything around you or anything about you to stand in your way. You will go to extraordinary measures to get what you need: freedom. You will not allow people or their opinions to discourage you. You will not allow stumbling blocks to keep you back. Instead, you will take those same blocks and make then stepping stones.

A person ready to be free will first and foremost acknowledge they have a problem. They will then get a vision of who or where they want to be. They will learn the necessary steps or changes that need to be made to accomplish their deliverance. And most importantly, they will embrace change. Even if it is uncomfortable or uncertain, when you are really ready to be free you will step off into the deep.

JULY 3
Celebrate Your Liberty!
EPHESIANS 2:1-7

And you hath He quickened, who were dead in trespasses and sins; Wherein in time past ye walked according to the course of this world, according to the prince of the power of the air, the spirit that now worketh in the children of disobedience: Among whom also we all had our conversation in times past in the lusts of our flesh, fulfilling the desires of the flesh and of the mind; and were by nature the children of wrath, even as others. But God, who is rich in mercy, for His great love wherewith He loved us, Even when we were dead in sins, hath quickened us together with Christ, (by grace ye are saved ;) And hath raised us up together, and made us sit together in heavenly places in Christ Jesus: - King James Version

There was time when you lived in bondage. Yes, you lived according to the desires of your flesh and the suggestions of the enemy. It was normal and natural for you to do and say ungodly and unholy things. But, God adopted you into the royal family and changed everything in your life.

Yes, your walk and talk have changed. You may still dance, but your dancing partner has changed. Your purpose for celebration has been altered. He has put a new song in your mouth, one that the angels don't know anything about. He has redeemed you by His precious blood. And now you are free!

Celebrate your independence from sin. Give God an awesome praise offering. Worship with an intensity you have not experienced before. Make a new vow and commitment to honor His Name and His Word like never before.

Be explosive for God in your zeal and excitement of your life with Him. Let your praise be louder and brighter than fireworks. Fill your calendar not with just holidays, but holy days. Celebrate!

Consider the lyrics recorded by the late great Milton Brunson and The Thompson Community Choir, *"I am free. Praise the Lord, I'm free. No longer bound! No more chains holding me! My soul is resting. It's just a blessing. Praise the Lord, Hallelujah, I'm free."*

JULY 4

Celebrate! Your Dependence On God!

ACTS 17:28

We live and move in him, can't get away from him! One of your poets said it well: 'We're the God-created.' – The Message Translation

Man was created to be dependent. God's design was for man to desire and embrace dependence upon Him. However, Satan offered a counterfeit dependence called sin. Ever since the fall in the garden of Eden, mankind has been subject to the improper dependence in life. The devil makes sin comfortable and attractive.

But, Jesus Christ showed great love by sacrificing His own life for you to free you from the bondage and penalty of sin. And with that sacrifice, the old dependence upon sin to live has been done away with. Now, you have a new dependence called holiness. With God's presence living within you, you can walk into the plan and purpose of God because of your allegiance to Christ.

Celebrate your liberty. You are no longer bound to the evil and sinful nature of your flesh. But, you are free to live an abundant life because of the blessing of your new nature in Christ Jesus. Don't let the devil fool you – you are free! For it is God's own Spirit within you prompting you and pushing you to do His perfect will. Celebrate your dependence on God!

JULY 5
Seize The Moment!
MATTHEW 5:6

Let your light so shine before men, that they may see your good works, and glorify your Father which is in heaven. – King James Version

Now that I've put you there on a hilltop, on a light stand - shine! Keep open house; be generous with your lives. By opening up to others, you'll prompt people to open up with God, this generous Father in heaven. – The Message Translation

Take every opportunity to allow the light of Christ to shine in your life. In every walk of life you have the opportunity to allow others to be delivered from darkness by your actions. When you live a transparent life, it gives hope to others. People should be able to see your flesh in its imperfections, yet at the same time see your spirit which illuminates God's glory in everything you do.

The mess that you have gone through in life should become your message. You do not have to be proud of your past, but you also should not be ashamed. For it was God's power, that delivered you. Proudly proclaim that the same power that freed you is still available to deliver others. Let people understand that you may be imperfect, but the God that lives within you is perfect and holy.

When you are doing the right thing, this should point people to Jesus. Let God be glorified in your conversation. In the songs that you sing, in the way that you dress, in the way you treat others – let others see the light of Christ. Don't take credit for doing things

right – give God the glory! Let the world know that it is because of the power of God that you live the life that you do!

JULY 6
God Has A Ram For You
GENESIS 22:13

Abraham looked up. He saw a ram caught by its horns in the thicket. Abraham took the ram and sacrificed it as a burnt offering instead of his son. – The Message Translation

It is quite evident that GOD always makes a way out of no way. He is a faithful God. He comes through "in time" and "on time" every time! He not only supplies needs, but He evens grants heart desires.

But, the question today is: What are you doing, feeling, thinking, and believing UNTIL He comes through? Are you pacing the floor? Are you stressing? Are you being temperamental?

The key to your blessing is obedience. Just do what God has instructed you to do, and watch God reward your obedience. Some people never get "rams" in their lives because they are afraid to make sacrifices. They are afraid to surrender everything to God in order to gain even more from God.

The ram represents God's provision for your righteousness to be fulfilled. When you simply learn to walk in obedience, you open the door for God to cause His Promises to come pass in your everyday existence. Trust God and try God today! He is Jehovah Jireh and He will provide!

JULY 7
Ask The Saviour To Help
ISAIAH 57:13

When thou criest, let thy companies deliver thee; but the wind shall carry them all away; vanity shall take them: but he that putteth his trust in me shall possess the land, and shall inherit my holy mountain; - King James Version

Go ahead, cry for help to your collection of no-gods: A good wind will blow them away. They're smoke, nothing but smoke. "But anyone who runs to me for help will inherit the land, will end up owning my holy mountain!" – The Message Translation

To be successful and victorious, you must make the right choices in life. Get out of the flesh realm and operate in the spirit. God has given you spiritual weapons that will prove advantageous in your warfare. You must simply seek His face and His help.

As a youth growing up playing street ball, the first thing you did was pick teams. You were very careful to pick the one with the most strength, the fastest speed, and the most experience. You wanted the best people on your side, so you would be guaranteed to win the game.

In this game of life, you must also carefully pick your team. Your educational degrees won't help you. Your people connections will be of little use. Your financial backing and bank account will not amount to anything. Even your own physical strength will be irrelevant. But, your trust in the Almighty God will be your safety.

He has promised that as long as He is on your side, it does not matter how many are against you. So, no matter how tough the trial, no matter how fierce the storm, no matter how aggressive the adversary is – you are guaranteed victory because He is your God. Ask HIM to help you!

JULY 8
Stop Blinding The Saints!
MATTHEW 5:16

Let your light so shine before men, that they may see your good works, and glorify your Father which is in heaven. – King James Version

Now that I've put you there on a hilltop, on a light stand - shine! Keep open house; be generous with your lives. By opening up to others, you'll prompt people to open up with God, this generous Father in heaven. – The Message Translation

Have you ever driven down a dark road and turned on your high beam in order to see better due to the darkness? What happened when another car came down that same road with its bright lights shining as well? That's it – both of you had to turn your high beams down to prevent blinding each other and causing an accident. This is the scenario is some churches today.

The light of Christ that is shining within you is not for the church – but it is for the world. Stop wasting time in the church trying to outshine each other. The real work is not within the four walls but in the dark world. Take your ministry to the streets where it is needed.

Stop wasting time "performing" for each other. There is nothing to prove to your brother or sister about God. Both of you should already have enough knowledge of God that to repeatedly rehearse to each other "who He is" and "what He does" yields very little productivity. God did not invest His power, glory and anointing in you for you to shine for each other.

The light is for the world! Stop blinding each other and go to a dark place and shine!

JULY 9
Are You Ready?
LUKE 12:40

Be ye therefore ready also: for the Son of man cometh at an hour when ye think not. – King James Version

So don't you be slovenly and careless. Just when you don't expect him, the Son of Man will show up." – The Message Translation

"People are dying who ain't never died before!" may be a comical statement but it is ever so true. Everyday people are making the transition from mortality to immortality. But, an important question remains: "Are You Ready?"

Not so much are you ready for Christ's return. There are many who will not live to experience the rapture. What happens if your time expires before then? What if you don't live to be 100? What if you don't have as much time as you thought? Are you ready?

You don't have to be sick to die. You don't have to live a "rough" life to die. Death comes to everybody. And then, everyone must stand before the judgment seat of God. Are you prepared for that conversation? Do you know what you will say?

Merely joining the church does not make you ready. Doing good deeds and trying to be a good person does not make you ready. The holy lifestyle of your parents doesn't make you ready.

Make sure that you are ready today, right now. Repent of sin. Confess (speak truthfully) that Jesus Christ is Lord and Saviour and welcome Him into your heart. Believe in your heart that the Virgin Born Saviour Jesus Christ of Nazareth died on Calvary for your sins. Believe that He was buried and rose again three days later with all power in His hands. Receive that same resurrection power in your life so you can walk in the newness of life. Experience water baptism and the Baptism in the Holy Ghost in your life. Connect with a local Bible-believing and teaching assembly. Live a life where you daily repent and thank and praise God for His grace and mercy. You can then be assured that you are ready!

JULY 10
Let God Use You!
MATTHEW 9:8

But when the multitudes saw it, they marvelled, and glorified God, which had given such power unto men. – King James Version

The crowd was awestruck, amazed and pleased that God had authorized Jesus to work among them this way. – The Message Translation

When the crowd saw this, they were filled with awe and praised God for giving such authority to humans. - God's Word Translation

Don't sell yourself short. You are a vessel and God wants to use you for His glory. No, you may not be perfect and you may not have it all together. That is why you are an earthen vessel! But, God loved you enough and trusted you enough to invest His power within you to be a blessing to others.

This is why it is important to obey God. When God gives you a message, speak it. Stop being afraid of people and quit worrying about what they will think or say. The message is not yours it is God's. When God directs you to pray for someone or lay hands upon someone, do it right then and there. Do not allow the spirit of procrastination to hinder you from being a blessing in someone else's life.

It is time for the world to be shocked. It is time for the saints to turn the heads of others. Let God use you. The power is in you.

The glory is for Him. The blessing is for humanity. Obey God today and recommit to be a willing vessel for His honor, glory, and praise!

JULY 11

Persistence Pays Off!

MATTHEW 9:27

As Jesus left the house, he was followed by two blind men crying out, "Mercy, Son of David! Mercy on us!" – The Message Translation

How bad do you want to be free? At what length will you go to get God's attention? How serious are you about your deliverance? What do you do when your "miracle" or your "blessing" is not manifested instantly? What do you do when you have to wait?

When you are determined to get God's attention and let Him know you mean business – your faith will cause you to persevere! You will not just pray, but you will fast as well. You won't just quote scriptures, but you will make application and walk in those same scriptures! You won't stay silent, but you will boldly and unashamedly praise God like never before!

Your faith will cause you to endure storm, wind and rain. Your faith will help you to "hang in there" until your wait is over. Your faith will strengthen and sustain you, even when it looks like nothing is happening.

What you are waiting on is on the way! Your faith will move God's hand and you will receive the grace and mercy you stand in need of. Just don't give up!

JULY 12
How Do "You" See You?
NUMBERS 13:33

And there we saw the giants, the sons of Anak, which come of the giants: and we were in our own sight as grasshoppers, and so we were in their sight. – King James Version

Why, we even saw the Nephilim giants (the Anak giants come from the Nephilim). Alongside them we felt like grasshoppers. And they looked down on us as if we were grasshoppers." – The Message Translation

Perception has strength! Not only does perception govern your feelings and actions concerning yourself, but they also translate into the opinions of others. The Word of God continually tells you to "have faith" and "believe". These directives compel you to trust what God has said concerning you. You must refute and ignore what you think, see or even feel.

God had made a promise to His people that victory belonged to them. But, they defeated themselves by allowing their perception of whom and what they were to be determined by the situation and not by God's promise. You must be careful not to be intimidated by your environment or your adversary.

If God said healing, stop embracing sickness. If God promised prosperity, stop holding on to lack. If God declared victory, stop expecting defeat. The key is to simply trust what God said and allow your faith to demonstrate that trust through your actions.

When others see you, often how you present yourself governs their opinion of you. When you have low self-esteem it makes it difficult for others to think highly of you. But, when you exuberate confidence in yourself and your abilities, people stop and begin to consider you in a different light.

JULY 13
The Struggle Is Not Always Bad!
JAMES 3:2

For in many things we offend all. If any man offend not in word, the same is a perfect man, and able also to bridle the whole body. – King James Version

And none of us is perfectly qualified. We get it wrong nearly every time we open our mouths. If you could find someone whose speech was perfectly true, you'd have a perfect person, in perfect control of life. – The Message Translation

It is refreshing to know that we still have room to grow. Some people boast about their deliverance in certain areas of their lives; however, they fail to mention the areas where there is still a struggle. The key is to understand that we all are still growing. His Word is perfecting us day by day. Every experience: good and bad, He causes to work together for our good.

So, praise God for the areas that are under control. And the areas where more grace is required, sing, "I need Thee every hour." He will not only bring deliverance but He will be with you through the times when you feel the most vulnerable and weak. Always practice growing in grace. Don't allow the mistakes or the "oops" of life to hold you back. Keep chasing after God and He will cause His anointing to change you into His image from glory to glory.

JULY 14

Don't Twist Your Liberty!
I CORINTHIANS 8:9

But take heed lest by any means this liberty of yours become a stumblingblock to them that are weak. – King James Version

But God does care when you use your freedom carelessly in a way that leads a Christian still vulnerable to those old associations to be thrown off track. – The Message Translation

Always keep in mind that your life no longer belongs to you. You have been bought with a price and you are no longer your own. You are an ambassador for the kingdom of God here in the earth realm on assignment. The actions you take and the steps you make must always be done with consideration of your brothers and sisters in the Body of Christ.

Understand that even though you are "free" – always remind yourself what that really means! You are free from sin! You are free from the penalty of sin. You are free from the power of sin. And soon you will be from the presence of sin! Your freedom is from the enemy.

You are not free to walk and talk anyway that you please. You are not free to look and dress anyway that you please. You are not free to attend church, praise, or give as you please. God has standards! You must live God's way! You must allow His Word and His Spirit to guide your life. You are free to live within the parameters established by God!

JULY 15
Nobody Like The Lord!
PSALM 89:6-8

6 For who in all of heaven can compare with the LORD? What mightiest angel is anything like the LORD? 7 The highest angelic powers stand in awe of God. He is far more awesome than those who surround his throne. 8 O LORD God Almighty! Where is there anyone as mighty as You, LORD? Faithfulness is Your very character. - New Living Translation

The God you serve is an awesome God. There is none like Him in the heavens above, in the earth below, or even in the sea below the earth. He is a God of mercy and faithfulness. No one has the power of God – He is omnipotent. What a mighty God you serve!

Mercy is the act of disregarding punishment and extending an opportunity to repent. God is not reactive, but He is proactive. He even forgives before repentance occurs. For Romans 5:8 declares: *"But God commendeth His love toward us, in that, while we were yet sinners, Christ died for us."* Mercy does not come because of your desire – but it is because of God's character and nature.

Faithfulness is the ability to always cause one's word or vow to be fulfilled. You serve a faithful God. The scriptures declare that God watches over His Word and hastens (runs) to perform it. He will not allow His Word to return unto Him void (empty). God's faithfulness is not conditioned by us – but by His very nature. This is why we you must stand on the promises of God – because of His faithfulness.

God has power over everything. Power belongs to God! It is God that keeps things in divine order. He has the ability to even change the hearts of man. When man who doesn't like you – blesses you – it is the power of God. When miracles occur – it is the power of God. When prayers are answered – it is the power of God. When doors are opened – it is the power of God. When people's hearts change – it is the power of God.

Go on and praise Him today! There is none like the Lord. Many have gone on searching expeditions in their life attempting to fill the void in their life, but come up empty-handed. No doctor --- can compare. No lawyer --- can compare. No friend --- can compare. No lover --- can compare. There is none like Him. He is a great and awesome God. He is wonderful.

JULY 16
A Multiple Choice Test
JOSHUA 24:15

"If you decide that it's a bad thing to worship God, then choose a god you'd rather serve - and do it today. Choose one of the gods your ancestors worshiped from the country beyond The River, or one of the gods of the Amorites, on whose land you're now living. As for me and my family, we'll worship God." – The Message Translation

When God created you – He gave you a free will. He allowed you the choice to serve Him because you wanted to and not because He forced or made you. God always gives you a choice. You can choose to obey His Will or you can obey your flesh or the deception of the enemy.

Joshua gathered the people together to remind them of what God had done in their life: He delivered their ancestors from serving false gods. He blessed their forefathers. He delivered them from slavery. He protected them from the enemy. He kept them from being cursed. He blessed them in and from war. He gave them a free land.

God has done the very same thing for you today. If you would look back over your life – you can see that just as God blessed the Israelites, He has also blessed you. So, today your choice is not difficult. 1) Remember – Who God is and what He has done. 2) Forsake tradition and false gods. 3) Refuse world standards. And 4) Choose to serve the true and living God.

Your choice is simple: Choose God or Reject God! The choice is yours today!

JULY 17
Deliverance Is In You

MATTHEW 1:21

And she shall bring forth a son, and thou shalt call his name JESUS: for he shall save his people from their sins. – King James Version

God has made a supernatural investment in you. The Christ (The Anointed One and His Anointing) in you is there to be a blessing in the earth realm for others. Just as Mary brought forth Jesus to save His people from their sins, the power and presence of God is in you to be deliverance for others.

God knows the thoughts and plans He has for you. He orders your steps and coordinates your life even when you make choices that are different than His original design. Don't allow what others say or think cause you to be worried or concerned. The gift in you is not yours it is God's.

He will bring confirmation to your heart and mind to let you know that you are in His will and that He is being glorified by your life. Whatever your life purpose – He will give you a passion in that area.

Remember, there is deliverance in your womb. So, do not abort, ignore or be afraid of that gifting that is within you. Somebody, somewhere is waiting on what has been invested in you. Get ready to be used of God.

JULY 18
When God Speaks!
LUKE 5:5

Simon said, "Master, we've been fishing hard all night and haven't caught even a minnow. But if you say so, I'll let out the nets." – The Message Translation

When you have struggled to do all you know to do, listen for the voice of God to speak in your life. God wants you to do all you can. He wants you to exhaust all of your resources. He wants you to go as far as you can go.

So, when He steps in others can see His glory show up in your life. No man can get the credit for what you are able to accomplish through the power of God. Your degree, your social status, your financial backing, not even your physical strength could bring to pass the miracle that God wants to make manifest in your life.

Do not be distressed or depressed. Just keep doing what you are doing and listen for the voice of God. He will speak to you. And even if He tells you to do the same thing you have been doing – don't doubt, argue or struggle with the will of God. What you fail to understand is that He is placing a special anointing on what you are doing this time – and watch what happens!

Get ready for the miraculous. Get ready for the supernatural. Get ready for an awesome move of God. And then you can truly declare: I CAN do all things through Christ which strengthens me"!

JULY 19
Don't Complain!
ECCLESIASTES 7:14

In the day of prosperity be joyful, but in the day of adversity consider: God also hath set the one over against the other, to the end that man should find nothing after him. – King James Version

On a good day, enjoy yourself; On a bad day, examine your conscience. God arranges for both kinds of days So that we won't take anything for granted. Stay in Touch with Both Sides. – The Message Translation

There will be good days and there will be bad days. There will be sunshine and there will be rain. There will be smiles and there will be frowns. There will be joy and there will be sorrow. These extremities are all a part of life.

Don't get bent out of shape when life deals you challenges that seem unbearable. Always remember that life is a cycle. And whatever you are going through is exactly that – you are "going through it". Tell yourself: "This too will pass".

Don't waste time complaining. That just makes the devil rejoice. When you complain you excite the devil to make him feel as if he is defeating you. But, the Greater One lives on the inside of you. So, even when it seems you have been defeated – the resurrection power of Christ manifests in every situation of life.

Take advantage of the good days, the full days, and the happy days. Enjoy them and live life to the fullest. And when the script is flipped and the days are not so cheery and bright continue to praise God in spite of what it looks like. Appreciate what He has done and have faith to know that He is preparing you for greater! Just don't complain!

JULY 20

Run! And Don't Look Back!

I CORINTHIANS 10:13

There hath no temptation taken you but such as is common to man: but God is faithful, Who will not suffer you to be tempted above that ye are able; but will with the temptation also make a way to escape, that ye may be able to bear it. – King James Version

No test or temptation that comes your way is beyond the course of what others have had to face. All you need to remember is that God will never let you down; he'll never let you be pushed past your limit; he'll always be there to help you come through it. – The Message Translation

In every life temptations will abound. Yes, you will be tempted to say or do things that do not necessarily line up with God's Word. The temptation itself is not a sin. The yielding to that temptation is where sin begins. Do not feel as though you are less than a Christian because you are tempted. Temptations come in everyone's life.

The devil's job is to distract you and delay you in your journey. He comes to place ungodly invitations before you to lead you away from God's intended plan and purpose for your life. You have to be wise and know when the devil has launched an attack against you. There is precious cargo within you and the devil wants to destroy it.

God has promised to be faithful unto you. He never said that He would take the temptations away. But, He did promise to give you an exit door for every temptation that comes your way. Yes, God will make a way of escape for you.

So, as you consider choice words to say to someone who has upset you, remember God has another way. When you are encouraged to go somewhere that you don't feel good about in your spirit, remember God has another way. At the time you are considering doing something that you and everyone else knows is sinful, remember God has another way.

There are points in life that you have to learn how to get up, run and don't look back. The Bible says to *flee even the appearance of evil*. If something does not check in your spirit – then you need to obey your heart and accept God's way out.

JULY 21

Walk On Water Again!

MATTHEW 14:28-32

28 "LORD, if it's you," Peter replied, "tell me to come to you on the water." 29 "Come," He said. Then Peter got down out of the boat, walked on the water and came toward Jesus. 30 But when he saw the wind, he was afraid and, beginning to sink, cried out, "LORD, save me!" 31 Immediately Jesus reached out His hand and caught him. "You of little faith," He said, "why did you doubt?" 32 And when they climbed into the boat, the wind died down. – New International Version

Sometimes you experience failure in life. Those are the times when your faith must kick in and hope must be embraced. Giving up is never an option for a Christian. You must believe that the same God that blessed you before will bless you again. Whatever promise you believe God made unto you, it will still come to pass.

Jesus allowed Peter to experience a miracle when he walked on the water to Jesus. Of course, he sank when he became fearful of the wind and waves. But, as he cried out to the Lord to save him, the scriptures declare that he and Jesus both walked back to the boat.

God will work the same miracle in your life. If you have faith enough to pursue the impossible, touch the intangible and see the invisible – God will provide the miracle to match your faith. Yes, after you have trusted God and the enemy brings fear – you can bounce back. Don't get lost in the waves of fear, failure or shame. But cry out to God to help you and walk in victory back to the boat to show others the miraculous wonder-working power of God.

JULY 22

God Blessing It Right...
HAGGAI 1:6

You have spent a lot of money, but you haven't much to show for it. You keep filling your plates, but you never get filled up. You keep drinking and drinking and drinking, but you're always thirsty. You put on layer after layer of clothes, but you can't get warm. And the people who work for you, what are they getting out of it? Not much - a leaky, rusted-out bucket, that's what. – The Message Translation

Everyone wants to blessed, but sometimes people don't operate in the right kingdom principles in order to be blessed. The bottom line is: the King is Supreme. That means He must be first! In Matthew 6:33 the principle is outlined by exhorting believers to seek FIRST God's Kingdom and His way of operating!

If you are selfish, you will hinder your blessing. If you are only concerned about what you want or need, you will contaminate the good that should be coming to your life. If you take care of your own wants and needs first, then you are operating out of order!

If you can make it happen at God's house – God will make it happen at your house! That's right. Make certain that the house of God is in order. Pay your tithes. Be faithful to the upkeep of God's house. Let corporate worship and fellowship become a priority. Learn to be a blessing to others before being concerned about yourself.

Then watch God work. Lack will disappear. Joy will be full. Peace will reign. The blessings of God will make you rich (spiritually, emotionally, physically, and financially) and add no sorrow. That's just how God operates. If you do it right, God will bless it right!

JULY 23

Stop Watering Weeds!

PSALM 19:14

Let the words of my mouth, and the meditation of my heart, be acceptable in thy sight, O LORD, my strength, and my redeemer.

Positive words are like seeds that grow into plants. But, negative words are like weeds that flourish on their own. Have you ever noticed how bad news always travels faster than good news? If somebody was mugged or killed at your church on Sunday it would be front page news on Monday Morning. But, if someone got healed or delivered it would probably not be deemed newsworthy. That is so sad!

Be careful not to be a tool of the enemy by engaging in unprofitable conversation. Run from gossip. Flee speculation. If it is not your business or directly related to your life – leave it alone. Negativity does not need any help in advancing itself. Change your thinking and the make sure that the words that you allow to come from your mouth be words that glorify God and edify others.

JULY 24

Let Your Praise Be Radical

II SAMUEL 6:14, 20-22

14 And David danced before the LORD with all his might; and David was girded with a linen ephod. 20 Then David returned to bless his household. And Michal the daughter of Saul came out to meet David, and said, How glorious was the king of Israel to day, who uncovered himself to day in the eyes of the handmaids of his servants, as one of the vain fellows shamelessly uncovereth himself! 21 And David said unto Michal, It was before the LORD, Which chose me before thy father, and before all His house, to appoint me ruler over the people of the LORD, over Israel: therefore will I play before the LORD. 22 And I will yet be more vile than thus, and will be base in mine own sight: and of the maidservants which thou hast spoken of, of them shall I be had in honour.

When God has been to you and you know it – give Him praise! Do not let anybody or anything hinder your praise. The enemy would have you sitting somewhere quiet in a corner. Your challenge is to praise Him like you never have before. Praise Him until you free yourself from every restraint that has held you back.

David danced before the Lord without restraint. Your challenge is to take your praise to a new level. Let your praise be so free that you abandon the care and concern of what others think. Leap, jump, dance and shout until you lose every inhibition that held you back.

This radical praise will usher in God's presence like never before. Others may get jealous, envious, or mad – but that is their problem not yours! Your praise is not for man, and may not be understood by man. But, your focus is on celebrating God for who He is, what He has done, and what your faith is expecting. Praise Him until His glory appears.

JULY 25

Say It – Until You See It

HEBREWS 10:23

Let us hold fast the profession of our faith without wavering; (for He is faithful that promised;) – King James Version

Let us hold firmly to the hope that we have confessed, because we can trust God to do what he promised. – New Century Version

What you said last week, say it again today. What you said yesterday, say it again today. The same Word that you trusted in before is still relevant today. Do not change or alter your confession. Speak the same word of faith, healing, and deliverance and trust God to do His part.

Do not be moved by your environment or situation. You must be aware that there will be challenges. Rain will fall. Winds will blow. Storms will rise. Family may forsake you. Friends may get few. But none of these change God's Word.

The saints used to sing: *"Time is filled with swift transition; naught on earth unmoved can stand..."* Everything around you is in transition. And if you are not careful you will find yourself battling emotions of depression, disgust and dismay when things don't go your way. You must understand that it is the intent of the enemy (your adversary) to derail your faith by encouraging you to give up.

Your challenge is to hold on to what you have already confessed. God will honor His Word. You need not worry about that. Do not stress if it seems that He is running late or not going to show up at all. *"He that shall come, will come and He will not tarry." (Hebrews 10:37).* That is God's Word and you can take that to the bank. Keep speaking God's Word!

JULY 26
Endure Until The End!
MATTHEW 24:13

"Staying with it - that's what God requires. Stay with it to the end. You won't be sorry, and you'll be saved. – The Message Translation

What you are enduring may seem tedious and impossible, but that has no bearing on God's ability. He can take the worst situation and turn it around in your favor. Your simple responsibility is to have faith and endure. Stay in the race!

Without enduring, there is no testimony. If Peter had never gotten off that boat and almost drowned he would not have the testimony of "walking on water" and "God saving Him". The three Hebrew boys had to go through the fire in order to be able to testify that God was a way maker and a deliverer as God joined them in the fire! Job lost everything he had just to be able to testify that God would bless you with "double" for your trouble. Even Lazarus had to actually die, only to be resurrected by Jesus and have the awesome testimony: "I was dead, but now I live again."

Today, your objective is to stand still and see the salvation of the Lord. Simply trust and obey. Know in your heart and confess with your mouth that victory belongs to you. And most importantly, Endure! No matter what pictures the enemy brings your way – endure. No matter what lies are told – endure! No matter how bad things look, seem, or feel – endure and watch God!

JULY 27
Don't Stop Believing!
NUMBERS 20:12

God said to Moses and Aaron, "Because you didn't trust me, didn't treat me with holy reverence in front of the People of Israel, you two aren't going to lead this company into the land that I am giving them." – The Message Translation

Always remember it takes FAITH to please God. Don't miss out on the blessings or His promises because of a lack of faith! And never get comfortable with the general blessings that everyone else receives.

Some people have the attitude that they are blessed already. It is true that God has general blessings that are extended just because He is a loving God. But there are also specific promises that are hinged on your obedience to God's Word.

Not trusting God can cause you to forfeit future opportunities. God is holy, righteous and true. You must honor and respect Him as such.

No matter how difficult the obstacle before you may be, God is able to do exceeding and abundantly above anything you could ask or think! But, it all comes to you based upon the power (the faith) that you release. Keep believing! Keep trusting! Keep receiving!

JULY 28
You're Just That Special
GALATIANS 3:14

And now, because of that, the air is cleared and we can see that Abraham's blessing is present and available for non-Jews, too. We are all able to receive God's life, his Spirit, in and with us by believing - just the way Abraham received it. – The Message Translation

Abraham's blessing did not stop with Isaac. But, you are also Abraham's heirs through faith and the blessings that were promised to Him and his seed also belong to you.

You were so special to God that He gave His only begotten Son that you could be adopted into the royal family and receive those same blessings and more by faith. No, you don't have to do any works of the law to qualify. Simply believe on the precious Lamb that was slain for your sins.

You were so special to God that He rescued you from your sins and gave you a brand new life. Restored your power and authority! Blessed you to walk in divine healing! Sent His Spirit to dwell in your hearts by faith! God really loves you and did that and much more just to prove His love to you.

How special you are! The next time you feel hopeless, worthless, or useless – remind yourself of how God feels about you! He has sacrificed much and invested much into you! Because you're just that special!

JULY 29
Benefits Of Connection
JOHN 15:5

I am the vine, ye are the branches: He that abideth in me, and I in him, the same bringeth forth much fruit: for without me ye can do nothing.

What you must always remember about connections is that whatever is in one part affects the other part. Being spiritually connected to God has so many benefits. Yes, the more you stay connected to God through His Word and His Spirit the more you become like Him.

When your Godly connection is made manifest others can see the assimilation to your Heavenly Father that is taking place. Your attitude undergoes change. Your actions are more holy. Your choices are more in line with God's Word.

You have a responsibility. Your job is to keep the connection secure. Don't let anyone or anything come between your relationship between God and you. Keep the spiritual flow free from obstruction. Lay away the sin and weight that hinders you. Continue to grow everyday. Look for progress and development.

Cherish the Godly connection. He is the true vine and you are the true branches. Yes, receive the sustenance that the vine provides. And allow the nutrition you receive in your branch to transfer to other branches connected to you so that you may be a vessel of honor used by the Lord.

JULY 30

The Bad News Ain't News

MARK 13:7

When you hear of wars and rumored wars, keep your head and don't panic. This is routine history, and no sign of the end. – The Message Translation

Some people live in panic mode as soon as they hear of another tragic event somewhere across the globe. Whether it is a natural disaster such as an earthquake, or violence such as wars, uprising or murders; they are unsettled and fearful. This is not a time to fear but have a sober understanding of what God's Word already foretold.

Don't be so concerned about the day and hour when Christ shall return. The end is near but it is not here today! The concern should actually be for you! Are you in His will? Are you part of the church (Body of Christ) for which He is returning? Have you completed your assignment here in the earth realm? Those are the questions that should concern you!

All that is going on today does not surprise or catch the true believers by surprise. God already informed us that these things would come to pass. The enemy desires to use these events to distract you from your true purpose or from making an impact in the earth realm. No longer gawk at the news reports! Stay focused and prayerful. Do all you can to make a difference in somebody's life! And when the end does come (or when your personal life's end comes), you will be ready and prepared to stand before God to hear Him say, "Servant, well done".

JULY 31

No More Sad Face!

I KINGS 18:41

And Elijah said unto Ahab, Get thee up, eat and drink; for there is a sound of abundance of rain. – King James Version

Elijah said to Ahab, "Up on your feet! Eat and drink - celebrate! Rain is on the way; I hear it coming." – The Message Translation

The Word of God declares that "Faith comes by hearing, and hearing by the Word of God!" When you hear a promise from God it is time for you to move on what you have heard. Even if you don't see the change – believe the change – and walk in it!

Your life may be in a drought or depression right now! Change your habits. Adjust your actions. Eat, drink and be merry! For what God promised is coming to pass! You don't have to see the rain coming, but if you hear the Lord decree it and declare it then you know it is so.

No longer allow the enemy to have you living and operating in fear and beneath your privileges. Whatever the devil said is a lie. Remind yourself of what God said concerning you. Know that He is running to ensure His Word comes to pass in your life. Meet Him with your faith! And celebrate!

AUGUST 1
Your Words Can Make It Happen!
MATTHEW 18:18-19

18 Verily I say unto you, Whatsoever ye shall bind on earth shall be bound in heaven: and whatsoever ye shall loose on earth shall be loosed in heaven. 19 Again I say unto you, That if two of you shall agree on earth as touching any thing that they shall ask, it shall be done for them of my Father which is in heaven.

What you have been praying about and asking God to do is in your hands. God made a promise to you which will allow your faith and actions to release His anointing and blessings in your situation. He is waiting on you to take the next move. You must learn to go beyond mere asking and pleading. He has given you dominion and authority. You must learn to use the tools He has invested within you.

His Word declares that when you decree a thing in the earth realm that is in accordance with His Word, He will concur in the spirit realm and make it begin to manifest. Yes, He is waiting on you to demonstrate your kingdom authority and "speak". If you take notice of your words, you will find that your lips produce fruit. So, if you are dissatisfied with what you see in your life, reflect and check out what you have been saying.

God has further promised that when you find a spiritual brother or sister that will stand in agreement with you, He will intertwine

Himself by the Spirit in your affairs. *"A threefold cord is not easily broken."* (Eccl. 4:12) There is power and strength in unity. You will be amazed at what happens when people come together for the same purpose and goal.

Today – make it happen! Set into motion the answers to your supplications and petitions. Begin to thank God in advance knowing that He has heard you and answered you. Rejoice in the ability to partner with someone in the earth realm to not only have your needs and desires met and fulfilled, but theirs as well.

AUGUST 2

Take That Off!

I SAMUEL 17:39

And David girded his sword upon his armour, and he assayed to go; for he had not proved it. And David said unto Saul, I cannot go with these; for I have not proved them. And David put them off him. – King James Version

David tried to walk but he could hardly budge. David told Saul, "I can't even move with all this stuff on me. I'm not used to this." And he took it all off. – The Message Translation

David strapped Saul's sword over the armor and tried to walk, but he couldn't, because he wasn't used to wearing them. "I can't fight with all this," he said to Saul. "I'm not used to it." So he took it all off. – Good News Translation

God loves you so much that He has already equipped you with what you need to be successful in life. He has placed within you His Spirit to empower you, to direct you, to teach you and to comfort you. Look back over your life, and you will recall how God has never left you and even at your lowest moments He caused victory to be made manifest in your life.

It is dangerous when people try to be like others and not themselves. You must understand that God works individually with people. What may work for one does not always work for other people.

When you pray, just pray. Don't be like a parrot and try and mimic others. When you praise, just praise. Don't have a "monkey see, monkey do" mentality. When you allow God to use you in spiritual warfare, just fight. Stop trying to learn the style and technique of others. God wants you to be yourself!

Celebrate your uniqueness! Praise God for your individuality. Use the tools and techniques that God has placed within you. When you live your life in this manner, you will experience a greater degree of victory in situations. People often fail because they refuse to be themselves and waste time being a cheap copy of someone else. Today, be the awesome original!

AUGUST 3
Be Aware Of The Kiss!
MATTHEW 26:49 AND II CORINTHIANS 13:12

He went straight to Jesus, greeted him, "How are you, Rabbi?" and kissed him. – The Message Translation

Greet one another with an holy kiss. – King James Version

Greet one another with a holy embrace. – The Message Translation

Having friends is a good thing. The Scriptures even declare that a friend loves at all times, even in times of adversity. (Proverbs 17:17) But, you must be wise enough to understand the difference between true friends and false friends. You must have spiritual discernment to know who is your blessor and who is your betrayer.

On the surface, people can say nice things and even do nice things. They can be part of your circle and go where you go and do what you do. But, do you actually understand their true motive? Are you spiritual enough to discern their destiny. Is it the same as yours?

An old adage says to keep your friends close, and your enemies closer! Don't push your enemies away. They are needed for your promotion. Remember, God said He would prepare a table for you "in the presence of your enemies". (Psalm 23:5) Just be wise enough to know the difference! Love everybody. Be nice to everybody. But, be aware of the truth of every relationship and know the true purpose of it.

AUGUST 4
For His Name's Sake!
EZEKIEL 36:20-25

And wherever they went among the nations they profaned my holy name, for it was said of them, 'These are the LORD's people, and yet they had to leave his land.' I had concern for my holy name, which the house of Israel profaned among the nations where they had gone. "Therefore say to the house of Israel, 'This is what the Sovereign LORD says: It is not for your sake, O house of Israel, that I am going to do these things, but for the sake of my holy name, which you have profaned among the nations where you have gone. I will show the holiness of my great name, which has been profaned among the nations, the name you have profaned among them. Then the nations will know that I am the Lord, declares the Sovereign Lord, when I show myself holy through you before their eyes. "For I will take you out of the nations; I will gather you from all the countries and bring you back into your own land. I will sprinkle clean water on you, and you will be clean; I will cleanse you from all your impurities and from all your idols. – New International Version

Consider your life. Be honest with yourself. How many times have your actions brought shame upon the Name of the Lord? How many times (since you have been saved) have you missed the mark and come short of His will? How many times have you reacted or responded in a way that brought your status as a Christian into question? If you are honest with yourself – the response would be too numerous to count or recall.

But, the awesome and wonderful God that you serve has not changed His mind on you. Yes, His gifts and callings are without repentance. He still blesses you. He still brings favour and increase your way. He still causes His face to shine upon you. But, understand that it is not just because you are so great and wonderful – but it is for His Name's sake.

When God's Word goes out on you it does not return void. But, it continues until it accomplishes what God said for it to accomplish. God is a God of restoration and reconciliation. For His glory and because His Name is out – He demonstrates agape towards you. He picks you up from your low place of sin and shame. He dusts you off and brings you into your proper place and position with Him again.

Today, thank Him and praise Him for His act of mercy and grace in your life. He parades you before the world to demonstrate that you are yet His child and that the covenant between you and Him is an everlasting one that cannot be broken. Yes, you are covered. You are delivered. You are forgiven. You are renewed. You are restored for His Name's sake.

AUGUST 5

Give God Praise!

PSALM 34:1

I will bless the LORD at all times: His praise shall continually be in my mouth. – King James Version

I bless God every chance I get; my lungs expand with his praise. – The Message Translation

In good times and bad, happy times and sad: you should always have "a praise" in your mouth. Your praise cannot be taken away from you! You may lose your job, your house, or even your car. But, you always have "a praise." Sickness can ravish your body, but you can still have "a praise." Your finances may suffer lack, but your praise can always be in abundance.

The enemy may bring situations, circumstances and conditions to encourage you to complain! Don't do it! Just start thinking about His goodness and praise Him in spite of. And when the blessings begin to pour in don't forget where your blessings came from. Praise Him when all is well and you don't have a specific prayer request.

Praise Him before you get out bed in the morning. Praise Him while driving down the street. Praise Him on the job or at school. Praise Him at the store or just around the neighborhood. Praise Him on vacation. Praise Him on the way to and from church.

Don't allow your mouth to be contaminated with complaint. But give God praise. Don't allow negativity to flow from your lips. But give God praise. Don't permit your tongue to talk of the ungodly or the unholy. But, give God praise.

AUGUST 6
Conviction Not Condemnation!

JOHN 16:8

And when He is come, He will reprove the world of sin, and of righteousness, and of judgment: - King James Version

"When He comes, He'll expose the error of the godless world's view of sin, righteousness, and judgment: - The Message Translation

Conviction and condemnation are not the same! As believers we should operate in the same spirit that God operates in. Conviction simply means to point out error, while condemnation brings guilt and negative feelings to those who have erred.

The Spirit of God brings conviction and draws us to God. In John 16:8, the Bible says, *"And when He is come, he will reprove the world of sin......"* When the Bible says that the Spirit of God will "reprove" the world, it means to bring under conviction. The Greek word for reprove is elegcho. This means to convince, refute, expose, or bring to shame the person being reproved. One of the Holy Spirit's job descriptions is to identify error and then lead and guide into truth! (John 16:13)

The Spirit of God is the agent by which the new birth occurs. In order to be a Christian, you must be born of the Spirit. You must undergo a spiritual birth. Religion offers a natural new birth, but God said it must be spiritual. Live for God and do it His way!

AUGUST 7
An On Time God!
HEBREWS 10:37

For yet a little while, and He that shall come will come, and will not tarry. – King James Version

It won't be long now, He's on the way; He'll show up most any minute. – The Message Translation

Today, do not allow yourself to stress over anything that you have committed to God. If God has made you a promise, He will keep His Word. Even if it seems you are being denied or delayed, do not permit those thoughts to prevail in your mind. Accept that God has all things under control. Believe that your life is in divine order.

God will show up on time every time. He will never arrive early. And, do not fear that He will ever be late. Often, God allows flesh to be completely exhausted before He manifests on the scene. Remember, He is not going to share His glory. He wants you and everyone around you to know that He has done great and marvelous things. There is none beside Him. He is God alone.

So live in the assurance that your steps are being ordered by Him. Accept the belief, that where you are God knows it and He cares. Believe God's Word and confess that if you do not faint (give up, or lose heart), you shall reap. He will not delay. He will deliver on time. Trust His Word!

AUGUST 8

He Hears and Responds!

PSALM 145:19

He will fulfil the desire of them that fear him: He also will hear their cry, and will save them. – King James Version

He does what's best for those who fear him - hears them call out, and saves them. – The Message Translation

Do not worry or fret that God has forsaken or forgotten you. He promised that He would never do that. He is an ever present God. He knows what's best for you and will not allow you to go through what He has not equipped you to be able to endure or handle.

Embrace the idea that God will be glorified in your life. When you are troubled or pressured allow your praise to ring louder than your lament. Let the world around you know that you yet trust the God who is able.

So, continue to love on God and pray that He will reveal His will to you for your life. Ask Him to continue ordering your steps. And when trouble comes – call His Name. Not only will He show up, but He will show out! You will walk in victory because He has already promised victory to you.

AUGUST 9

Stop Fussing!
PROVERBS 19:11

The discretion of a man makes him slow to anger, And his glory is to overlook a transgression. – New King James Version

Smart people know how to hold their tongue; their grandeur is to forgive and forget. – The Message Translation

A true sign of maturity is compassion in the face of offense. Having to have the last word or always fighting back is a work of the flesh. Strife and anger are tricks of the devil. True Christians learn to stand still and trust God.

Don't let the enemy push you into an ugly scene by speaking to your mind. The devil will have thoughts like, "They don't know who they are messing with; or "They don't know that I a child of the King and don't have to take that", running through your mind.

Rebuke the enemy and fool him by operating in love. Matthew 5:25 encourages you to *"agree with thine adversary"*. Pray for those who have done you wrong and ask God to bring deliverance to them. Be an example of Christ in the earth realm and strengthen your testimony.

AUGUST 10

Complete Confidence!

DANIEL 3:17

If it be so, our God whom we serve is able to deliver us from the burning fiery furnace, and He will deliver us out of thine hand, O king. – King James Version

If you throw us in the fire, the God we serve can rescue us from your roaring furnace and anything else you might cook up, O king. - The Message Translation

Things may look bad. Things may feel bad. Things may very well be bad. But, none of these things should shake your faith in the God you serve. Testify before all that you know God is able! There is nothing that can come against you that is too strong or powerful that He cannot usher in victory in your situation.

Keep speaking the word of faith to encourage yourself. Broadcast your confidence before your adversary. Praise God in the midst of the challenge and watch Him show up and show out. There is no "Plan B." God has ordered your steps and even if it seems like you are in a "valley of the shadow of death" environment – He is there!

Giving up is not an option. Turning back is not a choice. The only action for you is to fight the good fight of faith and remain encouraged in your inner man. Speak to your soul and keep your hope alive! *"He that shall come, will come. And He will not tarry"* (Hebrews 10:37).

AUGUST 11

God Will Cheer You Up!

PSALM 94:19

In the multitude of my thoughts within me thy comforts delight my soul. – King James Version

When I was upset and beside myself, you calmed me down and cheered me up. – The Message Translation

In the presence of the Lord, your joy is full and complete. He is so awesome. He is the lifter of your head. He is the comforter of your heart. He is the regulator of your mind.

In the time of storm, He brings peace to your emotions while the wind is still blowing and the rain is continuing to fall. In the midst of trouble, trial and confusion, He brings assurance to your mind while the adverse conditions still exist.

Perfect love casts out all fear. Fear is the response of your mind to what is taking place on the outside. Love (made manifest through your faith) is the response of your mind to what God is doing on the inside.

Let God cheer you up today! Let God bless you through His omnipresence in your life. No longer allow the antics and attacks of the enemy to control your emotions – but surrender to the omnipotent Spirit of the living God and experience peace like never before. God has it all under control!

AUGUST 12
Do The Right Thing For Those You Hurt!
LUKE 19:8

And Zacchaeus stood, and said unto the Lord; Behold, Lord, the half of my goods I give to the poor; and if I have taken any thing from any man by false accusation, I restore him fourfold. – King James Version

But Zacchaeus stood up. He said, "Look, Lord! Here and now I give half of what I own to those who are poor. And if I have cheated anybody out of anything, I will pay it back. I will pay back four times the amount I took." – New International Reader's Version

When you realize the errors of your way, true repentance is shown by the actions that follow. Tears and conversation mean very little. But, a manifested turn in a different direction shows a true change of heart.

Are you willing to go above and beyond to make your wrongs right? Are you willing to admit your humanity and frailty? Are you ready for true change and deliverance?

There is an old adage that says, "Put your money where your mouth is"! That is powerful. Because the Bible also says that money "answereth all things". When you can release your money to make restitution or be a blessing in someone else's life it shows spiritual growth and maturity.

If you have hurt anyone, go make amends with them. If you have cheated anyone, go and repay them more than what you took from them. If you have caused someone to suffer physically or emotionally, go and restore them and make life better for them. Do it because it is the right thing and the "God" thing to do!

AUGUST 13
Watch God Show Out!
PSALM 37:5

Commit thy way unto the LORD; trust also in Him; and He shall bring it to pass. – King James Version

Open up before God, keep nothing back; He'll do whatever needs to be done: - The Message Translation

Put your life in the hands of the Lord; have faith in Him and He will do it. – Bible In Basic English Translation

There is nothing impossible with God. If you have faith enough to believe it, He is God enough to help you achieve it. Dream big! Have high hopes! Live with great expectation!

Do not be afraid to talk to God about anything. Nothing is too small. Nothing is insignificant. You are very important and very special to Him. Tell Him your hopes, dreams, and aspirations. Ask Him to reveal His will to you. Ask Him to show you how to make your will line up with His. He is your heavenly Father and desires to make your life happy and abundantly blessed.

You cannot do everything on your own. All He asks is that you share your heart with Him. Trust Him. And then follow His plan and see His glory. He is ready to open doors for you. He is ready to bring peace and prosperity into full manifestation in every relationship. He is ready to bring to pass an awesome blessing as you have never experienced! He is ready to show Himself strong on your behalf! Just trust Him!

AUGUST 14

Get Busy! Now!

JOHN 9:4

We need to be energetically at work for the One who sent me here, working while the sun shines. When night falls, the workday is over. – The Message Translation

The God who exists outside of time gives assignments to those who live within time. Yes, God has work for you to do! Before you were even born, attached to your destiny and purpose were assignments. Every assignment has a timeline attached to it. It is important that you learn to seize the moment. Being lazy or slothful can cause you to miss some awesome blessings.

You cannot get so comfortable with your own agenda that you miss God's plan or intent. There are people that He wants you to come into contact with. The Word says that the steps of a good man are ordered or directed by the Lord. Sometimes when negative situations arise you immediately get upset and mad at the devil. But, often it is an opportunity for God to use you to demonstrate your faith and Christian maturity to bless someone else.

There is much work to be done in the earth realm. Never live your life where regret has power over your tomorrow. Dr. W.E. Jones often said, "Do all you can, while you can". And this is the way your life should operate every day. Embrace opportunities to be used of God. So, when the day is done you have the confidence in knowing that the words, "Well Done" are being said to and about you!

AUGUST 15

Hallelujah—All Day Long!
HEBREWS 13:15

Let us, then, always offer praise to God as our sacrifice through Jesus, which is the offering presented by lips that confess him as Lord. – Good News Translation

Today let your lips release nothing but praise. Command your tongue to sing and speak of His awesomeness and His power. Declare His splendor in the earth realm.

Your praise becomes sacrificial when it becomes a challenge. Storms of life can beat you down and encourage you to grumble or complain. Challenges of sickness, finances, relationships and even self-esteem can persuade you to be disgruntled. The enemy will do all he can to trick you into making negative confessions that promote what you may be going through.

Your challenge is to rise above what you are going through and remained focus on where you are headed and the God who is taking you there. Override your emotions and command your tongue to proclaim the Lordship of Jesus Christ in your life. Keep a "Hallelujah" on your lips all day long!

AUGUST 16
When You Have Changed!
I PETER 4:4

Wherein they think it strange that ye run not with them to the same excess of riot, speaking evil of you: - King James Version

Ungodly people think that it's strange when you no longer join them in what they do. They want you to rush into the same flood of wasteful living. So they say bad things about you. – New International Reader's Version

Of course, your old friends don't understand why you don't join in with the old gang anymore. But you don't have to give an account to them. – The Message Translation

Time often brings about change. There may have been a time in your life when you may have lived wild and carefree. However, since you began your walk with Christ things changed in your life. You no longer had a desire to live the way you used to live. Sometimes, people that you ran with "back in the day" may not understand your new walk.

You must recognize that everyone who started with you may not finish with you. Some people are only in your life for seasons. When the season is over – you must move on. You cannot allow yourself to be hindered in your spiritual walk by people who are not part of your change or your destiny. Even when they give arguments to the choices that you have made, with a committed mind you must press on.

Don't waste time arguing and defending your spiritual choices. When you are dedicated to walking a new walk with Christ, for you to entertain meaningless dialogue with others who are not walking with you is a distraction. You have no time for distractions in your life. Distractions delay your progress towards destiny.

Commit to living your new life by pleasing God, not man. Focus on reading, studying and applying His Word as never before. Don't feel the need to explain yourself to anyone. Just let your light shine – and let them see Jesus.

AUGUST 17

Time For Your Ministry

II CORINTHIANS 9:8

And God is able to make all grace abound toward you; that ye, always having all sufficiency in all things, may abound to every good work: - King James Version

God can pour on the blessings in astonishing ways so that you're ready for anything and everything, more than just ready to do what needs to be done. – The Message Translation

God has an assignment for you in the earth realm. You have to make a choice and decision to say "yes" to Him. He is not so much concerned about your ability as He is your availability. Don't let the devil keep you from your blessings by filling your mind with your frailties, shortcomings, and mistakes. God knew you had those before He issued the assignment.

God's grace is truly amazing. He will take who and what you are and utilize it for His glory. If you simply surrender to His Will and follow the leading of His Spirit, you will see Him do great and mighty things. His grace will equip and empower you to do exceeding abundantly over all you could have ever imagined.

There will be no more lack when the ministry is God's. He will take care of what belongs to Him. If you live totally committed and dedicated to Him, His plan, and His work – He will make sure that all the needs are supplied. And the blessings will be so great that He will cause you to be blessed for simply being a blessing. Always remember, the pipe that brings the water to the thirsty also gets wet.

AUGUST 18
Worship Must Be Willed
LUKE 7:45

Thou gavest Me no kiss: but this woman since the time I came in hath not ceased to kiss My feet. – King James Version

You gave Me no greeting, but from the time I arrived she hasn't quit kissing My feet. – The Message Translation

Don't be envious or jealous of the adoration and praise that you see others giving to God. You have the same opportunity. Nothing hinders or stops you from praising God except yourself.

Praising God is simply boasting about who He is. Making declarations about His awesomeness! Expressing thanksgiving and joy over His sovereignty! Everyone who has breath can and should praise God.

However, to move into worship it requires a denial of self and total devotion to Him. Worship is not just singing a slow song and waving your hands. But, true worship is a lifestyle of surrender and commitment to Him. Worship is the expression of single-hearted love and devotion to God.

No one can force or compel you to worship! True worship must come from the heart desire of one who is connected to God. Real worship has no boundaries. Time is not a constraint. Place is irrelevant. Situations and circumstances in life have no power to hinder true worship. Worship must be willed: it must be desired, longed for, embraced, and sought after by a believer.

AUGUST 19
Your Praise Ushers In His Presence
PSALM 22:3

But Thou art holy, O Thou that inhabitest the praises of Israel. – King James Version

And you! Are you indifferent, above it all, leaning back on the cushions of Israel's praise? – The Message Translation

Praise is boasting on God! It is declaring who He is, what He has done, and what you know He can do! Praise may be accomplished through singing, dancing, clapping, shouting, talking and other action words. It is a transport mechanism that takes you to worship.

Praise gets God's attention. And His presence is made manifest in praise! Yes, when you praise God, He shows up and He shows out. If you don't believe it – ask Paul and Silas who prayed and sang at midnight in a Roman jail. God's presence was made manifest to the extent that the earth shook and then the jailer's entire household got saved.

Whatever you are going through, praise your way through. Invite God into your situation through praise and not complaint. Stop worrying and fretting, but begin to sing and shout the victory that your faith has brought victory through Christ Jesus. If you praise Him, He will show up. And that right on time!

AUGUST 20

When Will You Believe?

JOHN 20:29

Jesus saith unto him, Thomas, because thou hast seen me, thou hast believed : blessed are they that have not seen, and yet have believed. – King James Version

Jesus said, "So, you believe because you've seen with your own eyes. Even better blessings are in store for those who believe without seeing." – The Message Translation

What do you have to experience or go through to know that God's Word is true? What has to happen in your life for you to simply believe that God is real? What will it take for you to know that He is yet alive and moving on your behalf?

You must graduate beyond a mere carnal knowledge and assent that what you hear is true. You must operate on the level of true faith – by walking in the truth of God's Word. Saints' spiritual growth and development is thwarted by consideration and not believing. Stop thinking and start trusting. Faith is simply agreeing with God.

Grow to the understanding that God is no respecter of persons. What others have received is also available for you. Prepare yourself for "due season" and learn how to wait on God. Be encouraged even when bad things happen understanding that all things are still working for your good.

There is a great blessing for exercising your faith. Know who He is without prior experience. Believe that God is a healer without having to get sick! Believe that He is a way maker without having your lights cut off! Believe that God is a provider without being hungry or broke! When you can simply trust and believe – your faith will deepen your relationship with God like never before! Oh the glory!

AUGUST 21
Celebrate With Others!

LUKE 15:9

And when she hath found it, she calleth her friends and her neighbours together, saying, Rejoice with me; for I have found the piece which I had lost. – King James Version

And when she finds it you can be sure she'll call her friends and neighbors: 'Celebrate with me! I found my lost coin!' – The Message Translation

It is troubling and unsettling to lose a possession. But, it is refreshing and rewarding to find the item which was lost. When you reclaim that which was precious to you – it can excite you enough to want to include others in your celebration.

People live such busy and hectic lives. Sad to say, but many times if people were placed under a microscope it might reveal many Christians living selfish lives. It is not God's will that people become so preoccupied with "us, mine, ours", that there is a failure to realize that God's real desire is fellowship.

God wants you to learn to weep with those who mourn. And He wants you to dance with those who rejoice. Embrace the lives of others as if they were your own. This not only encourages the other person but it develops and fosters a relationship whose bond will be proven in time of challenge or storm.

Involve yourself deeply and seriously in the intimate lives of others. Be an extension of God through your hands, your feet, your resources and your emotions. Always be willing to be a dance partner with others and help them to celebrate!

AUGUST 22

Embrace The God Life!

MATTHEW 10:39

If you cling to your life, you will lose it; but if you give it up for me, you will find it. – New Living Translation

If your first concern is to look after yourself, you'll never find yourself. But if you forget about yourself and look to me, you'll find both yourself and me. – The Message Translation

You have been bought with a price. Your life is not your own. So no longer should you live selfishly doing your own thing, but allow God to use you in the kingdom. Stop embracing what is temporal and cling to what is eternal. Stop focusing on your personal agenda and learn God's purpose and plan.

God's intent is that you make an impact in the earth realm. You are designed to be used for His glory to be a blessing in the lives of others. You are light for those in darkness. You are a voice for those in the wilderness. You are strength for those who are weak. You are hope for those who don't have the ability to believe on their own.

Embrace the intent of God in your life. Allow your prayer time, devotional time, and personal worship to position you to fully comprehend what God desires to do through you. Don't allow your flesh to take you in the wrong direction. Your career, your family and friends, your possessions must all be prioritized AFTER God! Tell self and others to "wait" and let God use you!

AUGUST 23
He's Still Working!
PHILIPPIANS 1:6

Being confident of this very thing, that he which hath begun a good work in you will perform it until the day of Jesus Christ: - King James Version

There has never been the slightest doubt in my mind that the God who started this great work in you would keep at it and bring it to a flourishing finish on the very day Christ Jesus appears. – The Message Translation

God's not through with you yet! You may have suffered a few setbacks and encountered some roadblocks. But, it's all good because God is still in control. He still has His hand upon you. He is yet pouring grace and mercy into your life to make up the difference.

There is a spiritual investment in you that God intends to be a blessing in the earth realm. He is allowing even things that seem to be bad to occur, so that you can see how He makes all things work together for good in your life.

Stay focused. Remain committed. Do what He has called and anointed you to do. Not only will your life be made better for it, but someone else will be blessed because of what God is doing in your life. He's still working on you. Be patient and simply participate by being obedient!

AUGUST 24
Did You Hear The Question?
JOHN 5:6

When Jesus saw him lie, and knew that he had been now a long time in that case, He saith unto him, Wilt thou be made whole? – King James Version

When Jesus saw him stretched out by the pool and knew how long he had been there, He said, "Do you want to get well?" – The Message Translation

Sometimes when God is attempting to bring the miraculous into manifestation in our lives – we all of a sudden allow False Evidence to Appear Real (FEAR)! Instead of just giving God a simple yes, we begin to give reasons of why it can't happen. God has no time for your excuses. He is the miracle worker. He is the deliverer. He is the way maker. There is nothing too hard for God.

No longer allow your condition or situation to dominate your thinking. Of course God moves in mysterious ways. Yes, He will speak and offer what seems to be an impossibility. But, that is because He is God. He makes the impossible possible. He makes the invisible visible. He makes the intangible tangible.

The question is simple: Do you want to be blessed? Do you want to be healed? Do you want to be delivered? Do you want to prosper? Do you want to be free? All God needs you to do is trust

Him and believe. Take your eyes off the problem and focus on the Provider! He is a Promise Keeper. He will do what He says.

He is not taking a survey of your situation. He already knows your condition. That is why He is offering you a way out! Hear the voice of God and release your faith today! And, watch God turn it around!

AUGUST 25
Each Victory Will Help
DEUTERONOMY 7:22

And the Lord your God will drive out those nations before you little by little; you will be unable to destroy them at once, lest the beasts of the field become too numerous for you. – New King James Version

God, your God, will get rid of these nations, bit by bit. You won't be permitted to wipe them out all at once lest the wild animals take over and overwhelm you. – The Message Translation

Have you ever heard the expression: "How Do You Eat An Elephant?", with the response, "One bite at a time!" This is the same principle you should utilize in establishing and maintaining victory in your walk with God. Some areas of deliverance may be immediate but there are some things that you will have to walk out by faith. Stop defeating yourself by creating unrealistic goals and then finding yourself in a pity party when you fail.

If there is a habit you cannot break or an adverse action that you cannot stop doing: apply this principle. Tell yourself today, "I will not...". And if that seems too much, tell yourself for the next hour, "I will not...". And when you are successful in your short goal – celebrate. This accomplishment should give you the encouragement needed to extend your goal.

Stop looking for a cheering section. Be your own cheerleader and encourage yourself. Pat your own self on the back when you have walked in the deliverance that you sought. Others will catch up later. All that really matters at this point is what you and God know is true. Sing the words of the hymn writer Horatio L. Palmer to yourself today, *"Each victory will help you some other to win. Fight manfully onward. Dark passions subdue. Look ever to Jesus, He will carry you through."*

AUGUST 26

The Value Of His Name!

PSALM 106:8

He saved them because of His reputation so that He could make His mighty power known. – God's Word Translation

God is not going to be out done. When He makes a promise, He guarantees that it will be fulfilled. In the words of the old folk, "His Word is His bond". He will not allow His Name to be put to shame.

You receive the benefits of God because of His great love for you. But, also He hastens to perform His Word in your life because He has attached His Name to it. It is impossible for Him to lie. He always makes good on what He has spoken.

In this day and time, many people don't respect their own name. They operate in foolish ways to cause their credit to need repair. They participate in activities that cause others to gossip and tarnish their reputation. They even tell lies or fail to fulfill obligations to such an extent that others don't believe what they say.

God refuses to function in this manner. His Name is holy. His Name is sacred. His Name is true. And He makes certain that anything that His Name is attached to fulfills His will. Your healing, your blessings, your deliverance, your prosperity all come because God demonstrates His power and shows the strength of His Name!

AUGUST 27
Not Yours! But God's!
PSALM 24:1

The earth is the LORD'S, and the fulness thereof; the world, and they that dwell therein. – King James Version

Everything and everybody belongs to God – including you! Nothing belongs to you. You have simply been given authority and control over things in the earth realm. God has supreme control!

You are only a steward. Everything that you have – including ability and potential – comes from God. You simply choose how you use or invest that which the Lord has entrusted unto you. Some are good stewards and some are poor stewards.

Good stewards use every available opportunity to allow God to use them. They willingly give of themselves regardless of the personal sacrifice that they may have to make. But, there are others who are cold and stagnant. Poor stewards come up with excuses in refusing to allow God to do anything through them.

Practice loving people. If you learn to sow into the lives of people, God will take good care of you. But, you must have pure motives. You must love people simply because of God's love that is within you. If you pretend to love people because of the potential reward in the future, you will miss the blessing. Be a good steward of "God's love" and great will be your reward!

AUGUST 28
Living Off The Interest
GALATIANS 6:7

Be not deceived; God is not mocked: for whatsoever a man soweth, that shall he also reap.

Preparation is the key to living a successful life. In all aspects of life, you must learn to prepare. Spiritually, you prepare for heaven by accepting Jesus. Educationally, you prepare for a career by studying. Financially, you prepare for prosperity by wise sowing and saving. Physically, you prepare for a healthier body by exercising and dieting.

When you make sufficient deposits in your preparation – you can live off the interest! Wouldn't it be wonderful if your bank account balance was sufficient for the bank to simply send you a monthly interest check and it covered all of your needs and some of your desires? Well, your spiritual life can be like that when you learn to make sufficient deposits of prayer, praise and power.

Prayer is simply communication with God. Learn to dialogue with Him everyday and not just in cases of emergency. Praise is fellowship with God. He inhabits the praises of His people. His presence is constant in your life because His praise continually fills your mouth. Power is partnership/unity with God. There are signs that God wants to follow you. Lay hands on the sick. Cast out demons. There are lives that need to be impacted by the manifestation of God's word in your life.

Although, life has seasons you can be certain of the benefits of the principles of God. When you do it God's way – God will bless it. Learn to invest in every area of your life. Whatever it is that you want to reap, you need to sow that very same thing. And learn to sow in abundance. Don't eat all your fruit. When God blesses you – learn to be a blessing. When you operate in the principles of God, you will see the rewards of God.

AUGUST 29
Don't Be So Shocked!
HABAKKUK 1:5

"Take this most seriously: A yes on earth is yes in heaven; a no on earth is no in heaven. What you say to one another is eternal. I mean this. – The Message Translation

Don't fool yourself! Your words, thoughts, and actions do matter and have far reaching consequences. God's power operating in you gives you the authority to speak and create your destiny. Basically, He is saying that as you release your faith for a particular thing, He would stand behind your word and agree with you.

Stop limiting yourself. And quit allowing the enemy to distract you. Even if things are not working in your favor at the moment – you have the power to change things. Keep standing on God's Word. Keep believing. Keep hoping. Keep trusting. And most of all, keep speaking into the atmosphere your faith statements so they may go beyond your finiteness and move into the spiritual realm of infinity.

Do not waste time with trivial matters such as what you will eat, wear or how you will lodge. As you seek God's way of doing things and His righteousness, He already promised to add these things to your life. Take spiritual authority over things in your life and decree and declare that all things align themselves with God's Word and God's will. You will be amazed at how God will show up and show out on your behalf.

AUGUST 30
God: Your Deliverer!
PSALM 34:19

Many are the afflictions of the righteous: but the LORD delivereth him out of them all. – King James Version

Anyone who does what is right may have many troubles. But the LORD saves him from all of them. – New International Reader's Version

Challenges may exist in your life, but those serve only as great opportunities for God to show up and show out in your life. Stop allowing people and your mind to push you into gloom and despair. The presence of negative adversity does not signal the absence of God nor does it dictate the denial of your destiny.

Doing the right thing can and often does provoke the enemy. As long as you are playing on his team, you are not a threat. But, when you decide to get on God's roster – then you become an enemy to "the enemy". And he takes that opportunity to launch unfair and unexpected attacks towards you.

God (in His awesomeness) has already "fixed the fight" so that no matter what happens in your life, He causes all things to work together for your good. So, even when you seem overwhelmed by life just embrace God's promise. The more attacks and the more adversity, consider yourself a valuable asset in the kingdom of God.

Utilize your praise weapon and watch God cause your enemies to begin to destroy each other. Employ the sword of the Spirit, which is the Word of God, to negate every seed sown and counter every offensive attack. So, no matter the area of attack (your health, your finances, your relationships, and everything else) just know that God is bringing healing and restoration to your situation and condition. He is your deliverer!

AUGUST 31
God Is Always There!
DEUTERONOMY 4:31

God, your God, is above all a compassionate God. In the end He will not abandon you, He won't bring you to ruin, He won't forget the covenant with your ancestors which He swore to them. – The Message Translation

You can always count on God. He won't leave you neither will He forsake you. Even when you feel all alone in the midst of your challenges and adversities it is God Himself sustaining you. He will keep you in the midst of the storm and then bless you as He brings you out.

The same God that blessed your parents, grandparents and forefathers is the same God who reigns in your life. His promises do not fail. They are still yes and Amen! So, stay encouraged to know that you serve a God who is ever present. He is not far away! All you have to do is call Him and He will remind you through the presence of His Holy Spirit that He is still ready, willing, and most of all ABLE to do what you need the most.

You are never alone. The Greater One lives on the inside of you. Through your praise, you make His presence manifest. Through your prayer, He hears your cries and pities your groans. Through your worship, He fellowships and communes with you and makes you oblivious to whatever is going on around you! He is your ever-present strength! Your ever-present joy! Your ever-present peace!

SEPTEMBER 1
Trouble Ain't All That Bad
MATTHEW 7:25

And the rain descended, and the floods came, and the winds blew, and beat upon that house; and it fell not: for it was founded upon a rock. – King James Version

Rain poured down, the river flooded, a tornado hit - but nothing moved that house. It was fixed to the rock. – The Message Translation

Change your attitude regarding trouble. Trouble can take you to new beginnings. Trouble may test you – but at the same time trouble can bless you. Trouble is not always bad! Just make certain that you have the Word of God as a foundation in your life.

When some hear that trouble is approaching – their automatic response is usually fear and apprehension. They often find themselves stressed out and flesh driven in their response. This is not the will nor is it the intent of God. All throughout the Bible, the people of God respond to trouble.

Abraham willingly took his only son Isaac to be sacrificed. Joseph endured the pit and prison on his way to the palace. Daniel slept comfortably in the lion's den. Shadrach, Meshach and Abednego walked in the fiery furnace. Job maintained his integrity even though he lost everything he had and his health was gone. What kept them was their connection and trust in what God had promised and said.

Remember these points when trouble comes in your life: There is a safe place that God prepares for you. God will keep you, if you want to be kept. Trouble will always come. You can rise above your circumstances when you trust in God's Word. Others will perish. The only difference between you and others is the Word of God. Those who are not connected to Word of God will perish. God brings you to a new beginning. Your trouble can bless you to start over. You have the opportunity to rid yourself of excess: sin and others who hinder your walk with God.

SEPTEMBER 2
You Are Not The Only One
I CORINTHIANS 10:13

There hath no temptation taken you but such as is common to man: but God is faithful, who will not suffer you to be tempted above that ye are able; but will with the temptation also make a way to escape, that ye may be able to bear it. –
The King James Version

No test or temptation that comes your way is beyond the course of what others have had to face. All you need to remember is that God will never let you down; He'll never let you be pushed past your limit; He'll always be there to help you come through it. – *The* Message Translation

How often are you challenged with the choice of right or wrong, good or bad, your way or God's way, your will or God's will? If you are honest, it is everyday – actually many times everyday. Eventhough, your spirit man may be born again – you must understand that the enemy will still come to tempt your body and soul.

Stop feeling like the Lone Ranger! Whatever, your struggle or temptation is not reserved just for you alone. You would be surprised at how many other people have the same challenges and struggles. Yes, others go through what you go through.

However, many don't discuss their personal issues. This is another trick of the enemy. If he can keep you silent, he isolates you and then has more of an opportunity to conquer you. "Divide and conquer" is a war tactic. As children of God, learn to live transparent lives and connect with people who will compassionately share with you the grace of God.

You need to remember two truths: First, you are not alone! Second, God has a way out for you!

Jesus is your first example that you can walk in victory. Yes, He has already demonstrated in the flesh that you can be tempted and still not yield. There is no sin in being tempted, the sin is in yielding. Second, whatever the enemy brings to make you fall always know God has prepared an escape route for you. Yes, God has a way out and this is why you must continue to pray, praise and worship and maintain a fellowship with the Father so that you may understand His will and direction for your life!

SEPTEMBER 3

Yes, You Can Be Nice!
ROMANS 12:18

Do everything possible on your part to live in peace with everybody. – Good News Translation

This is interesting. How honest will you be with yourself? Are you saved? Are you born again? Are you a spirit-filled believer? If your answer is yes, that means you have the Spirit of God dwelling on the inside of you. And, you can be nice!

It may seem as if there are some people placed on the planet just to challenge your peace. But, you can walk in victory in this relationship challenge. Stop being aggravated. Stop saying things that are hurtful or that you later regret saying. Stop being short tempered. Stop fussing!

You must learn to allow the Spirit of God within you to be in control. You must stop putting Him on hold and on pause. You must allow Him to help you as He desires to do. He will show you how to walk in true love (not hypocrisy) with others. He will show you how to live a peaceful existence and be nice.

Don't fool yourself. You can be nice. It is the enemy telling you that you can't. Allow God to bring the peace that passes even your own understanding as you demonstrate patience, compassion, forgiveness, and understanding to others in your life.

SEPTEMBER 4
The Heart Of Worship
PHILIPPIANS 3:3

The real believers are the ones the Spirit of God leads to work away at this ministry, filling the air with Christ's praise as we do it. We couldn't carry this off by our own efforts, and we know it. – The Message Translation

What a wonderful feeling and knowledge to know who you are in Christ Jesus. When you realize the awesome sacrifice that God made for you through His only Son, it will change your life forever. No longer will you find yourself lost in meaningless rituals and practicing patterns that accomplish little. Your spirit has been made alive in Christ!

By yourself – you are nothing. But, with Him not only can you do all things, but you are an awesome vessel of honor to His glory and praise. You can worship God in spirit and in truth. You can enter that secret and special place of communion and fellowship with Him. The Sunday School song takes on new meaning as you experience Him "walking with you, and talking with you, and telling you that you are His own".

Your flesh may get tired, but you will always have a YES in your spirit. When you are a true believer, a special part of you will always cry out to God and hunger and thirst for more of Him. Bask in true worship. Long for His presence! Worship Him like never before!

SEPTEMBER 5

The Living Word Manifest Via You!

II CORINTHIANS 3:3

Christ himself wrote it - not with ink, but with God's living Spirit; not chiseled into stone, but carved into human lives - and we publish it. – The Message Translation

The Word of God should be evident through the lives of believers. You are "living epistles"! When people in the earth realm come into contact with you, they should experience every dimension of God's Word.

They should see a miracle first-hand. They should encounter someone whose life has been miraculously changed by the power of God's Word. They should come into touch with someone who has been washed in the saving and cleansing blood of the Lamb of God. They should see someone with the testimony of God as a healer, deliverer, sustainer!

The DNA of your father should be replicated in your life. You should exude the fruit of the Spirit and the gifts of the Spirit in your everyday life. God's love should prevail in every experience. His grace and mercy should be reproduced in all your dealings. The Bible is not just in print – It is living and breathing, walking and talking, impacting others' lives through you!

SEPTEMBER 6

Daily Living Habits

ROMANS 12:12

Rejoicing in hope; patient in tribulation; continuing instant in prayer; - King James Version

cheerfully expectant. Don't quit in hard times; pray all the harder. – The Message Translation

You are in control of your life. God has given you a free will. Never allow your circumstances to dictate your actions — that relinquishes control. Never allow an individual to "make you mad or glad" — again that gives them power over you.

Determine that you will be who God has called you to be. Identify with what God's Word says about you. Read it, believe it, speak it, and walk in it! When you live like this, you learn how to not allow a temporary challenge to get the best of you.

Keep believing that the best is on the way. Hang in there during tough times. Keep sending "knee-mail" to God by praying and praising without ceasing.

SEPTEMBER 7

Simply Forgive!
LUKE 17:4

And if he trespass against thee seven times in a day, and seven times in a day turn again to thee, saying, I repent; thou shalt forgive him. – King James Version

Even if it's personal against you and repeated seven times through the day, and seven times he says, 'I'm sorry, I won't do it again,' forgive him." – The Message Translation

It does not feel good to be offended or wronged, but you must operate in the same action you desire that God would take towards you. Forgive those who have hurt you, lied on you, or done any type negative action against you.

How many times have you messed up with God? How many times have you disobeyed Him? How many times have you not done all that He instructed or desired you to do? But, each time you have come short of His will – He has yet forgiven you! That is the same action God desires that you take towards others.

Forgiveness gives the recipient the opportunity to be restored and get their life together. Being angry and mean is unproductive and only fuels the fires of the enemy's intents. Shut the devil down by simply forgiving!

SEPTEMBER 8

Just Stop!

EXODUS 16:30

So the people rested on the seventh day. – King James Version

Life is filled with challenges every day. Stress when not managed properly can wear a person down physically and mentally. When your body and soul are out of order, you will also see manifestations of imbalance in the spirit realm. The key is simple – rest.

Some people have struggled to grow spiritually and have not identified that the cause could be a simple balancing issue. Bring balance to your life! Your praise, your worship, your study of the Word, your understanding of the Word, and most important your application of the Word will undergo improvement.

Learn to say "No"! You can't go everywhere all the time. Learn to sit down! Turn off the television and radio and just have some quiet time. Learn to shut up. Yes, refuse to even engage in conversation. Take an opportunity to free your mouth and mind so God can renew and refresh you.

Take the opportunity to get honest rest. It will position you to be more beneficial in every aspect of life. God rested on the seventh day. You must create pockets of "seventh days" in your life and learn to rest.

SEPTEMBER 9

Don't Let Others Hinder Your Praise!

MATTHEW 26:10

When Jesus realized what was going on, he intervened. "Why are you giving this woman a hard time? She has just done something wonderfully significant for me. – The Message Translation

Have you ever been to a worship experience and observed people just sitting around looking while others were clapping, singing, dancing and expressing praise to God? Have you ever heard people complaining about the emotional and spiritual zeal and exuberance of others? How many times have you heard the expression, "It don't take all that!"? Why waste time worrying about the actions of others?

Praise is important to God and should be a desire of your heart and mind. Everything and everybody that has breath has the same right and privilege to praise God. Worship is an intimate experience that should have no parameters or boundaries. Worship is personal. It should be extravagant and sacrificial.

Don't miss out on the opportunity to express your love and devotion to God by focusing on the actions of others. Be like the woman with the alabaster box and pour out your praise and worship upon Him with no regard for cost or sacrifice. Give Him your everything! Don't allow by-standers or on-lookers to hinder your praise or deter your worship!

SEPTEMBER 10
Keep Up Your Momentum
HEBREWS 10:35

Cast not away therefore your confidence, which hath great recompence of reward. – King James Version

So don't throw it all away now. You were sure of yourselves then. It's still a sure thing! – The Message Translation

The same gusto, drive and enthusiasm you had at the beginning must be kept until the end. That's right. No matter what it looks like or feels like, your job is to stay focused on your victory. This attitude is your faith. Don't allow your faith to be shipwrecked. Keep it afloat by believing against all odds.

God does not change. God will not fail. You must be just like him. Never change. Don't allow your faith to fail. Keep smiling. Keep believing. Keep trusting.

It is the devil's job to try and distract you. It is his primary objective to attack your faith and get you to stop believing. He knows that God won't change his mind on sending your blessing. So, He targets you to get you out of place and position. He wants to create an atmosphere in your life where you stop believing that your blessing is coming.

Stay focused. Ignore negativity. Keep pushing forward. And know that what God promised at the beginning, it will be delivered at the end. Don't get side-tracked while you are "in the middle of it"! Just keep trusting.

SEPTEMBER 11
Do You Know The Season?
ECCLESIASTES 3:1

To every thing there is a season, and a time to every purpose under the heaven.

Life occurs in seasons! Naturally, there is summer, fall, winter and spring. But, in the spirit there are many more seasons. There are seasons of joy and times of sorrow. There is a time to sow and a time to reap. There are points of complete health and times that we look for the manifestation of healing. Yes, understand that life is full of seasons.

A danger in not acknowledging a season is to miss the benefit of that season. For in the time of harvest, if you do not gather – then a season of lack and famine will soon appear. You must stay spiritually connected and sensitive to what God is saying and doing in your life – so that you will be aware of the season.

When it is time to dance, cease from mourning. When the season of peace has come, don't allow the enemy to confuse your mind and have you in disarray. Always pray that your steps be ordered by the Lord. Always seek that the words that flow from your mouth are acceptable in His sight. Your words have power and can bless or curse your season.

Do you know what time it is in your life right now? Do you know what season is manifest in your life today? Busy yourself with the things of God and walk into your divine destiny.

SEPTEMBER 12

Commit To The Constant

MALACHI 3:6

For I am the LORD, I change not;... - King James Version

I am God - yes, I Am. I haven't changed. – The Message Translation

Stop connecting to variables and learn to connect to the constant. Frustrations abound in life when you feel safe and secure, but then all of a sudden what you have connected to has changed its mind. It throws your life in a tizzy and uproots your ability to trust.

Friendships, marriages, and varied other relationships suffer crisis because of misplaced commitment. When two people come together it should be because the Lord has brought them together. To maintain sanity especially in troubled times, you must look to God and not to the other person. God never changes. However, the other person has the same propensity to change as you do!

Stay focused on God – The Faithful! His Word never fails. He promised to keep you in perfect peace if you keep your mind on Him. He will never leave, nor forsake you. He will cause all things to work together for your good. You can count on all of that!

SEPTEMBER 13
A Faith Conversation!
GENESIS 22:5

And Abraham said unto his young men, Abide ye here with the ass; and I and the lad will go yonder and worship, and come again to you. – King James Version

Abraham told his two young servants, "Stay here with the donkey. The boy and I are going over there to worship; then we'll come back to you." – The Message Translation

Only Abraham knew what he was really up against. Isaac, nor the servants knew that God had commanded Abraham to take Isaac to the mountain to sacrifice him. But, Abraham knew that God was his friend and that he was a friend of God. He was confident that God would not allow defeat to come to him. Nor would God allow him to suffer tragic loss.

What you must learn from this conversation is that Abraham did not allow his situation to alter his faith or his conversation. He told the servants that he and the lad were going to the mountain to worship and that THEY would be back. How could "they" come back if he killed Isaac? Evidently, his faith would allow Him only to speak faith and trust in the God that he served.

Change what you say! Learn to expect the best and speak only the best. Do not allow what you are going through to sway your conversation. Come out of defeat, depression and gloom. Rise up and embrace your faith, hope and peace. God will honor His Word and your word as you stand on His promises! Know and show that God always has your back!

SEPTEMBER 14
Praise Him For Yourself!
LUKE 8:35-39

35 A crowd soon gathered around Jesus, for they wanted to see for themselves what had happened. And they saw the man who had been possessed by demons sitting quietly at Jesus' feet, clothed and sane. And the whole crowd was afraid. 36 Then those who had seen what happened told the others how the demon-possessed man had been healed. 37 And all the people in that region begged Jesus to go away and leave them alone, for a great wave of fear swept over them. So Jesus returned to the boat and left, crossing back to the other side of the lake. 38 The man who had been demon possessed begged to go, too, but Jesus said, 39 "No, go back to your family and tell them all the wonderful things God has done for you." So he went all through the city telling about the great thing Jesus had done for him." – New Living Translation

In this passage of scripture, a man who had been under the control of evil spirits was healed by Jesus. After he was delivered, the Bible says that the man was found sitting at the feet of Jesus. However, the crowd of people reacted with fear instead of joy and excitement.

Understand, in your life that not everyone will always be excited about the move of God in your life. Sad to say, some people get joy from seeing you as dependent and needy. It gives them the ability to talk about how much they have done for you and how you would not have made it without them. Just as soon as you get up on your own feet their response changes. They are upset because they have lost the control they had over your life.

You would think they would be happy for you. But they are not. Many times people have ulterior motives. You do not have time to worry about people and whether or not they are excited about your blessings. You must be as the delivered man. Stay close to Jesus and thank Him for being in your right mind.

Your testimony of who God is and what He has done should be a witness everywhere you go. When people who knew you back then can see the change in you today, souls will be won for the kingdom. Practice being a walking praise report! Let the world see the change that God has made in your life!

SEPTEMBER 15
Don't Waste Time Fussing!
II TIMOTHY 2:23

But foolish and unlearned questions avoid, knowing that they do gender strifes. – King James Version

Refuse to get involved in inane discussions; they always end up in fights. – The Message Translation

Life is too short to get lost in meaningless and wasteful discussions. Some people enjoy arguing over things that often they have little or no knowledge of. Often the subject of the arguments have very little to do with salvation and are merely cultural or personal differences.

Especially when it comes to God's Word – work hard to avoid disputes with others. Study God's Word and show yourself approved unto HIM! Don't waste time trying to prove yourself to others. Share your faith with others, but never fall into the trap of fighting over God's Word.

The Bible admonishes you to live peaceably with all men. Find commonalities to share with each other. And when you experience differences learn to live respectful of the opinions and feelings of others. The ministry of love supersedes all.

SEPTEMBER 16
Just What He Said!
NUMBERS 23:19

God is not man, one given to lies, and not a son of man changing his mind. Does He speak and not do what He says? Does He promise and not come through? – The Message Translation

The reason it is so important to know God's Word and to discern His voice is because of the validity of what He says. You don't have to wonder if what He tells you will come to pass. In Isaiah 55:11, God decrees that His Word cannot return unto Him until it has accomplished what He has purposed in the earth realm.

So when doubt arises in your mind, dismiss it and embrace God's promise. The only question that should remain is when? If God tells you that it will come to pass, it will! Your responsibility is to not get weary in well doing, but encourage yourself that "due season" will come and you will reap if you don't give up.

Yes! You can take it to the bank! When God decrees your healing, your blessing, your breakthrough, your deliverance – just know that it is on the way. When His Word tells you that you are the righteousness of God and that you are holy as He is holy – ignore the deception of your own mind and learn to walk in what God has said concerning you. When things around you look bad and cause you to feel like giving up – that is the time to press even harder towards your goal – God will always keep His Word and come through for you!

SEPTEMBER 17

Let God Use You – His Way!

ROMANS 9:21

Hath not the potter power over the clay, of the same lump to make one vessel unto honour, and another unto dishonour?
– King James Version

Isn't it obvious that a potter has a perfect right to shape one lump of clay into a vase for holding flowers and another into a pot for cooking beans? – The Message Translation

Many people get bent out of shape because of how God chooses to use different people. But, if care would be taken to learn the Scriptures many would understand that all parts of the body glorify God and are important. Whether you have the microphone leading praise, or if you have the broom sweeping trash – both duties are important.

Don't complain about another person's gifts or anointing. Just be grateful that God chooses and uses you. It may not be as He uses others, but that is His choice. Consider a football team. It does not matter if you are the star quarterback or if you ride the bench, at the end of the season if the team wins the championship you all are celebrated. That is the way you should consider your position in the kingdom of God. As long as all work together for His glory that is all that matters. All are winners!

Always remember that the gifting that is within you does not belong to you – it is God's! And He chooses when and how it is to be a blessing in the earth realm. So, learn to just be a willing vessel for His glory.

SEPTEMBER 18

Holy For Him!
II CORINTHIANS 7:1

Having therefore these promises, dearly beloved, let us cleanse ourselves from all filthiness of the flesh and spirit, perfecting holiness in the fear of God. – King James Version

Holiness is not what you wear. Holiness is not what you say. But, true holiness is characterized by a life-style that emulates the life of Christ. True love for God is depicted not in rituals or traditions but in obedience to His Word. His living Word breathes brand new life into you.

God just made an awesome promise in the 6th chapter of II Corinthians. He has promised the blessings of relationship. And, because of your relationship with Him your lifestyle is changed.

Have you ever noticed in the natural that you change things about yourself when you are "in love" with someone? Even more so in the spirit, now change everything for the lover of your soul. No longer seek to please your flesh, but strive everyday to please Him.

He is such a wonderful God. God has blessed you with a marvelous and wonderful life. He is always a constant help in good and bad times. He desires that you disconnect yourself from the enemy and those who align themselves with evil tactics and ways. He wants you all for Himself. Be ye Holy – just for Him!

SEPTEMBER 19

God Don't Wanna Hear That

JEREMIAH 1:6

Then said I, Ah, Lord GOD! behold, I cannot speak : for I am a child. – King James Version

But I said, "Hold it, Master God! Look at me. I don't know anything. I'm only a boy!" – The Message Translation

Stop making excuses about your limitations. God already knows your handicaps, your issues, and your shortcomings! But, He did not allow those things to stop Him from giving you an assignment. So, you must stop using those as excuses to not obey God.

God knows all about you. Because He is the Creator, He uniquely created you for His glory and purpose different from others around you. What you sometimes may view as deficiencies – God does not see them as hindrances for you to be successful.

So stop making complaints! Just thank God for who and what you are and get busy. Do what He anointed and appointed you to do. There is someone waiting on the gift in you. Don't waste time talking about what you can't do. Get busy doing what you can. You will be surprised at how God's anointing on you for that purpose will not only bless others but you as well.

SEPTEMBER 20
Blessing In Waiting!
ISAIAH 40:31

But they that wait upon the LORD shall renew their strength; they shall mount up with wings as eagles; they shall run, and not be weary; and they shall walk, and not faint. – King James Version

But those who wait upon God get fresh strength. They spread their wings and soar like eagles, They run and don't get tired, they walk and don't lag behind. – The Message Translation

Some have said that the mentality of many people today is that of a microwave society. People have been accustomed to getting what they want, when they want it, and how they want it - right now! Quick and in a hurry is the order of the day. However, there is a blessing in learning to wait on God. He is the God of due season. At the appropriate time, He will deliver.

Yes, there is a blessing in waiting. God has promised in His Word that your strength will be renewed. So, if you are challenged in any area of your life – don't be discouraged. Allow God's Word to encourage you to understand that even in your weakness, His strength is made perfect. Waiting really prepares you for the awesome blessing that God has in store for you.

Waiting is not sitting idly by. But waiting is synonymous with serving. When you go to a restaurant and you have a waiter this is the person that takes care of your order. When you wait on God you must consume yourself with pleasing Him. Praise Him!

Worship Him! Adore Him! Honor Him! And at the end of the day, watch Him renews your strength and bless you.

God has not forgotten you – change your focus. Do not focus on your problems and your needs. Focus on the awesome God that you serve. Think on His magnificent power. Meditate on His promises. And you will experience an awesome renewal and revival as never before.

SEPTEMBER 21
Get Right With God!
I CORINTHIANS 11:31-32

If we get this straight now, we won't have to be straightened out later on. Better to be confronted by the Master now than to face a fiery confrontation later. – The Message Translation

As a young child growing up, the saints used to sing a song and the words said, *"Get right with God, and do it now..."* God is such a compassionate and merciful God that He will withhold judgment and extend grace and mercy to you. Your job is to confess, repent and live a new life before Him.

God uses His Word to help you understand His will. And as His child, your love for Him should cause you to obey His Word and live right before Him. As I reflect back to my great-grandmother, Dear, she never physically chastised me. But, she had a way with her words that cut so deep that I would be in tears. Her words made an impact upon me because I loved her.

Your love for God should be the same way. When you find yourself out of order, He will send His word to correct you. Even though, it is not always comfortable it is always right! So, make a decision today to learn to hear His Word and obey His Word. Listen for His voice and obey that voice. Sense the move of His Spirit and allow your life to line up with the Spirit of God. "Get right church and let's go home!"

SEPTEMBER 22
Who Will You Encourage?
HEBREWS 3:13

But exhort one another daily, while it is called Today; lest any of you be hardened through the deceitfulness of sin. – King James Version

Life offers daily challenges for everyone. There are many times people don't talk about what they are battling with or dealing with in their personal life. But, God often positions you to intersect in others' lives so that you may be a blessing. Yes, God will use you to encourage someone.

You don't have to pry into people's lives to be an encouragement. Just learn to be sensitive to the Spirit of God and He will not only position you around the people who you need to encourage but He will also tell you what to say to them. But, you must be a willing vessel.

Stop waiting for people to come to you! It is ridiculous if you see your brother fall in a ditch that you would not be proactive and do what you can to assist him. Why would you be so self-centered to wait for him to ask for help if you saw him fall in the ditch? That type of egocentricity is dangerous because it makes you appear to be better than others.

Make time to stay focused in life to be a blessing to someone every day. Tomorrow, you might be the one challenged and need someone to rescue you through a Word from God.

SEPTEMBER 23

Glad That Ain't Your God

I KINGS 18:27

By noon, Elijah had started making fun of them, taunting, "Call a little louder - he is a god, after all. Maybe he's off meditating somewhere or other, or maybe he's gotten involved in a project, or maybe he's on vacation. You don't suppose he's overslept, do you, and needs to be waked up?" –
The Message Translation

You ought to be so glad that you serve the one true and living God! He is never busy. He does not go on vacation or take breaks. He never slumbers or sleeps. He is always listening for your call.

There are some who do not believe. They put their faith in other things or even in themselves. But the danger in living like that is when the need for help comes, there is none to help. Alone, you do not have the power to heal yourself, bless yourself, deliver yourself, or anything.

But, the God you serve has the power. He loves you so much that when you call Him, not only will He show up but He will show out. He will not allow you to be put to shame. He will bless you in front of others who never believed you would make it. He will heal you against the doctor's orders or diagnosis. He will free you and deliver you against the whims and desires of the unjust judge or jury. He will bless you and extend favor in your life in front of those who tried to hold you back and keep you from advancing. That's the God you serve! You ought to rejoice and be exceedingly glad!

SEPTEMBER 24

No More Hunger!

JOHN 6:35

And Jesus said unto them, I am the bread of life: he that cometh to Me shall never hunger; and he that believeth on Me shall never thirst. – King James Version

Jesus said, "I am the Bread of Life. The person who aligns with me hungers no more and thirsts no more, ever. – The Message Translation

Sometimes a void exists in people's lives that can only be filled by God. No matter how you seek to satisfy that hunger and quench that thirst, you will simply waste time attempting to utilize other resources to address the issue. The search may be natural, but the answer is spiritual.

Stop looking in the natural for what can only be fulfilled in the spirit realm. The abundance of things will not bring joy. But, the presence of God will. The absence of your adversary's attacks will not bring peace. But, the presence of God will. Some physical sensual relationship will not bring true love. But, the presence of God will.

When you embrace God and His Word through the acceptance of Jesus as your Lord and Saviour, you will experience a fullness and wholeness that is quite unexplainable. Your life will undergo transformation like never before. So, call off the endless search when all you need to be filled and refreshed is found in God.

SEPTEMBER 25

Let Jesus Lead You!

ISAIAH 55:8

For my thoughts are not your thoughts, neither are your ways my ways, saith the LORD. – King James Version

"*I don't think the way you think. The way you work isn't the way I work." God's Decree.* – The Message Translation

Can you recall when you were a child and you knew everything? And then you became a teenager and you really knew everything and didn't need anybody to tell you anything. And you grew up and became a young adult, and realized that when you were a child you didn't really know it all, but now that you are grown you have it all together. Keep living and what you will discover is that you never know everything!

This is what God wants you to realize in your walk with Him. Stop trying to be in charge and learn to listen to Him. He is Alpha and Omega, the beginning and the ending. He already knows your destiny. He knows the thoughts He has concerning you, and His plans to bring you to an expected end.

Learn to live by trusting God, even when you don't have all the answers. Stop having to be in total control. Learn to seek His face for wisdom and guidance even on simple choices and decisions in your everyday life. Through prayer and worship, practice listening for and hearing His voice. As the old folk used to sing, "Let Jesus lead you. He's a mighty good leader."

SEPTEMBER 26
What Road Are You On?
ISAIAH 35:8

And an highway shall be there, and a way, and it shall be called The way of holiness; the unclean shall not pass over it; but it shall be for those: the wayfaring men, though fools, shall not err therein. – King James Version

There will be a highway called the Holy Road. No one rude or rebellious is permitted on this road. It's for God's people exclusively - impossible to get lost on this road. Not even fools can get lost on it. – The Message Translation

Times may change but the Word of God remains the same. It's still holiness or hell! Yes, everyone does not just die and go to heaven. There are choices that must be made during life that determine your eternal home. If you accept the salvation and lordship of Jesus Christ, heaven belongs to you. But, if you reject Jesus who is the only way to the Father then in hell will you lift your eyes.

Holiness is not a denomination. It is a lifestyle. Holiness means that you have patterned every part of your public and private life after God's Word. Holiness produces spiritual fruit and spiritual gifts. Holiness brightens the light of Christ within you and shines for others to see your good works and give God the glory.

Do not fool yourself. Merely attending church does not put you on the right road. Trying to do good deeds and being nice to people does not put you on the right road. But, when you repent of your sins, accept Jesus as your Lord and Savior and allow His

Spirit to fill you and lead, guide and direct you then you are on the right road!

SEPTEMBER 27

Ignore The Spectators
I CHRONICLES 15:29

When the Chest of the Covenant of God entered the City of David, Michal, Saul's daughter, was watching from a window. When she saw King David dancing ecstatically she was filled with contempt. – The Message Translation

Do not allow spectators and non-participators to sway you. When God blesses you it is right for you to celebrate. You should praise Him with all of your might. Whoever is standing by watching on – if they won't join you – Don't let their actions (or rather inaction) stop you from praising Him!

Your blessing comes from your thankfulness. When you praise God, He will show up and show out. And if you thought what you were praising Him for was awesome – just wait and see what He has in store for you. Eyes have not seen, nor ears heard about the good things God has prepared for you because you love Him!

However, for those who refuse to give God praise – the scenario plays out differently. The seed of contempt that they may be sowing as they simply watch you or talk about you will also bring in a harvest for them. Remember, negative seeds sow weeds!

Don't slow down. Don't stop. Don't ask any questions. Just keep shouting. Keep dancing. Keep praising!

SEPTEMBER 28
God Will Take Care Of You
GALATIANS 6:7

And why take ye thought for raiment? Consider the lilies of the field, how they grow; they toil not, neither do they spin: - King James Version

All this time and money wasted on fashion - do you think it makes that much difference? Instead of looking at the fashions, walk out into the fields and look at the wildflowers. They never primp or shop, - The Message Translation

Don't stress and don't complain about physical things that you feel may be lacking in your life. God has your back! Remember, you were created in His likeness. He adopted you into the royal family. So, He definitely is concerned about your well-being and your welfare.

If He shows care and concern for the things of nature, He assuredly will make certain that you are taken care of. Learn to focus on spiritual things and see the benefits and blessings that are made manifest in your life.

A few verses later, the key is revealed. If you learn to seek God's way of operating and His righteousness you will find that God will add to your life the things that so many others waste time focusing on. You don't have to look for blessings – they will find you!

SEPTEMBER 29

What Are You Doing With Your Gift?

LUKE 19:13

And he called his ten servants, and delivered them ten pounds, and said unto them, Occupy till I come. - King James Version

Before he left, he called his ten servants and gave them each a gold coin and told them, "See what you can earn with this while I am gone.' – Good News Translation

God has made an investment in your life. He desires to observe your stewardship of the gifts, talents, abilities, and resources with which He has blessed you. Increase comes when you begin to unselfishly share yourself with others. Look for ways to be a blessing in the lives of others.

You have no time to observe the blessings of others. But, you must learn to focus on what God has placed in you. Some people complain because of their "lot" in life. These people fail to understand the true power of faith and prayer. Little becomes much when it is placed in the Master's hand.

Your prime objective is to use whatever God has given you for the benefit of the kingdom. God will bless you and bring increase as you sow into the lives of others. Sow your time, talent and even your treasure. Invest wisely. Don't cast pearls to the swine. But, pray for guidance from the Holy Spirit and make the best of your actions.

Don't sit down. Get up and use what God has given you. Stop looking around. Look within you and determine what is the next thing within you that you will bring forth to be a blessing. When God returns, will He be pleased with your stewardship?

SEPTEMBER 30

Just Be The Original You
GALATIANS 6:4

But let every man prove his own work, and then shall he have rejoicing in himself alone, and not in another. – King James Version

Make a careful exploration of who you are and the work you have been given, and then sink yourself into that. Don't be impressed with yourself. Don't compare yourself with others. – The Message Translation

When God created you, He gave you a specific purpose! Keep that purpose at the forefront of your mind. That should be your focus and your goal. Don't allow anything or anybody to stand between you and your divinely appointed destiny. You may experience challenges in life – but keep pressing forward. Every stumbling block must be viewed as a stepping stone.

God has already given you what you need to succeed. When the Father created you, He placed within you a seed of greatness to become His intent for your life. Jesus Christ manifested as your pattern so that you would know how to be who God called you to be. And the Holy Spirit is ever-present to serve as your guide to make certain that you understand how to navigate through this thing we call life.

Concentrate on allowing your individuality to color and define the gifting that God designed you to share with the world. Don't cheapen yourself by trying to be a carbon copy of others. It lessens your value and your impact. But strive to allow who you are (imperfections and all) to be utilized for God's glory and man's edification in the earth realm. There is something in you that someone in the earth realm needs. Don't contaminate the gift by patterning yourself after flesh.

OCTOBER 1
Work The Word!
I CORINTHIANS 4:20

For the kingdom of God is not in word, but in power. — King James Version

God's Way is not a matter of mere talk; it's an empowered life. — The Message Translation

Talk is cheap. Actions speak louder than words. It is better to see a sermon than hear one. All of these are true adages that encourage action over conversation.

As God's child, you don't have to simply run around quoting scriptures and talking about what God can do! You can bring the Word of God off the pages of the Bible and demonstrate the power of God's Word. God has empowered you to be a manifestation of the gospel.

Go and lay hands on the sick, and God will heal them. Go and speak encouragement to the bereaved and disheartened, and God will bring comfort. Go and help the poor and needy, and God will bless them and you for your liberality.

Yes, you can! You can walk on water. You can sleep in the lion's den. You can go through the fire. You can lose everything and recover double. God is the same yesterday, today and forever. He does not have picks and chooses. What He did for one, He will also do for you. Just walk in God's Word and let it flow out of your life today.

OCTOBER 2
Put Your Praise First!
II CHRONICLES 20:21

And when he had consulted with the people, he appointed singers unto the LORD, and that should praise the beauty of holiness, as they went out before the army, and to say, Praise the LORD; for His mercy endureth for ever. – King James Version

After talking it over with the people, Jehoshaphat appointed a choir for God; dressed in holy robes, they were to march ahead of the troops, singing, Give thanks to God, His love never quits. – The Message Translation

Life is an on-going, never ending battle. Because of the awesome treasure that God has deposited within you, the enemy considers you a threat and has made you his target. But, you have to continually remind yourself that this is not a physical war! You are not wrestling against flesh and blood. Even though your challenges seem to be flesh driven, they are not flesh originated.

In order to fight effectively and win the battle, you need the right tools and tactics. Praise is your answer. Praise is a weapon and a practice. Praise confuses the enemy. Praise also ushers in the very presence of God. Praise must be on-going and multi-faceted. Praise Him when you feel like it and praise Him when you don't. Praise Him in song, in dance, in declarations, and prayer. Praise works!

So, stop wasting time getting bogged down in verbal and even physical altercations with people. Don't try to get even with them because of what they have done to you. Break out in "a praise" and watch what happens. Praise will change the atmosphere and cause them to self-destruct. You won't even have to fight when you learn how to effectively and fervently praise God. Put your praise first!

OCTOBER 3

Giving Up – Is Not An Option

LUKE 18:1-8

And He spake a parable unto them to this end, that men ought always to pray, and not to faint; Saying, There was in a city a judge, which feared not God, neither regarded man: And there was a widow in that city; and she came unto him, saying, Avenge me of mine adversary. And he would not for a while: but afterward he said within himself, Though I fear not God, nor regard man; Yet because this widow troubleth me, I will avenge her, lest by her continual coming she weary me. And the Lord said, Hear what the unjust judge saith. And shall not God avenge his own elect, which cry day and night unto him, though he bear long with them? I tell you that he will avenge them speedily. Nevertheless when the Son of man cometh, shall he find faith on the earth?

Persistence is a by-product of faith. Faith does not give up because of the lack of an immediate physical manifestation. Faith does not quit because of an appearance of denial or delay. Faith believes that the spirit realm already contains what is en route to the natural realm. And faith pushes and presses until the manifestation of the belief is brought forth.

Cry unto God and tell Him your heart's desire. Get up and trust that He heard you and begin walking in it. Thank Him for what you are trusting in Him for, even when you don't see it. Praise Him when the enemy tries to fill your heart with False Evidence Appearing Real "FEAR". Your praise will do three things.

Your praise will arrest the attention of God. He inhabits the praises of His people. So, when you praise Him – you invoke His manifested presence into your atmosphere. Praise will confuse the enemy. The devil expects you to have negative emotional responses to challenges and trials. He is confounded when you give God glory even in adversity. Praise will lift you. Praise will change your attitude, outlook and disposition. The saints used to sing: "The more I praise God, the better I feel".

So, press your way and persevere. Let praise drive your faith to the victory and blessing that has already been prepared for you. Your persistence will position you for your blessing. The woman with the issue of blood had to change her position. The four lepers at the gate had to change their position. For the blessing that is yours – persevere and position yourself for the glory!

OCTOBER 4
When My Friend Falls!
I PETER 4:15

But let none of you suffer as a murderer, or as a thief, or as an evildoer, or as a busybody in other men's matters. – King James Version

Suppose you suffer. Then it shouldn't be because you are a murderer or a thief. It shouldn't be because you do evil things. It shouldn't be because you poke your nose into other people's business. – New International Reader's Version

People are so quick to run to judgment when something negative happens to a member of the Body of Christ. However, if you live by God's Word you really have only two choices when a negative accusation or event occurs in someone's life. Either you believe the accusation and pray for restoration or you don't believe the accusation and treat it as a spiritual attack.

But, many people choose a third option that basically places them outside of the will of God – they choose to gossip and be judgmental.

If you believe a brother or sister has fallen, then you have a spiritual obligation to embrace Galatians 6:1. *Brethren, if a man be overtaken in a fault, ye which are spiritual, restore such an one in the spirit of meekness; considering thyself, lest thou also be tempted. (King James Version). Live creatively, friends. If someone falls into sin, forgivingly restore him, saving your critical comments for yourself. You might be needing forgiveness before the day's out. (The Message Translation).*

However, if you believe that someone has lied on your brother or sister and that the negative situation is an attack from the enemy, then you have a spiritual obligation to embrace Isaiah 54:17. *No weapon that is formed against thee shall prosper; and every tongue that shall rise against thee in judgment thou shalt condemn. This is the heritage of the servants of the LORD, and their righteousness is of me, saith the LORD. (KJV). But no weapon that can hurt you has ever been forged. Any accuser who takes you to court will be dismissed as a liar. This is what God's servants can expect. I'll see to it that everything works out for the best." God's Decree. (The Message Translation).*

It is unfortunate that many people have not become spiritually mature in order to Biblically and correctly deal with issues in life. Just as bad as the accusation itself is the response some people take. Gossiping, tale bearing, judging and discussing other people's business puts you at a great spiritual disadvantage. I Timothy 5:13 describes how being a meddler in other people's lives also places you outside of the will of God.

OCTOBER 5
You Are Not In This Alone
PSALM 23:4

Yea, though I walk through the valley of the shadow of death, I will fear no evil: for thou art with me; thy rod and thy staff they comfort me. – King James Version

Even if I go through the deepest darkness, I will not be afraid, Lord, for you are with me. Your shepherd's rod and staff protect me. – Good News Translation

"And He walks with me and He talks with me, and He tells me I am His own..."

Those were the blessed lyrics that many grew up singing in Sunday School and Church. But, they are more than just lyrics – they are truth. No matter what you are facing or going through in life God promised to never leave you nor forsake you. Yes, Jehovah Shammah, "The Lord is there", is ever present to bring the manifestation that you need in your life.

Everyone has different paths to travel. No matter what your personal "valley" is, you are never alone. Just like God was with the Hebrew boys, He will be with you. Paul and Silas were not alone in the prison, but the Lord was there and made the earth shake them free. You may experience some challenging scenes and settings in life – but God is always there and He has your back!

Your responsibility is to simply trust God and have no fear. For there is nothing that can come against you that your "Big Daddy" is not able to protect you from. Always know that your steps are ordered by God. So, if you are on the mountain top or in the valley low – it's okay. Just keep holding His hand and The Shepherd will lead you to the green pastures. His Word and His Spirit will provide you with the comfort and strength you need to endure anything.

OCTOBER 6
Don't Stop Doing Good
GALATIANS 6:9

And let us not be weary in well doing: for in due season we shall reap, if we faint not. – King James Version

So let's not allow ourselves to get fatigued doing good. At the right time we will harvest a good crop if we don't give up, or quit. – The Message Translation

God has a calendar and watch in the spirit realm to determine the appropriate time in your life to allow the manifestation of your blessing to appear. You cannot allow the challenges of your own flesh, the attitude and actions of others, nor the trick of the enemy to stop you from doing good. Your responsibility is simple: don't lose heart!

Quitting is the easy way out. However, if you quit you deny your own self the sweet taste of victory. An old song's lyrics said, "The road is rough, the going is tough, and the hills are hard to climb…" Make up in your mind that you will endure to the end and get God's best.

He has already equipped you with what you need to endure the storm and come out safe. You may go through the fire but you won't be burned. The waters may threaten you, but you will not drown. Keep doing God's will and watch God work on your behalf. Just – never quit!

OCTOBER 7
God Will Do Even More!
PSALM 46:1

God is our refuge and strength, a very present help in trouble.
— King James Version

God is a safe place to hide, ready to help when we need him. —
The Message Translation

It's okay when you find yourself in a difficult situation or in the midst of trying times. Always remember, you are never alone. God promised in His Word that He would never leave you nor forsake you. Not only is He with you in the midst of your challenges, but He is your help.

Stop fighting and struggling and just trust Him. Once you retire from attempting to "fix" everything, He is more than ready, willing and able to do for you what you cannot do. He won't usurp authority over your will. But, He will wait patiently for you to stop trusting yourself and trust in Him.

He will be a hiding place for you so the enemy cannot find you. He will be your offense and defense to keep you safe no matter how fierce the attack. And, He will be your deliverer and bless you with true victory and a testimony. God will do all of that and more when you learn to simply relax and trust in Him.

OCTOBER 8
He Will Show Up!
MATTHEW 14:27

But straightway Jesus spake unto them, saying, Be of good cheer; it is I; be not afraid. – King James Version

But Jesus was quick to comfort them. "Courage, it's Me. Don't be afraid." – The Message Translation

There are numerous places in the Word of God where you are exhorted to not fear or be afraid. II Timothy 1:7 reminds you that fear is a spirit and it does not come from God. Fear can paralyze you and cause your life to be in great turmoil. You must learn how to allow peace which comes from God to manifest in every situation.

It does not matter what challenges you face in life. God is omnipresent. He is always there. However, even though He is all places at all times, He has an awesome way of manifesting Himself according to your present needs. When you are sad, He reveals Himself as the Comforter. When sickness invades your body, He manifests as Jehovah Rapha, God your healer. When sorrow is a prevailing force in your life, He will be your joy and that same joy will be your strength. He will be the Mighty Counselor and give answer to the questions in your life. He is an awesome God.

So, do not over stress because of what you are going through in life. Always know that you are not alone and that God is your very present help. He will come to wherever you are and do whatever is needed to bring peace and tranquility to your situation. He will change the atmosphere. He will adjust the climate. But, most importantly, He will deliver you!

OCTOBER 9

God Gives Green Lights!
I SAMUEL 30:8

And David enquired at the LORD, saying, Shall I pursue after this troop? shall I overtake them? And he answered him, Pursue: for thou shalt surely overtake them, and without fail recover all. – King James Version

Then David prayed to God, "Shall I go after these raiders? Can I catch them?" The answer came, "Go after them! Yes, you'll catch them! Yes, you'll make the rescue!" – The Message Translation

At some point or time, everybody suffers loss. The Word of God in John 10:10 declares that the "thief comes for but to steal, to kill, and to destroy..." However, when you pray God will tell you when and where to "go get your stuff!"

Recovery is a blessing from God. You must learn the distinction between release and recovery. It is called simply trusting God. God knows what you are going through. He understands the pain that you endure. When you suffer any type loss, you must learn to simply commit it to God and trust Him.

Some things need to go because they are not part of your destiny. But, there are some things that the enemy has illegally confiscated. God will enlighten you and empower you to make full recovery. Whether it is your health, relationships, finances, or spiritual growth and development every loss is not permanent. Don't take every loss sitting down. Talk to God and ask Him, can you go get your stuff back? God will give you the green light to go and recover all.

OCTOBER 10
God Gets All The Praise!
II CORINTHIANS 4:15

For all things are for your sakes, that the abundant grace might through the thanksgiving of many redound to the glory of God. – King James Version

Every detail works to your advantage and to God's glory: more and more grace, more and more people, more and more praise! – The Message Translation

Keep giving God praise! In the good times thank Him! In the bad times bless Him! At all times praise His Name! For He is God; and He causes all things to work together for your good. Even when you don't see it or understand it, God still has everything under control.

Share your life story with others. Many are blessed and encouraged to know that they are not alone in their struggle. Much of what you go through is not even really for or about you, but it is for ministry sake. Somebody needs your track record, your praise report, your deliverance!

And God gets glory and praise from all when you continue to let your light shine! So, keep smiling on the bad days. And let that smile equate the same smile of the good days. And He gets all the praise!

OCTOBER 11
Another Way He Blesses!
JOSHUA 6:1

Now Jericho was straitly shut up because of the children of Israel: none went out, and none came in. – King James Version

Jericho was shut up tight as a drum because of the People of Israel: no one going in, no one coming out. – The Message Translation

God will always fulfill His Word. He will put life on pause just to bring His promise to fruition in your life. When God decides to bless you, there is nothing anybody else can do about it. Yes, God will put life on hold just to make His Word come to pass for you.

When God brings you to a place of promise, there are certain actions you should take. Learn to thank God in advance, trust Him for the complete manifestation and worship Him so you are not distracted during the process.

Live your life with an "attitude of gratitude"! Remind yourself of the "good" in the things that have happened in your life. God's promise that all things would work together for your good, is still true. See God's undeserved blessings in your life. See the times He blessed you – in spite of!

You must trust and obey God. Learn to hear and obey God's voice. Remember God's Word supersedes everything. Know that nothing is impossible with God – He can bless you over and over again (Matt. 6:33).

Your "lifestyle" must be one of worship – it must honor the King. Your life should be a living testimony of who God is and what God can do! There are things in your past that God has allowed you to come in contact with that cannot go with you into your promised future. Whether they are good or bad – let go of yesterday so you can embrace the place God has prepared for you!

OCTOBER 12
True Believers – Wait!
ISAIAH 40:31

But they that wait upon the LORD shall renew their strength; they shall mount up with wings as eagles; they shall run, and not be weary; and they shall walk, and not faint. – King James Version

But those who wait upon God get fresh strength. They spread their wings and soar like eagles, They run and don't get tired, they walk and don't lag behind. – The Message Translation

For the true believer – Giving up is never an option. The only recourse for the people of God is to learn how "to wait." Waiting is not just sitting idly by. But effective waiting is busying one's self in serving God.

When you give up it makes statements that are inconsistent with being a believer. First, it says that the devil was right. You know that cannot be true! For, John 8:44 declares that the devil is a liar and the father of lies. Second, giving up says that your faith is weak. You must exercise your faith and make it strong. This is done by learning how to agree with God's Word through your actions. Third, if you give up you really are declaring that God was wrong. How could God ever be wrong? He can't! He is God. His Word never fails. He even watches over it and hastens to make sure it produces what He promises.

Christians learn how to wait. You must learn to wait in patience. Luke 21:19 says, "In patience possess ye your souls." Developing patience in your life will help you become more emotionally stable. You cannot allow nouns (people, places, things or ideas) to control your soulish man! You also must learn how to wait with expectation. Know that whatever God has promised you will come to pass. Live everyday looking for the manifestation of God in your life. And third, learn to wait with thanksgiving. Before you see it, touch it, or possess it – thank God for it. This demonstrates your faith in action.

Learn to wait on God. Stop stressing over "microwave" fixes for issues in your life. Sometimes you may see an instant move or miracle, but often times in life you must learn to see a progressive work in your life. In regards to your situation: learn to treat your situation as seed. Answer these three questions. 1. Did you plant? 2. Have you watered? 3. Do you believe? If your answer is "yes" to all three – then simply wait because your blessing is on the way!

OCTOBER 13

Call Jesus Louder!

MATTHEW 20:31

The crowd tried to hush them up, but they got all the louder, crying, "Master, have mercy on us! Mercy, Son of David!" – The Message Translation

God is who He says He is! He is the healer. He is the deliverer. He is the waymaker. He is the keeper. He is the miracle worker. The same works that He performed in the Bible days are still being done by Him today! Don't let people fool you and tell you that He doesn't operate like that anymore.

And because He is God – and because you need Him – you have a right and an obligation to call Him! When you need Him – call His Name! Don't worry about who is around you or where you may be! If you need Him in a public place – don't be afraid to praise Him and call on Him in a public place. If there are non-believers or naysayers around – don't let them hinder you in your relationship with your God.

Never keep silent. If anything – allow your situation to serve as a witnessing tool. Let others see that your God is real and He loves you enough to come to your rescue. Let Him bring you bread in a starving land. Let Him bring you water in the desert. Let Him open closed doors for you. All you have to do is acknowledge that you need Him and call His Name!

OCTOBER 14
Getting God's Best
PSALM 37:4

Delight thyself also in the LORD; and He shall give thee the desires of thine heart. – King James Version

Delighting yourself in the Lord is more than a superficial display of emotional contentment. Delighting yourself in the Lord demands that change erupts in every area of your life. You can no longer exist the same way when you totally surrender. There is a reward for living this kind of life. He blesses you with His very best. There are some prerequisites to receiving His very best.

You must learn the art of self-denial. You cannot be the center of attention. God must have that spot. You must ask God to perform heart surgery on you. You need Him to create a clean heart and renew the right spirit within you. You must fall so much in love with Him that He consumes every thought and every action. Your priority must undergo drastic rearrangement. He has to be first. No questions asked. And you must be a worshipper. He is looking for worshippers.

When you live like this, you position yourself for God's very best. Your heart changes and is aligned more with His will than your own. His desire has become your own. And because He watches over His Word and His will shall be accomplished you are ready for the blessing. You can open your mouth and the creative power of God will become manifest. All of a sudden you will begin to see what you say. Keep delighting yourself in Him, and He will continue blowing your mind and leaving you amazed!

OCTOBER 15

Don't Rejoice – In Others' Mistakes!

JOHN 8:7

So when they continued asking Him, He lifted up himself, and said unto them, He that is without sin among you, let him first cast a stone at her. – King James Version

They kept at Him, badgering Him. He straightened up and said, "The sinless one among you, go first: Throw the stone." – The Message Translation

It seems to give some people joy to revel in the faults and failures of others. Some people celebrate the fall of others. You must remind yourself that no one is perfect. There is some spot or blemish somewhere in everyone that needs to addressed.

Be careful about people who like to shine flashlights. They enjoy shining the light on the error of others while still living in the dark. The appropriate action is to turn on the overhead light so that everyone is exposed. All stand in need of the grace of God in some area of life.

The scriptures encourage you to bring restoration to those who have fallen into sin. It is your Christian duty and responsibility to express the agape of God towards others. Every action that you take in life is simply seed sown. When you sow criticism and unforgiveness, that same harvest will manifest back in your life.

God does not want you to validate sin. He does not expect you to encourage the acceptance of error. But, you must learn to sow the same mercy and compassion that you would desire that God would extend to you. Be careful about throwing rocks when you dwell in a glass house!

OCTOBER 16
Where To Place Your Trust
PSALM 44:6-7

For I will not trust in my bow, neither shall my sword save me. But thou hast saved us from our enemies, and hast put them to shame that hated us. – King James Version

I don't trust in weapons; my sword won't save me - But it's you, you who saved us from the enemy; You made those who hate us lose face. – The Message Translation

There will come a time in your life that you will come to terms with opposition and discover that by yourself you are no match. When God created you, He made you dependent upon Him and His resources. He gave you the ability to work and power to achieve, but He also conditioned you that you would always partner with Him for victory and success.

Remember Philippians: You can do "all things" THROUGH Christ that strengthens you. No matter how many degrees you have on the wall, without Christ they mean very little. There will come a point where even your financial resources, no matter how vast, will not profit you in your challenge. Your friend and family connections will even prove futile.

Put your trust in God and in Him alone! Thank Him for every resource. Praise Him for every blessing. Appreciate Him even for favor. But always remember that your victory is through Him alone.

OCTOBER 17
Forgiving Is Fruitful!
LUKE 17:4

And if he trespass against thee seven times in a day, and seven times in a day turn again to thee, saying, I repent; thou shalt forgive him. – King James Version

Even if it's personal against you and repeated seven times through the day, and seven times he says, 'I'm sorry, I won't do it again,' forgive him." – The Message Translation

Each day that you awaken, God has new mercies awaiting you. Being that you have been created in His image, you should function and operate in His likeness. Your relationships will be better blessed as you embrace the ministry of forgiveness. Your intentional production of agape will bless you and others. You will be filled with the joy and peace of knowing that God's Spirit has equipped you to demonstrate the greatest love. Others who have brought offenses will experience grace and mercy and release.

Forgiveness is a wonderful fruit with seed within itself. The intent of God is that forgiveness would replicate itself in the lives of people. What has been sown from God in your life, now you should sow that same seed in the lives of others. The fruit that will be made manifest will produce wholesome, healthy and thriving relationships and enduring friendships. Forgive someone today!

OCTOBER 18
God Will Speak Through You
LUKE 12:12

For the Holy Ghost shall teach you in the same hour what ye ought to say. – King James Version

The right words will be there. The Holy Spirit will give you the right words when the time comes." - The Message Translation

God wants to use you. He wants you to be a vessel of honor for His glory. Do not worry or be afraid of "what to say"! He will let you know at the appropriate time what to say and even how to say it. You just must be ready and willing.

You do not have to be a walking Bible. You may not even know where all of the Scriptures are located. However, God will position you to still speak a word of encouragement and blessing to someone without ever directly quoting a verse of Scripture. And the blessed part about it is that it will still be anointed.

Yes, change will come because of your obedience to God. Someone will be healed, delivered, set free and encouraged because of the words that you say. Wherever you go, always be sensitive to the Spirit of God. He will place people in your path that need to hear from Him. And He will use your tongue to speak. Open your mouth and let God speak!

OCTOBER 19

Thank You Lord!

LAMENTATIONS 3:22

It is of the LORD'S mercies that we are not consumed, because his compassions fail not. – King James Version

God's loyal love couldn't have run out, his merciful love couldn't have dried up. – The Message Translation

Make today your personal praise day! Thank and praise God for His unfailing love, mercy, and grace He has extended to you down through the years. It was not your good deeds or anything that you have done to earn even the breath you are breathing right now. It is only because He is so good and so kind.

Your heart's desire should be to be HIS vessel for HIS glory and to leave a legacy for others. This is only possible through His power!

Reflect upon your life, the truth of the matter: You have done some right and you have done some wrong. You have operated in His will and you have detoured on your own path. You have helped others and you have hurt others. You have brought glory to His Name and you have brought shame and dishonor to His Name. So, the summation is that you are completely dependent upon His grace and His mercy.

For your life, thank Him and give Him praise. Yes, for the good and the bad – because He has caused all things to work together for your good. Thank the Lord today!

OCTOBER 20

Just Be The Original You!

GALATIANS 6:4

But let every man prove his own work, and then shall he have rejoicing in himself alone, and not in another. – King James Version

Make a careful exploration of who you are and the work you have been given, and then sink yourself into that. Don't be impressed with yourself. Don't compare yourself with others. – The Message Translation

When God created you, He gave you a specific purpose! Keep that purpose at the forefront of your mind. That should be your focus and your goal. Don't allow anything or anybody to stand between you and your divinely appointed destiny. You may experience challenges in life – but keep pressing forward. Every stumbling block must be viewed as a stepping stone.

God has already given you what you need to succeed. When the Father created you, He placed within you a seed of greatness to become His intent for your life. Jesus Christ manifested as your pattern so that you would know how to be who God called you to be. And the Holy Spirit is ever-present to serve as your guide to make certain that you understand how to navigate through this thing we call life.

Concentrate on allowing your individuality to color and define the gifting that God designed you to share with the world. Don't cheapen yourself by trying to be a carbon copy of others. It lessens your value and your impact. But strive to allow who you are (imperfections and all) to be utilized for God's glory and man's edification in the earth realm. There is something in you that someone in the earth realm needs. Don't contaminate the gift by patterning yourself after flesh.

OCTOBER 21
Multiply Don't Magnify
COLOSSIANS 1:10

That ye might walk worthy of the Lord unto all pleasing, being fruitful in every good work, and increasing in the knowledge of God; - King James Version

We pray that you'll live well for the Master, making him proud of you as you work hard in his orchard. As you learn more and more how God works, you will learn how to do your work. – The Message Translation

God has placed you in the earth realm on assignment. It is His will and desire that you make an impact. He has equipped you with His power to produce fruit and operate in gifts. You must be careful that you are actually accomplishing what He has given you to do and not merely appear to be doing a great work.

There is a distinct difference between multiplying and magnifying. When you multiply an actual increase occurs. However, when you magnify no increase takes place. Magnification only gives the perception that something is getting bigger. God wants you to do more than give the perception of being fruitful.

Don't get lost in just going to church. But, become a vibrant member of the Body of Christ. Your life should be changing and the lives of others in your atmosphere should be affected by that change as you grow in the knowledge, wisdom, and grace of our Lord. This is well pleasing to God, when you busy yourself working in His kingdom and producing great fruit.

OCTOBER 22
God Deserves More!
ROMANS 6:19

I speak after the manner of men because of the infirmity of your flesh: for as ye have yielded your members servants to uncleanness and to iniquity unto iniquity; even so now yield your members servants to righteousness unto holiness. – King James Version

I'm using this freedom language because it's easy to picture. You can readily recall, can't you, how at one time the more you did just what you felt like doing - not caring about others, not caring about God - the worse your life became and the less freedom you had? And how much different is it now as you live in God's freedom, your lives healed and expansive in holiness? – The Message Translation

(I use everyday language because of the weakness of your natural selves.) At one time you surrendered yourselves entirely as slaves to impurity and wickedness for wicked purposes. In the same way you must now surrender yourselves entirely as slaves of righteousness for holy purposes. – Good News Translation

Can you remember when you were living in sin? Do you remember the sacrifices and allowances you made for your flesh? Can you recall how you would push yourself to do certain things even if you were tired or not feeling well? Well, God deserves more!

It is amazing at the lame excuses people produce when it comes to serving, praising, or living for God. People will refuse to do what is right or even necessary when it is inconvenient to their own personal agenda. Have you ever been guilty?

When you were a sinner, have you ever partied all night long but still showed up to work the next day? Have you ever gone to a sporting event, and came back hoarse from yelling and screaming to support your team? Have you ever pushed yourself to go out with family or friends even though you were not feeling well?

God deserves more! Christians must learn to live sacrificial lives and honor God. Sick or well: Go to church! Broke or not: Pay your tithes! Tired or not: Give God praise! Happy or sad: Share the good news! Remember, if you pushed and pressed your way for your own agenda before you were saved – Now, push and press even more for God since you are saved!

OCTOBER 23
Minister Don't Mingle!
PROVERBS 25:26

A righteous man falling down before the wicked is as a troubled fountain, and a corrupt spring. – King James Version

If the godly compromise with the wicked, it is like polluting a fountain or muddying a spring. – New Living Translation

A good person who gives in to a bad person is a muddied spring, a polluted well. – The Message Translation

It is God's will and desire that you be a light shining in this dark world. He expects you to be salt in the earth. He has placed you IN the earth realm to make a difference. He does not expect light to have "fellowship" with darkness, but He intends that you allow His glory to shine in the midst of the darkness.

You must be careful in your dealings with non-Christians. You are never to present yourself as being better than them or having a "holier-than-thou" attitude. But, you are to represent to them that the same grace that saved you has already been made available for them. Don't get caught in trying to be too friendly. God's desire is that you minister and be an example.

You are holy and you are clean. God expects you to remain in that condition until He returns. While in the earth realm, He does not expect you to be like the world – but He wants you to transform and change the world to be like Him!

OCTOBER 24

Which Eye Are You Using?

II CORINTHIANS 5:7

"For we walk by faith, not by sight:..." – King James Version

Is the glass half empty? Is the glass half full? How interesting, two people looking at the same thing but visualizing two completely different concepts. Life is basically the same way. The way you view or see a thing dictates your feelings, beliefs and actions.

When you are born again, you have to fight the desire of your flesh to control your vision. It is so easy to allow what you see in the natural to navigate your life. You must learn to employ your spiritual vision to see what God desires you to see.

If you see yourself as weak, you will not fight. If you do not fight, you will not win. Yet, if you see yourself as *strong in the Lord*, you will go to the fight and He will fight the battle for you. If you see yourself as sick, you will lose hope. If you lose hope, you will die. But, if you see yourself as *healed by His stripes,* you will turn your face to the wall and trust God and live.

You cannot allow the challenges, adversities and distractions of life to overwhelm you. When the enemy shows you a picture of how bad things are. Remember, the God you serve causes all things to work together for good because you love Him and are called to "purpose". You must allow faith to show you victory. You must allow faith to cause you to see the hand of God at work in your life for your good and your benefit.

Don't let your natural eye cause you to live beneath your promises and privileges. Use your spiritual eye and walk into the impossible, intangible and incredible. The glass is always half full!

OCTOBER 25
Do You Realize What You Have?
II PETER 1:4

Whereby are given unto us exceeding great and precious promises: that by these ye might be partakers of the divine nature, having escaped the corruption that is in the world through lust. – King James Version

We were also given absolutely terrific promises to pass on to you - your tickets to participation in the life of God after you turned your back on a world corrupted by lust. – The Message Translation

The power and presence of God in your life equips you to not only live a holy and righteous life, but to enjoy the manifold blessings and benefits of being in the kingdom of God. It is impossible for God to lie. His Word is sure and steadfast. Practice embracing the promises given to you in His Word. Even though you may endure challenges in the earth realm, keep in mind that you are a spiritual being simply living in the natural world.

Don't allow the distractions of the enemy to hold you back or slow you down. You have power over all of the devil's plans and tactics. The "God" in you empowers you to live victoriously. So practice living the abundant life that belongs to you. Healing, deliverance, peace, prosperity, and so much more are all yours simply because of who you are and Whose you are!

OCTOBER 26
Prepare For Plenty!
PROVERBS 30:25

The ants are a people not strong, yet they prepare their meat in the summer; - King James Version

ants - frail as they are, get plenty of food in for the winter; - The Message Translation

You don't have to have great physical strength to achieve great things. But you must have a vision and a plan. You must also be consistent enough to follow through and bring your dream into reality.

The key to success is having a vision, developing a plan, following through on your plan and celebrating your accomplishments. Success is not based upon how much money you gain or other people's approval or estimation. Success comes from the inner satisfaction of bringing vision to manifestation.

Make a decision today to see an aspiration. That's right! See into the spirit realm and see what you desire. Develop small objectives to reach small attainable goals. Each time you accomplish a goal encourage yourself and celebrate. Thank and praise God for what He has empowered you to do – and then get back to work!

The season of winter will come – but you won't starve! When you have worked hard and made accomplishments – you will be able to rest in the success you have achieved. It came not because of your strength but because of your diligence. Proverbs 13:4

reminds you that, *"The soul of the sluggard desireth, and hath nothing: but the soul of the diligent shall be made fat."*

OCTOBER 27
You Don't Need Money!
ISAIAH 55:1

Ho, every one that thirsteth, come ye to the waters, and he that hath no money; come ye, buy, and eat; yea, come, buy wine and milk without money and without price. – King James Version

Hey there! All who are thirsty, come to the water! Are you penniless? Come anyway - buy and eat! Come, buy your drinks, buy wine and milk. Buy without money - everything's free! – The Message Translation

God has a great love for you. He wants you to receive His Spirit and His Word so they may bless your life. The price tag is your faith. If you can simply trust God and believe He will bless you beyond measure!

Wine is symbolic of the spirit of God. God wants His Spirit to fill you and influence your life like never before. He wants to lead, guide, and direct you. He wants His Spirit to empower you to live a victorious life and be an effective witness in the earth realm.

You must desire the sincere milk of the Word of God so that you may grow. God's Word always works. It never fails. God wants you to live by His Word so that you may obtain the benefits of His Word.

All you have to do is act upon your faith. That's right – walk in what you believe. You can have God's best!

OCTOBER 28

You Have A Cross Too!

MATTHEW 16:24

Then Jesus said to his disciples, "If anyone would come after me, he must deny himself and take up his cross and follow me. – New International Version

Then Jesus went to work on his disciples. "Anyone who intends to come with me has to let me lead. You're not in the driver's seat; I am. Don't run from suffering; embrace it. Follow me and I'll show you how. – The Message Translation

The cross represents suffering. Jesus willingly endured the cross to satisfy the sin debt for the world. He endured not only the suffering but the shame as well. He had done no wrong, yet he was convicted of every sin from days past and days to come.

You identify with what he did on Calvary by willingly embracing suffering. Life can be challenging – but your Christian foundation ensures that you will stand no matter how fierce the storm. The challenges that you go through are not always for you. Don't be so self-centered and selfish in your thinking and actions that you feel everything is about you.

Deny yourself. Put your own feelings and emotions on the back burner. Whatever you have to go through in life; endure it so you can be a living testimony for others. Learn to allow your life to be an example just like Jesus.

OCTOBER 29

Now Tell God "Thank Ya"
I THESSALONIANS 5:18

In every thing give thanks: for this is the will of God in Christ Jesus concerning you. – King James Version

Thank God no matter what happens. This is the way God wants you who belong to Christ Jesus to live. – The Message Translation

Admit it. Life does offer challenges. Sometimes there are days when you question if your prayers are actually being heard. The enemy delights in your frustration and desires that you begin to murmur and complain. But, this is exactly the time that you must only allow "a praise" to spring forth from your lips.

It is God's will and desire that you learn to be thankful in every situation you find yourself. Good days and bad days, happy times and sad times – you must learn to not allow your emotions to be conditioned by the climate or atmosphere. But, you must allow your faith to command your soul and body to be thankful and grateful always.

David was not worried about valley situations because he realized He was not alone, the Lord was with Him. Jehoshaphat learned that every battle in life was not one that He had to fight because His God would fight the battle for Him when He learned to stand still. Relationships on the rock or solid as a rock, bills paid in advance or bills past due, body racking with pain or body feeling just fine – learn to simply tell God: "Thank Ya!"

OCTOBER 30

Be Proud Of Fellow Believers

II CORINTHIANS 1:14

You'll now see the whole picture, as well as you've seen some of the details. We want you to be as proud of us as we are of you when we stand together before our Master Jesus. – The Message Translation

Exhort and encourage fellow believers in their spiritual walk with God. Don't waste time looking for faults or tearing people down because of your personal judgment or opinion. Realize that it was Jesus Christ who shed His blood for all. And that His blood covers you as well as your brothers and sisters in the Lord.

Each day speak into the atmosphere words of encouragement and admonition that their lives be holy and sanctified. Take opportunity to personally bless someone with words that affirm their position in Christ. Consume your conversation with positive things to say about others.

There will come a day when all shall be gathered before the Lord. As all gather, it will be grace and mercy that comes through Jesus Christ that will enable all to stand in true holiness and righteousness. So, exhaust all your energy in pushing your brothers and sisters to greatness. Encourage them to stay focused and pursue destiny.

OCTOBER 31
Celebrate The God Gifts
II TIMOTHY 1:7

God did not give us a spirit that makes us afraid but a spirit of power and love and self-control. – New Century Version

Focus your energy and effort on the "God-gifts" and not the tricks of the enemy. God has blessed you with power, love and a sound mind. Do not waste time celebrating or embracing works of the flesh that encourage fear.

God wants you to live in the abundant life He has promised you. He has given you His Spirit to empower you to be victorious. He wants to abide in you and bless you to reproduce His character and fruit of love. Your obedience to His Word will help you to discipline yourself to do those things that are pleasing unto Him.

When these areas become your focus, you won't have time for the frivolity that others involve themselves. Your desire and corresponding actions will be holy and righteous. The best way to defeat the devil is to ignore him. The power he has is to influence. So, if you don't give in to his suggestions and invitations – you will find that he will have to flee. The Bible says to resist the devil and he will flee.

So celebrate: God's power in you, His love made manifest through you, and good sense to know that all He does in, for and through you is right and good! Celebrate!

NOVEMBER 1

I Want More Milk!

I PETER 2:2

As newborn babes, desire the sincere milk of the word, that ye may grow thereby: - King James Version

Now, like infants at the breast, drink deep of God's pure kindness. Then you'll grow up mature and whole in God. – The Message Translation

When babies are hungry – they cry. When they are given milk – they settle down. When sinners are lost – they cry. When they are given the Word of God – they settle down.

Crying is manifested through sin and iniquity. Sometimes in their frustration with life, people turn to the flesh to look for hope. Turning to the flesh is similar to giving a pacifier to a hungry baby. It may keep the baby quiet for barely a moment. It cannot substitute for milk when the baby is hungry. You cannot substitute a natural answer to solve a spiritual problem. God's Word is the only answer to the cries of humanity.

As you allow God's Word to fill your life: strength, development and maturity come. God's Word will strengthen you to weather any storm that life can throw your way. God's Word will cause you to grow and you will see the actual transformation in choices and decisions you make, and in the way you respond to challenges. Your growth will cause you to mature into a settled child of God – not moved by wind or erroneous doctrine.

As a true child of God – desire milk! Yearn for more of God! Seek to grow through reading His Word, studying His Word, praying His Word, memorizing His Word, meditating upon His Word, and even more so by applying His Word!

NOVEMBER 2

Go Bless Somebody!

LUKE 10:33-35

"A Samaritan traveling the road came on him. When he saw the man's condition, his heart went out to him. He gave him first aid, disinfecting and bandaging his wounds. Then he lifted him onto his donkey, led him to an inn, and made him comfortable. In the morning he took out two silver coins and gave them to the innkeeper, saying, 'Take good care of him. If it costs any more, put it on my bill - I'll pay you on my way back.' – The Message Translation

Do the unexpected and bless someone who least expects it. How easy is it for you to help a friend? How simple is it for you to do something nice for a family member or church member? Today, break out of your comfort zone and bless someone who least expects it. Go beyond social class, racial boundaries, religious barriers, or anything else that separates people.

When you learn to live sacrificially and be a blessing in others' lives, you are setting yourself up to be awesomely blessed of God. If you help someone who does not have the ability to repay you, God will be your rewarder. Now, don't mess up your repayment. Whatever you do, you do not need to sound an alarm or blow a horn to let the world know how wonderful you are. Just do what you do discreetly, and God will reward you openly.

Your life will be made better by blessing someone else. The emotional feeling and spiritual benefit of your kind deed is indescribable. Actually, when you learn to live like this from the heart – you will experience an abundance of joy, peace and contentment that you have never known. Go be a blessing today!

NOVEMBER 3

Everybody Doesn't Need A Microphone!

ROMANS 9:21

Isn't it obvious that a potter has a perfect right to shape one lump of clay into a vase for holding flowers and another into a pot for cooking beans? – The Message Translation

Members of the Body of Christ must not allow the fleshly spirit of competition, rivalry, or jealousy to creep into their lives. God decides how we best can make an impact in the earth realm. Learn your position and stay on your post. Understand that every member of the body is important.

The enemy desires to bring damage and destruction to the kingdom of God. Even though it is impossible for him to do, it does not stop him from trying. He will encourage people to be jealous of other people's assignment. When the enemy can keep you focusing on what someone else is doing, he succeeds in keeping you from doing what you should be doing. This is how progress is sometimes hindered.

Be happy with what God blesses you to do. If you have the microphone and stand before the people – do it for the glory of God! If you have the mop and broom and keep the house clean – do it for the glory of God. God is always in charge. Be grateful for the mere fact that He loves you enough to still use you and choose you. You don't have to be up front in the spotlight – to be used of God and be a blessing in the kingdom and the earth realm.

NOVEMBER 4
Cease And Desist!
PSALM 46:1, 10

God is our refuge and strength, a very present help in trouble. Be still, and know that I am God: I will be exalted among the heathen, I will be exalted in the earth. – King James Version

God is a safe place to hide, ready to help when we need him. Step out of the traffic! Take a long, loving look at me, your High God, above politics, above everything." – The Message Translation

You have done all you can and now you are frustrated. You seem to be proverbially just "spinning your wheels". You are marking time, wasting your energy and resources, marching but going nowhere. The solution is simple. Let God be God!

Take your hands off the problem and allow Him to be God. He is God, you are not! Yes, there are steps that He wants you to take. There are actions that He wants you to engage. But, there comes a point and time that He wants you to remove your hands off the situation so He can show up and be God!

He will not share His glory with anyone! He is well aware of the obstacles that you face. He knows, cares, and feels the pain and frustration in your heart and mind. Now, He wants you to simply trust Him to be all that you have prayed for Him to be. He won't let the enemy triumph over you or Him. But, He will bring victory to your situation – in His time and in His way!

NOVEMBER 5

The Key To Prevailing Prayer

JAMES 5:16

Confess your faults one to another, and pray one for another, that ye may be healed. The effectual fervent prayer of a righteous man availeth much. – King James Version

Make this your common practice: Confess your sins to each other and pray for each other so that you can live together whole and healed. The prayer of a person living right with God is something powerful to be reckoned with. – The Message Translation

Clear the prayer path by clearing your heart and mind. Whenever you hold onto something, that thing which you hold onto captivates you and enslaves you. Don't allow the enemy to deceive you into harboring thoughts and deeds. Get a prayer partner and free your mind of guilt, sin, and shame. God has already provided His grace and mercy to cover whatever it is that you have done.

Your connection or relationship with God gives you access to the throne room. So, when you pray make sure that your prayer is effectual and fervent and the benefits will be astounding. An effectual prayer is one that is based upon God's Word. God's Word cannot fail. So, if you want God's best – speak His Word into the atmosphere. A fervent prayer is one that is empowered by the Holy Ghost. Allow the Spirit *"which searcheth all things, even the deep things of God"* to do His job and serve as your intercessor and helper.

God has already done His part – now it is your time to do yours. His blood was for yesterday, today and tomorrow. So, in effect your sin has already been forgiven before God. But, you have to forgive yourself through confession and repentance. Then you can live a life with a clear conscience to receive God's unlimited blessings.

NOVEMBER 6
When God Speaks!
II CHRONICLES 20:20

And they rose early in the morning, and went forth into the wilderness of Tekoa: and as they went forth, Jehoshaphat stood and said, Hear me, O Judah, and ye inhabitants of Jerusalem; Believe in the LORD your God, so shall ye be established; believe his prophets, so shall ye prosper. – King James Version

They were up early in the morning, ready to march into the wilderness of Tekoa. As they were leaving, Jehoshaphat stood up and said, "Listen Judah and Jerusalem! Listen to what I have to say! Believe firmly in God, your God, and your lives will be firm! Believe in your prophets and you'll come out on top!" – The Message Translation

How many times have you heard someone give you directions only to turn around and disobey what you heard? How many times has your mind been made up and you figured it was best to do it your own way? Especially in times of crisis, you may find yourself at a cross road of decision. You have the choice to either do what you heard or follow your mind and your own thoughts.

God has a funny and strange way of bringing victory in your life. The Word of God says that He often chooses the foolish things to confound those who think they are wise. (I Corinthians 1:27) This is where trusting and obeying has to kick into gear in your daily life.

Don't go to church to hear a sermon and walk out of the door doing the complete opposite. Stop reading books and magazines that God allowed to come into your presence at the right time to speak to your situation, to only turn around and follow your gut feelings or emotions. No longer listen to messages on the television, radio or tapes and then decide that what you heard is not for you! You are wasting time!

God promises that if you believe Him (His Word) and follow the directions of those He assigns to speak into your life (apostles, prophets, evangelists, pastors, teachers – *and anyone else He desires to anoint with a Word for your situation)* you will be successful.

Don't waste anymore time! Just walk by faith and not sight and obey the Word of the Lord and walk into your blessing. You may find yourself doing strange things – just do it and be blessed!

NOVEMBER 7
Keep Following The Light
JOHN 8:12

Then spake Jesus again unto them, saying, I am the light of the world: he that followeth me shall not walk in darkness, but shall have the light of life. – King James Version

Jesus once again addressed them: "I am the world's Light. No one who follows me stumbles around in the darkness. I provide plenty of light to live in." – The Message Translation

An old gospel song said, "Follow Jesus, take no chance getting lost..." This is a true statement. For on your own you are like a man walking in darkness in a strange place. However, when Jesus "The Light Of The World" appears there is no place where He leads you that you cannot successfully navigate.

The problem with many people is self-sufficiency. You must be delivered from the Burger King mentality of having it your own way on this Christian walk. God's Word reminds you that there is a way that seems right but the end results are death. God has a plan and in order to achieve success you must follow His plan and not another.

When times of uncertainty or confusion arise, look to Jesus. He will shine a light on every situation and circumstance. Oftentimes, He will not only show you where you are going but also explain why you are where you are! Yes, His Spirit reveals things that eyes have never seen nor has even entered your heart. Your responsibility is to simply trust Him and follow Him.

NOVEMBER 8
Don't Be Distracted!
NEHEMIAH 4:3

Now Tobiah the Ammonite was by him, and he said, Even that which they build, if a fox go up, he shall even break down their stone wall. – King James Version

At his side, Tobiah the Ammonite jumped in and said, "That's right! What do they think they're building? Why, if a fox climbed that wall, it would fall to pieces under his weight." – The Message Translation

Do not listen to foolishness from the lips of others. When you have an assignment from God, if you do it God's way it will work. Too often people allow the petty conversation of others to discourage them and cause them to second guess themselves. Life is too short and your assignment is too important for you to waste time with others.

Everyone has opinions. And everyone has a right to their own opinions. But, you cannot allow the opinions of others to control and dictate the actions in your life. You must realize that everyone that you know does not have your best interest at heart. Some want to see you fail. Others just don't want you to be better than them. Do not empower people to speak negativity into your life.

If God gave you an assignment, complete the task. If what you are doing is a "God thing", then He will bless it and cause it to stand. Doctors have told people that they were going to die, but God said they would live. Guess what? They can't die until God says so. Family members have told people that relationships would not last. Even with the high divorce rate of society, there are many who are holding on to "till death do us part". There are ministries that some have "prophe-lied" and said they were not ordained by God and would not last, however – sinners are still being saved, backsliders are still returning, sick people are still being healed, and the list goes on.

The bottom line: Do not allow anyone to tell you something different than what God told you. Let God be true and every man a liar.

NOVEMBER 9

The Peace Of God
PHILIPPIANS 4:7

And the peace of God, which passeth all understanding, shall keep your hearts and minds through Christ Jesus. – King James Version

Then God's peace, which goes beyond anything we can imagine, will guard your thoughts and emotions through Christ Jesus. – God's Word Translation

Before you know it, a sense of God's wholeness, everything coming together for good, will come and settle you down. It's wonderful what happens when Christ displaces worry at the center of your life. – The Message Translation

You don't have to understand it. Just receive it!

Everyday, the challenges of life bring new and interesting items for your agenda. Sometimes you have the power to refuse to allow the item to be placed on your agenda. But, there are some things you have no control of. They are a part of life and you are going to have to deal with them.

Pray won't reverse it. Praise won't make it as if it never happened. Worship won't cause it to disappear. But, your prayer, praise and worship together will usher in the manifested presence of God – *called the anointing* – to lift your spirit and soul above the challenge.

It may look bad. It may feel bad. It may sound bad. It may even be bad. But the peace that God will bring to your heart and mind will cause the challenge to lose its spiritual and emotional power over you. You will be like Hebrew boys and walk through the fire and not be burned. You will be like David and Job after seemingly losing everything, recover all and often double for your trouble. You will be like the Shunammite woman who instead or grieving and bereaving decreed "it is well" and see things resurrected in your life.

Today, embrace the peace of God and be excited. Don't try to understand it. That will only bring needless frustration. Simply thank and praise God for it – and enjoy the blessing of serving a God who keeps your heart and mind in perfect peace as you keep your mind focused on Him.

NOVEMBER 10

Be A Channel Of Blessing!

PROVERBS 11:25

The liberal soul shall be made fat: and he that watereth shall be watered also himself. – King James Version

A generous person will be made rich, and whoever satisfies others will himself be satisfied. – God's Word Translation

The one who blesses others is abundantly blessed; those who help others are helped. – The Message Translation

God has an awesome principle in place to ensure blessings upon His people. It is the simple law of sowing and reaping. Whatever it is that you desire, you must plant that same thing. And then trust God to bring fruition and harvest to the matter.

Don't be stingy. Don't be selfish. But, learn to go out of your way to be a help and a blessing to others. Remember, if you are a faucet bringing water to others, you can't help but always get wet yourself.

Always remember, you are only a channel. You are not the source! God is the source and He is the One who gets the praise! Just be ready, willing, and able for God to use you in His service to bless somebody!

NOVEMBER 11

The Future Is Still Bright!

JEREMIAH 29:11

For I know the thoughts that I think toward you, saith the LORD, thoughts of peace, and not of evil, to give you an expected end. – King James Version

I know what I'm doing. I have it all planned out - plans to take care of you, not abandon you, plans to give you the future you hope for. – The Message Translation

Life is life. Challenges abound. And sometimes your emotions get the best of you when it seems like everything is spinning out of control. But that is all part of the Christian journey you travel.

Homes catch on fire. Marriages fall "off the rocks". Cars are carjacked. Sickness invades bodies. Children get hooked on drugs. You cannot allow the works of the enemy (stealing, killing, and destroying) to control your faith. Build a new house. Revisit the honeymoon. Buy a new car. Stand on God's Word for healing. Pray for deliverance for your child.

You cannot allow situations or circumstances, no matter how dark or grim, to define who you are. You are not a by-product of your circumstances. You are a product of the mind of God. When He created you, He did so with purpose and gave you a destiny. Even though roadblocks and pitfalls have come along the way, those things only cause delays not denials.

Rise up and declare boldly who you are. Tell sickness you are healed in the name of Jesus. Speak to your finances and say that you prosper and have no lack. Command that every relationship in your life will no longer be in disarray but will come into divine order. Call confusion, envy, strife, worry, sadness, jealousy and all of their co-workers in for a staff meeting and dismiss them. Let them know they are being replaced with love, peace and joy.

Sing to yourself. Speak to yourself. Remind yourself. "I am what God says I am".

NOVEMBER 12

Walk, Leap and Praise!
ACTS 3:8

And he leaping up stood, and walked, and entered with them into the temple, walking, and leaping, and praising God. – King James Version

He jumped to his feet and began to walk. Then he went with them into the temple courts, walking and jumping, and praising God. – Today's New International Version

Have you ever been given directions on how to respond when winning a prize, or getting a raise, or seeing your favorite sports team win the game? Not likely! But, sad to say there is usually more exuberance in the celebration of those things than a visible excitement about what God has done! This should not be so.

God gave you emotions and emotions are not bad. It is okay to "make a joyful noise", "to praise him "in the dance", to "shout with a loud shout". The same way that you yielded your members to unrighteousness, now learn to yield those same members unto righteousness and holiness.

When God has blessed and moved in your life – change positions. Respond to God's blessing by undergoing change. Wherever and however God found you – it is time to move to a different beat. Don't allow the enemy to tempt you to live in a pity party or attempt to hold onto the past. Release yesterday and embrace tomorrow. Get into God's order. Begin operating in the way that best pleases God and best advances you in the kingdom.

And then respond! Jump up and walk, leap, and praise. Show the world how excited you are about what God has done. Let God know how much you appreciate His goodness.

NOVEMBER 13
Focus On Your Function!
LUKE 10:40

But Martha was cumbered about much serving, and came to Him, and said, Lord, dost thou not care that my sister hath left me to serve alone? bid her therefore that she help me. – King James Version

But Martha was pulled away by all she had to do in the kitchen. Later, she stepped in, interrupting them. "Master, don't you care that my sister has abandoned the kitchen to me? Tell her to lend me a hand." – The Message Translation

People sometimes become frustrated with others and their choices. But, everyone is responsible for their own actions. Mary chose to worship and Martha chose to serve. Both were important responsibilities.

When believers in the body of Christ begin to see themselves in this light the Body will be even more blessed. Everyone has a part to play. One is not any more important than the other. So, don't get frustrated over someone else's gift, talent, or assignment. Focus on doing the best job at your assignment and all shall be well.

When you begin to get upset over someone else's actions you lose productivity in your own assignment. Do your job. And concentrate on doing an excellent job! Remember – if you are a hand, the foot has nothing on you! If you are the eye, the nose cannot see better than you. Focus on what you do and see how blessed everyone will be.

NOVEMBER 14
Choose Your Song Wisely
EPHESIANS 5:19

Speaking to yourselves in psalms and hymns and spiritual songs, singing and making melody in your heart to the Lord;
- King James Version

Sing hymns instead of drinking songs! Sing songs from your heart to Christ. – The Message Translation

Some people don't think that it is very important when it comes to the type music you listen to. However, care must be taken because music is a powerful tool that heavily influences the emotions and ministers to the soul. "You are what you eat" is very true when it comes to music. Studies have shown that people's actions have been greatly influenced by music.

Music is a powerful instrument. It can lift your spirit, change your mood, and even guide your actions. A song does so much in a person's life. Recall the relationship between David and Saul. Whenever Saul was in a negative mood, David would be called upon to play and deliver Saul from the evil spirit which was upon him.

When you allow songs based upon God's Word to fill your life, the results are blessed. Your day can be brightened and you can be encouraged to keep fighting and moving forward when you allow spiritual songs to minister to your life. Be blessed and encouraged by the music you play.

NOVEMBER 15

God Is Focused On The Inside

JEREMIAH 17:10

But I, God, search the heart and examine the mind. I get to the heart of the human. I get to the root of things. I treat them as they really are, not as they pretend to be." – The Message Translation

Stop wasting time trying to prove yourself to man. God is the one who really matters. Man can only see the outside and make a judgment call on the inside. However, God can see the truth about the outside and the inside. There is nothing hidden from God.

When others have given up on you and have lost hope in your ability, God looks beyond all of that! He sees not just what you are actually doing, but he sees the true intent of your heart. This is why even when you make mistakes you cannot throw in the towel. You have to learn how to fall down and get back up again!

Focus on making sure that your heart is right. If you are really trying to please God, start working on the part of you that controls all of you. Dressing up the outside is only a pretense. But, when you allow the inside to change, you have then positioned yourself to change everything about you. True deliverance is nigh!

NOVEMBER 16

Partnership With God

I CHRONICLES 19:13

Be of good courage, and let us behave ourselves valiantly for our people, and for the cities of our God: and let the LORD do that which is good in his sight. – King James Version

Courage! We'll fight might and main for our people and for the cities of our God. And God will do whatever he sees needs doing!" – The Message Translation

Get rid of that "sit back and see what happens" attitude. God has invested His power in you to accomplish victory in the earth realm. Your faith is your weapon. It is made evident through your praise, worship, intercession and lifestyle.

Just because you are under attack does not mean that you are defeated or that God has forsaken you. Do your part. Do what God blessed and equipped you to do. And then God will do the rest.

The old folk used to say, "If you make one step, He'll make two." There is a bit of truth in that revelation. When you operate in faith, faith moves God. He will begin to work on your behalf when you walk according to His Word. His Word cannot and will not lie. God is hurrying to make certain of that!

NOVEMBER 17

Your Faith Glorifies God!
I PETER 1:7

That the trial of your faith, being much more precious than of gold that perisheth, though it be tried with fire, might be found unto praise and honour and glory at the appearing of Jesus Christ: - King James Version

Pure gold put in the fire comes out of it proved pure; genuine faith put through this suffering comes out proved genuine. When Jesus wraps this all up, it's your faith, not your gold, that God will have on display as evidence of his victory. – The Message Translation

No matter what you suffer or endure keep your head up and always have a good attitude. Faith is simply agreeing with God. So, keep your faith active and alive. This is the challenge in your life. When you can live by faith, victory will come to you and God will get the glory out of your life.

It's okay to endure a hardship. If you suffer, then eventually you will reign. God is completely aware of all that you are going through. He is pleased when you don't give up, but continue to trust Him and to stand on His Word. God will not and cannot lie. All things will work together for your good.

If the enemy can get you to abandon your faith, he knows that he can defeat you. But, you must be wise and courageous. Stay in the fight. Keep running the race. Victory has already been declared for you. Hang on and get the prize. God wants to put it in His heavenly trophy case.

NOVEMBER 18

Seize The Moment

JOHN 9:4

I must work the works of him that sent me, while it is day: the night cometh, when no man can work. – King James Version

We need to be energetically at work for the One who sent me here, working while the sun shines. When night falls, the workday is over. – The Message Translation

A well-known and beloved pastor, Dr. W.E. Jones, used to make the statement, "Do all you can, while you can!" And it is biblically sound and practically sensible. You should not wait on a tomorrow that is not promised, when you have been blessed with a "present" called today! The choices that you make today often lay the foundation for the future.

Learn to live your life to the max every day, so that you never live a life of regret. Don't ever put off a challenge because of fear. Go and get what God says belongs to you. The devil will attempt to derail your destiny by telling you lies and making you feel as if you can't accomplish what is in your heart.

Live your life as if there was no tomorrow. Praise Him now, not wishing you could when you are on a bed of affliction. Pay your tithes and give an offering now, not wishing that you had been more faithful when you find yourself financially challenged. Take hold of your life and live for God everyday! Life will be full and complete when you live each day to the fullest!

NOVEMBER 19
Unlikely Help!
LUKE 10:31-33

And by chance there came down a certain priest that way: and when he saw him, he passed by on the other side. And likewise a Levite, when he was at the place, came and looked on him, and passed by on the other side. But a certain Samaritan, as he journeyed, came where he was: and when he saw him, he had compassion on him, - King James Version

Luckily, a priest was on his way down the same road, but when he saw him he angled across to the other side. Then a Levite religious man showed up; he also avoided the injured man. A Samaritan traveling the road came on him. When he saw the man's condition, his heart went out to him. – The Message Translation

During times of tragedy and testing, help is a welcomed friend. However, the strange thing is that help does not always come from the likely source. It would seem natural that the priest or Levite would have come to the rescue of their Jewish brother – but it was not so. However, a Samaritan that was an outsider was the one to come to the rescue and help.

As you grow spiritually, you will discover that talk and walk are not always the same. Some people talk a good game, but usually that is what it ends up being: "a game." Looking and sounding religious do not make one a Christian. The word says that they'll know we are His disciples by our love. We must practice what we preach.

Have you ever found yourself in a position to help? When your heart is in the right place you don't allow differences: racial, religion, gender, economic, or any other categories to stop you from providing assistance. You will cross borders and barriers to be used of God to be a blessing. And once you decide to help, you will sacrificially do whatever it takes to ensure that your help is full and complete.

Look at the examples of the characters in this parable. The priest saw the pending potential to have to change his agenda and help someone, and immediately changed his route. The Levite was curious to get close enough to the situation, but did nothing to help. However, the Samaritan disregarded the differences between himself and the victim and responded by helping. Ask yourself: Are you are priest, a Levite or a Samaritan?

NOVEMBER 20

Let Your Joy Be Full!

PSALM 16:11

"Thou wilt shew me the path of life: in Thy presence is fulness of joy; at Thy right hand there are pleasures for evermore."

Paul described a challenging life (in II Cor. 4:8) when he said, *"we are troubled on every side, but not distressed, perplexed but not in despair…."* Life sometimes can be overwhelming. However, when you become a worshipper and allow God to be God you will discover a joy that is indescribable.

The late Elder James Simon would always declare that, "Joy is not the absence of sorrow, but it is the presence of the Lord." Oh, how true is that declaration!

What you must come to terms with is that oftentimes, things around you may not change. But, God in His awesomeness and goodness will change you for the things around you. When the Hebrew boys were thrown in the fiery furnace, God did not take the heat out of the flames. For the Scriptures declare that the ones who threw them in perished in the fire. But, God protected them and even showed up with them in the midst of their affliction.

God makes the same promise to you today. Real joy is the contentment of knowing that God is always in control and that your life is in his hands. Never confuse joy with happiness. Happiness occurs as a result of something good happening to you. But, joy occurs because of who God is in your life.

Worship God today. Welcome His presence in every situation and circumstance that you encounter. Smile. Speak positive words. Have confidence that victory belongs to you. And see your joy flow like rivers of living water.

NOVEMBER 21
Don't Be Distracted!
II KINGS 7:3

Now Tobiah the Ammonite was by him, and he said, Even that which they build, if a fox go up, he shall even break down their stone wall. – King James Version

At his side, Tobiah the Ammonite jumped in and said, "That's right! What do they think they're building? Why, if a fox climbed that wall, it would fall to pieces under his weight." – The Message Translation

Do not listen to foolishness from the lips of others. When you have an assignment from God, if you do it God's way it will work. Too often people allow the petty conversation of others to discourage them and cause them to second guess themselves. Life is too short and your assignment is too important for you to waste time with others.

Everyone has opinions. And everyone has a right to their own opinions. But, you cannot allow the opinions of others to control and dictate the actions in your life. You must realize that everyone that you know does not have your best interest at heart. Some want to see you fail. Others just don't want you to be better than them. Do not empower people to speak negativity into your life.

If God gave you an assignment, complete the task. If what you are doing is a "God thing", then He will bless it and cause it to stand. Doctors have told people that they were going to die, but God said they would live. Guess what? They can't die until God says so.

Family members have told people that relationships would not last. Even with the high divorce rate of society, there are many who are holding on to "till death do us part".

There are ministries that some have "prophe-lied" and said they were not ordained by God and would not last, however – sinners are still being saved, backsliders are still returning, sick people are still being healed, and the list goes on.

The bottom line: Do not allow anyone to tell you something different than what God told you. Let God be true and every man a liar.

NOVEMBER 22
Praise Him For Yourself
LUKE 8:35-39

35 A crowd soon gathered around Jesus, for they wanted to see for themselves what had happened. And they saw the man who had been possessed by demons sitting quietly at Jesus' feet, clothed and sane. And the whole crowd was afraid. 36 Then those who had seen what happened told the others how the demon-possessed man had been healed. 37 And all the people in that region begged Jesus to go away and leave them alone, for a great wave of fear swept over them. So Jesus returned to the boat and left, crossing back to the other side of the lake. 38 The man who had been demon possessed begged to go, too, but Jesus said, 39 "No, go back to your family and tell them all the wonderful things God has done for you." So he went all through the city telling about the great thing Jesus had done for him." – New Living Translation

In this passage of scripture, a man who had been under the control of evil spirits was healed by Jesus. After he was delivered, the Bible says that the man was found sitting at the feet of Jesus. However, the crowd of people reacted with fear instead of joy and excitement.

Understand, in your life that not everyone will always be excited about the move of God in your life. Sad to say, some people get joy from seeing you as dependent and needy. It gives them the ability to talk about how much they have done for you and how you would not have made it without them. Just as soon as you get up on your own feet their response changes. They are upset because they have lost the control they had over your life.

You would think they would be happy for you. But they are not. Many times people have ulterior motives. You do not have time to worry about people and whether or not they are excited about your blessings. You must be as the delivered man. Stay close to Jesus and thank Him for being in your right mind.

Your testimony of who God is and what He has done should be a witness everywhere you go. When people who knew you back then can see the change in you today, souls will be won for the kingdom. Practice being a walking praise report! Let the world see the change that God has made in your life!

NOVEMBER 23

Gratitude Determines Altitude

II CORINTHIANS 2:14

Now thanks be unto God, which always causeth us to triumph in Christ, and maketh manifest the savour of his knowledge by us in every place. – King James Version

When you express thanksgiving for what has not occurred it displays a level of faith. Faith is the act that moves God. God begins to stir things in the earth realm because He refuses to allow His Word to not perform.

Thank God for what you do not see and do not have, yet you desire so strongly within your heart. Allow your thanks to include the testimony of His Word. Decree and declare who He is and how you expect Him to manifest in your situation.

While yet sick, thank Jehovah Rapha for your healing – and watch God work. While still experiencing lack, praise Jehovah Jireh for providing – and watch God work. When you feel lonely and all alone, thank Jehovah Shammah for being everpresent – and watch God work!

That type praise will raise you out of your emotional slump. Your emotional man will connect with your spirit man and your physical man will follow suit. Give Him praise in advance. And watch your praise take you to new heights!

NOVEMBER 24
The Way To Please God!
HEBREWS 11:6

But without faith it is impossible to please him: for he that cometh to God must believe that he is, and that he is a rewarder of them that diligently seek him. – King James Version

It's impossible to please God apart from faith. And why? Because anyone who wants to approach God must believe both that he exists and that he cares enough to respond to those who seek him. – The Message Translation

Read God's Word and agree with God's Word. This is the core of your faith. Walk in what you read and that is faith in action. When you live a life based upon the truth of God's Word you will see the power and favor of God manifest in your life.

Exercising your faith is what gets God's attention. Believing that He exists and living a life that demonstrates that belief is the first step. Learn to worship Him, respect Him and acknowledge Him in everything you do.

You must not only believe that God's Word is true, but you must believe that it is true for you. Your actions should depict your confidence as God as your healer, your deliverer, your redeemer, your blessor, your everything!

When you walk by faith – GOD WALKS WITH YOU! When you live by faith – GOD LIVES THROUGH YOU!

NOVEMBER 25

Real Relationship!

PROVERBS 17:17

A friend loveth at all times, and a brother is born for adversity. – King James Version

Friends love through all kinds of weather, and families stick together in all kinds of trouble. – The Message Translation

"No man is an island," is a famous quote by the English poet John Donne. Stop trying to live all by yourself. God has placed you here on the planet to be helped and be blessed by others and to likewise be a blessing to others.

Real friends don't have to be in your face 24-hours a day to prove their friendship. But real friends are those who are there when you need them most. They are there to show unconditional love. When you are at your lowest moments, a true friend comes along to walk through your valleys with you!

And when the bottom falls out, real family steps up. It is so good to never have to fight a battle alone. God will bless you with both spiritual and natural family members who will "have your back".

Understand that real relationship is not determined by who is in your face on a daily basis. But when the storms of life are raging and the winds are blowing in your situation, the strength of the relationship is made manifest. Remember, a raincoat is not needed when the sun is shining but when the rain is coming down. A fur coat is not required in the summer when it is hot, but during the winter when it is cold.

The true value of friends and family is made evident when the chips are down. Thank God for placing you in someone's life to be a real friend or family member. And, rejoice that when you are going through your difficult season, God will position the right people to come alongside to help you!

NOVEMBER 26

Just Do Your Part!

MATTHEW 10:14

And whosoever shall not receive you, nor hear your words, when ye depart out of that house or city, shake off the dust of your feet. – King James Version

If they don't welcome you, quietly withdraw. Don't make a scene. Shrug your shoulders and be on your way. - The Message Translation

Your responsibility is to simply spread the good news. Tell anyone and everyone who will listen all about how God so loved everybody that He gave His Son Jesus to die on Calvary to save all. And tell how God loves us so much that He allows His Spirit to indwell believers who will surrender and yield. That is your job! That is your assignment.

However, you will encounter some who do not want to listen or obey. When your heart is filled with compassion for those you see headed for destruction it can be an emotional challenge. When you are connected to people and care about their eternal security, it can really be frustrating when they seem not to care.

But, God already knows that some will not listen. Also, you must understand your purpose in the overall plan. Some who appear not to listen are not part of your specific assignment. Simply do your part. Plant the seed of God's Word in others' lives. Water the seed that has already been sown by someone else. God knows the correct timing and due season for the harvest of that soul.

Once you have done your part – move on. You are not God! God is God! Do what God directed you to do. When it is received – rejoice! When it is not received – pray and move on!

NOVEMBER 27
Today – See His Goodness
PSALM 27:13

I had fainted, unless I had believed to see the goodness of the LORD in the land of the living. – King James Version

I am still confident of this: I will see the goodness of the LORD in the land of the living. – New International Version

Here is something I am still sure of. I will see the Lord's goodness while I'm still alive. – New International Reader's Version

"Something good is going to happen to you, this very day..." were the lyrics of the theme song of Oral Roberts' television program for years. These words are a powerful confession. It is a declaration of trust in an all-powerful and loving God. Regardless of what else is happening around, victory is still the end result.

Challenges do come every day. But, Christians have learned that this is simply a part of life. God promised you an abundant life – however, you have an adversary that desires to steal, to kill and to destroy. Learn to ignore the devil's temptation for you to give up or lose heart. Stay focused and remain prayerful.

Good things are happening in your life. Yes, God awakened you this morning. But, He has even more wonderful and great miracles to bring into manifestation in your life today. Look for God. Be a God chaser today. Pursue Him in your praise. Woo Him in your worship. Embrace him in your prayers and study of His Word. He is bringing good things to light for you today!

NOVEMBER 28
Holy For Him!
II CORINTHIANS 7:1

Having therefore these promises, dearly beloved, let us cleanse ourselves from all filthiness of the flesh and spirit, perfecting holiness in the fear of God. – King James Version

Holiness is not what you wear. Holiness is not what you say. But, true holiness is characterized by a life-style that emulates the life of Christ. True love for God is depicted not in rituals or traditions but in obedience to His Word. His living Word breathes brand new life into you.

God just made an awesome promise in the 6th chapter of II Corinthians. He has promised the blessings of relationship. And, because of your relationship with Him your lifestyle is changed. Have you ever noticed in the natural that you change things about yourself when you are "in love" with someone? Even more so in the spirit, now change everything for the lover of your soul. No longer seek to please your flesh, but strive everyday to please Him.

He is such a wonderful God. God has blessed you with a marvelous and wonderful life. He is always a constant help in good and bad times. He desires that you disconnect yourself from the enemy and those who align themselves with evil tactics and ways. He wants you all for Himself. Be ye Holy – just for Him!

NOVEMBER 29

God's Job Opening Just For You!

MATTHEW 4:19

And he saith unto them, Follow me, and I will make you fishers of men. – King James Version

Jesus said to them, "Come with me. I'll make a new kind of fisherman out of you. I'll show you how to catch men and women instead of perch and bass." – The Message Translation

If you pay close attention, the people that Jesus approached to utilize in the kingdom were already active and busy. It did not matter whether their profession was morally correct or if there was some shadiness about their business. He used people who had a mind to be productive. Matthew was a tax collector, Paul was a tentmaker, Luke was a physician, and James, John, Simon, and Andrew were fishermen.

When Jesus becomes the Lord and Saviour of your life, He changes you into a productive vessel for the kingdom of God. You may have skills you acquired in the world, but He will show you how to use those same parts of your body for God's glory. If you have a past that you are not extremely proud of – that's okay. God already knows about it. But, evidently He saw something in you to still cause Him to make plans to utilize you in His service.

There is work for you to do in the earth realm. He already has your assignment "job duties and details" prepared for you. He is the one who qualifies you and certifies you. Stop allowing flesh (people) to attempt to validate you. Man cannot stamp an approval (or voice a disapproval) on what God has already declared and decreed. Stop with the excuses and get busy for God!

NOVEMBER 30
It's Not All About You!
ROMANS 12:10

Be kindly affectioned one to another with brotherly love; in honour preferring one another; - King James Version

Be good friends who love deeply; practice playing second fiddle. – The Message Translation

Be kind to one another with a brother's love, putting others before yourselves in honour; - Bible In Basic English Translation

These present times promote selfishness. However, it is the will of God that you learn to be selfless and live to be a blessing to one another. Do not even allow your lack or present struggle stop you from helping someone else in need. Practice not allowing your agenda to be written in stone. Permit yourself to stop what you are doing to push someone else to destiny.

Jesus thought nothing of adjusting his itinerary when he was on the way to the ruler's house to raise his daughter from the dead, to stop long enough to address the woman with the issue of blood. (Matthew 9:18-20) You should pattern your life in the same manner. Don't ever be so busy that you cannot stop long enough to be used of God in other areas. Remember, it's not all about you – it is about the King and the Kingdom!

DECEMBER 1
Neither Do I!
JOHN 8:10-11

When Jesus had lifted up himself, and saw none but the woman, he said unto her, Woman, where are those thine accusers? hath no man condemned thee? She said, No man, Lord. And Jesus said unto her, Neither do I condemn thee: go, and sin no more. – King James Version

Jesus stood up and spoke to her. "Woman, where are they? Does no one condemn you?" "No one, Master." "Neither do I," said Jesus. "Go on your way. From now on, don't sin." You're Missing God in All This – The Message Translation

The Church of God must adopt the phraseology of Jesus *"Neither Do I"* and encourage people who are struggling by adopting the pattern of the Spirit of God. Too often believers become judgmental and overly critical of people who are doing the same thing that they used to do. The Bible says that the Spirit comes to convict of sin, but never to condemn.

Believers preach about, sing about and talk about grace and mercy. They embrace it for their own lives. But, it is time for believers to stop pointing fingers and learn to extend arms.

Sinners don't need to be notified that they are in sin and headed to hell. They are already well aware of that. They need a news bulletin to let them know about a loving God who loves them and cares for them right where they are, right how they are, and right who they are!

The love of God will cover a multitude of faults. Yes, the same grace and mercy that blessed changed your life will save and change the lives of others. Today, find someone who is lost in the struggle and "love them to life". Show them a more excellent way. Show them how their life can be better with Christ. This can be done in love without condemnation.

DECEMBER 2

How Persistent Is Your Faith?

ACTS 9:26

I tell you that he will avenge them speedily. Nevertheless when the Son of man cometh, shall he find faith on the earth? — King James Version

I assure you, he will. He will not drag his feet. But how much of that kind of persistent faith will the Son of Man find on the earth when he returns?" — The Message Translation

Faith is not the act of just "naming and claiming" or "calling and hauling". It is not saying a nice prayer with "In Jesus' Name" attached to it and turning around to always see the immediate physical manifestation. But, faith is being confident that what you believe has already been accomplished in the spirit realm. The absence of a physical manifestation does not cause your excitement or confidence to diminish. But, rather stirs you up to wait with greater expectation.

In the world there are those who will go to casinos or other gambling venues and consistently keep pushing buttons and pulling levers. Why? Because they believe that their number is about to show up! Some have participated to the extent that financial ruin has taken over their life. My point is NOT whether their activity is right or wrong! My point is simply the persistency of their belief made manifest by their actions!

Your healing, your deliverance, your blessing, your open door is just a FAITH away! That's right! Stand on God's Word and walk in His promises! When you don't see the manifestation of what you are believing God for, give Him an advance praise Him knowing that it is on the way. Don't give up! Don't give in! Don't let go! Don't surrender! If you endure – you will see victory!

DECEMBER 3
Why Are You Looking?
MARK 16:6

He said, "Don't be afraid. I know you're looking for Jesus the Nazarene, the One they nailed on the cross. He's been raised up; he's here no longer. You can see for yourselves that the place is empty. – The Message Translation

The women came to the tomb looking for the dead body of Jesus the Christ. They were sad and disheartened but their love drew them to the cemetery. They were in for a surprise!

You must learn to embrace the promises of God! He will do what He said. Situations and circumstances will encourage you to look for dead things. The enemy wants you to allow negativity and impotence to prevail. Disappointment will strive to be your manifested emotion in the face of defeat and denial. However, shake yourself and remind yourself of what God said!

Although, you have suffered loss; the loss was necessary. The death and burial was needed in order for God to bring the resurrection to pass in your life. Relationships may fail. Finances may suffer loss. Physical bodies may be challenged with sickness and disease. But, in all this you must remember that you are more than a conqueror.

Look for the newness of the resurrection in every area of your life. God is restoring. You are reclaiming. Look for the promise of God made manifest in the earth realm!

DECEMBER 4
Ministry Of Disconnect
PROVERBS 1:15

My son, walk not thou in the way with them; refrain thy foot from their path: - King James Version

Oh, friend, don't give them a second look; don't listen to them for a minute. – The Message Translation

God wants you to love everybody. You must be like your heavenly Father. He loves the sinner, he hates the sin. You must learn to embrace people. But, He also wants you to learn to love without fellowshipping. Your responsibility to God is to live a holy life. Your responsibility to others is to allow your light to shine.

There are people who may be part of your past, but they have no place in your future. They are not part of your destiny. Keep yourself from being contaminated by learning the ministry of disconnect.

Disconnecting does not mean being rude. It does not mean that you do not speak. But, what it entails is you learning how to distinguish spiritual from physical. There are conversations that you should refrain from with certain people. There are activities that are off limits with people who are not part of your destiny.

DECEMBER 5

Your Blessing Will Bless Others!

PSALM 23:5

Thou preparest a table before me in the presence of mine enemies: thou anointest my head with oil; my cup runneth over. – King James Version

You serve me a six-course dinner right in front of my enemies. You revive my drooping head; my cup brims with blessing. – The Message Translation

The blessing of the Lord makes rich and adds no sorrow. God knows when and how to bless you. Your responsibility is to simply remain humble. The Scriptures declare that if you stay humble, He knows the appropriate time to exalt you.

It does not matter who is around you or who is watching. God is so awesome, He will bless you even in front of those who dislike you or desire to do you harm. Yes, He will bless you in front of your haters.

But, the beautiful part of it all. His blessings will overflow in your life. When you get your "love" life together – God's blessings will be so powerful that even your enemies will be at peace with you because of the overbearing presence of God's anointing in your life.

You cannot contain all of God's goodness. This is why connections are so important. Others who are connected to you will be blessed along with you. Yes, hearts and lives will be changed. Healing, deliverance, peace, prosperity, and favor are on the way. Enjoy the overflow!

DECEMBER 6
At The End Of The Day!
II KINGS 7:3

So I sent messengers back with this: "I'm doing a great work; I can't come down. Why should the work come to a standstill just so I can come down to see you?" – The Message Translation

No matter what challenges you face on a daily basis – none of that changes who you are. You are not defined by your condition! You are not shaped or fashioned by the opinions of others. But, it is God who created you inside and out!

What appears on the outside is simply a work in progress for what is going on inside of you. Don't allow the word or the opinions of others to cause you to lose focus on the finished project. Stay committed to being who and what God ordained you to be.

God has a specific purpose for your life. So, don't lose yourself attempting to fit other people's agendas. Live for God and Him alone. At the end of the day, you must give account for how well you fulfilled the role that God chose you for.

Ignore adversity. And stop allowing trials and tribulations to change your confession. Keep your eyes open, your head up, and continue doing what you know in your heart you have been commissioned by God to do! When it is all said and done, at the end of the day you must be pleased to know that you and God are satisfied with your progress and your status.

DECEMBER 7
Know Who You Are!
ACTS 28:6

They kept expecting him to drop dead, but when it was obvious he wasn't going to, they jumped to the conclusion that he was a god! – The Message Translation

Be careful of "after the fact" prophets. There are some people who can't see until the storm is over. They don't see your true value or worth until you have successfully made it through a challenge. Wouldn't it be wonderful if these silent partners and silent spectators would learn to be encouragers in the middle?

But, you must learn to be like Paul. Know who you are for yourself. Encourage yourself. And when the critical challenge comes, just do what you know to do – exhibit faith. And let the onlookers just look!

It is sad to say but most people expect you to fail. They may smile and say nice religious words but often their hearts are in a different place. You must be able to stand on your own two feet. An old adage says, "It's a sorry tub that can't stand on its own bottom".

So, don't wait for other people to define you. God created you. God designed you. Let God define you. Your responsibility is to simply walk in who God created, anointed and appointed you to be.

DECEMBER 8
Watch Your Words!
PROVERBS 18:21

Death and life are in the power of the tongue: and they that love it shall eat the fruit thereof. – King James Version

What you say can preserve life or destroy it; so you must accept the consequences of your words. – Good News Translation

What you see around you is the result of a seed sown. Nothing just happens. Life is set into motion by thoughts and words. God said, "Let there be" and it was. You are created in the image of your Father the Creator. Your words have power and authority. For good or bad, what you say comes to pass.

Be careful about idle words or conversation. Be careful about trite expressions that you think mean nothing. Stop saying what everyone else says. Stop reiterating what you see. Those are all tricks of the enemy. He knows that if He can get you to put words out in the atmosphere they will manifest.

Practice saying what God says. It does not matter if you see it or not. Because it is God's Word, it cannot and will not return unto Him void or empty. It will fulfill its purpose. Only allow the positive things that you want to see made manifest flow from your lips.

For the negative that you have spoken, now speak and pray crop failure. For every time you were disappointed and you told yourself how you would not, could not make it. Speak crop failure to those word seeds sown. For those instances that you were frustrated and said harsh, cruel and mean things about others – repent and command that the words spoken would wither and be destroyed from the seed.

Today, focus on speaking life. Speak positive, uplifting, edifying words that promote success. Keep saying it until the manifestation comes. Only decree and declare what you are prepared to obtain. Watch your words!

DECEMBER 9
It Will Still Happen!
HABAKKUK 2:3

For the vision is yet for an appointed time, but at the end it shall speak, and not lie: though it tarry, wait for it; because it will surely come, it will not tarry. – King James Version

For the vision is still for the fixed time, and it is moving quickly to the end, and it will not be false: even if it is slow in coming, go on waiting for it; because it will certainly come, it will not be kept back. – Bible In Basic English Version

Patience to keep the faith and simply wait can sometimes be a challenge. However, what you have to understand is that God's Word cannot and will not lie. There is a season called due season. This is God's appointed time for the manifestation of His promise. He will always fulfill His word.

So do not be anxious when time passes and nothing seems to change. Sometimes the promise that you are waiting on is like a seed in the ground. You don't see anything until it is time for the manifestation of the plant. Just keep watering the ground. Remove the weeds. Allow patience to prevail in your life.

Your responsibility is to keep the faith by continuing to thank and praise God for the promise. Do not allow present circumstances or situations change your mind. Have confidence that what you desire will still come to pass. Create an atmosphere of worship which welcomes God's manifested presence in your life. And watch God show up and show out!

DECEMBER 10
God Shows His Awesomeness Via You!

PSALM 139:14

I praise you because I am fearfully and wonderfully made; your works are wonderful, I know that full well. – New International Version

I will give thanks to you because I have been so amazingly and miraculously made. Your works are miraculous, and my soul is fully aware of this. – God's Word Translation

Stop and look in the mirror! Look beyond you face, your hair, your body and look within. God is so awesome to have created and fashioned you as He did. There is none like you! He made you different from everyone else with a special treasure on the inside.

Give Him praise for His awesomeness. Others may look at you and discuss your faults, failures, imperfections and shortcomings. God looks within you and blesses you! Yes, in the midst of those same faults, failures, imperfections and shortcomings - to carry His glory. Yes, there is a light shining within you where you can impact the world as no one else. Only God could do this. Only God would do this.

So sing praises all day long. Boast and brag on His awesomeness all day long. Write Him a love letter. Read His Word and allow it to impact you as never before. Encourage others to also look within their mirror and give Him praise for His awesomeness in their life!

DECEMBER 11

Don't Look Back!

GENESIS 19:26

But his wife looked back from behind him, and she became a pillar of salt. – King James Version

The purpose of your walk with God is transformation. You should always be evolving from the old nature to the regenerated nature. The biggest challenge is regression. Some people have a big problem with letting go of yesterday.

There is a distinction between "longing" and "remembering". To long for something is to have a strong desire to return and embrace what once was. However, to remember a thing can be as simple as utilizing the event or experience as a learning tool.

If you are ready to grow and go with God, you must take pattern after the Apostle Paul and "forget those things which are behind and press toward the mark of the prize..." There are better things ahead for you. However, holding on to the weight of the past will hinder your acquisition of the good things of the future.

Don't delay an awesome destiny. Stagnancy and procrastination hinder progression. Don't just sit around talking about "the good old days". This is the day that the Lord has made – and it is a good day. Use it to propel yourself into a greater glory of God's anointing and power.

DECEMBER 12

From Bitter To Better!

RUTH 1:20

And she said unto them, Call me not Naomi, call me Mara: for the Almighty hath dealt very bitterly with me. – King James Version

And she said unto them, "Call me not Naomi [that is, Pleasant]. Call me Mara [that is, Bitter], for the Almighty hath dealt very bitterly with me. – Third Millennium Bible Translation

Sometimes life has a way of making you emotionally bankrupt. After you have done all that you know to do and it seems as if instead of getting better, things get worse – you are faced with the challenge of pressing on. God has a way of still showing up and showing out to bless you. That is the beauty of covenant, favor and just being blessed.

God keeps His word with His people. He will not change His mind on His promises to you. His love for you will cause favor to come and bless your life. Even at times when it seems as though failure has been served for your dinner, you can trust that God's faithfulness will show up at the same dinner table.

Encourage yourself through praise and worship and draw nearer to God. Don't get stuck in the trap of past problems or current challenges. There is a fantastic future that has your name on it. There is nothing that can happen in your life that God is not able to cause to still work in your favor. Remember, all things will still work together for your good.

DECEMBER 13

Concealed From Calamity!

PSALM 32:7

Thou art my hiding place; thou shalt preserve me from trouble; thou shalt compass me about with songs of deliverance. Selah. – King James Version

You are my safe and secret place; you will keep me from trouble; you will put songs of salvation on the lips of those who are round me. (Selah.) – Bible In Basic English Translation

God is all that and more! He will not only cover you and hide you from the evil one, but He will place the right people in your presence. He will surround you with singers whose mouths are filled with praise and thanksgiving. He will deliver you from those filled with doom and gloom.

What looked bad – God will adjust your vision. He will show you His hand of mercy at work on your behalf. Stop fretting over what could happen and what somebody said would happen. Remind yourself of the God that you serve.

Keep allowing God to order your steps. Whatever evil that was meant for your bad, God will turn it around and cause it to work in your favor. Decree and declare to the world who He is! Tell everyone that you serve a God who not only is able, but He is willing and He demonstrates it every day.

DECEMBER 14

They Need You! Not Your Money!

ACTS 3:6

Then Peter said, Silver and gold have I none; but such as I have give I thee: In the name of Jesus Christ of Nazareth rise up and walk. – King James Version

Peter said, "I don't have a nickel to my name, but what I do have, I give you: In the name of Jesus Christ of Nazareth, walk!" – The Message Translation

Within you, God has made an investment. The gift of His Spirit is not just for external manifestations such as shouting, dancing and speaking in other tongues. But, God declared that you would receive power after that the Holy Ghost had come upon you. This power, known as dunamis, is the very ability of God. It is explosive, life-altering and life-changing. The manifestation of spiritual gifts in your life are not just for you, but they are given to make an impact in the earth realm.

You must be spiritually sensitive to the move of God in your life. When you encounter others with needs, you need to be prayerful in offering assistance. You want to be a deliverer and not an enabler. Often, the one who is hungry does not need a fish sandwich, but they need a fishing pole, some bait and a quick lesson in fishing.

Today, remember these six powerful keys to being a blessing! God uses people who are BUSY. God works through people CONNECTED to Him. God will POSITION you to be used of Him. God expects your spiritual maturity to DISCERN true needs. God will EMPOWER you to operate signs and wonders when you trust and obey. God will be GLORIFIED by your actions.

Now go and bless somebody today – they don't need silver or gold, they need the gift of God that is operating in your life.

DECEMBER 15

Keep Going!
PSALM 34:19

Many are the afflictions of the righteous: but the LORD delivereth him out of them all. – King James Version

Disciples so often get into trouble; still, God is there every time. – The Message Translation

The words of a popular song say, *"Though trials come on every hand, I feel like going on."* Live every day with these sentiments. With full knowledge that adversities may come, stay committed to believing that God will still make everything alright.

It is no secret that this life is a warzone. Your faith is under constant attack. And even though things may get bad, look ugly, and feel hopeless – you must continue to trust the God you serve. The enemy has seen your destiny and will do anything he can to get you off track.

God has made you a promise that you are a victor. You have been assured that God is fighting on your behalf. Favor rises up and blesses you. Mercy shows up and suits your case. Grace embraces and clothes you. So, don't give up and don't give in – you might as well shout now because in the end you will win.

DECEMBER 16
He Will Fight Your Battle
HEBREWS 13:6

So that we may boldly say, The Lord is my helper, and I will not fear what man shall do unto me. — King James Version

we can boldly quote, God is there, ready to help; I'm fearless no matter what. Who or what can get to me? — The Message Translation

Have you ever felt under attack? Have you ever felt as if you were fighting a losing battle? Have you ever felt that your enemy had an advantage over you? Well, when you find yourself in Christ Jesus those days are over and are no more!

It is always good to have protection. And when your protector is bigger than your adversary it gives you a great calm and peace. God is bigger than anything or anyone that can come against you.

Can you recall a time when you were out-numbered or overpowered by your adversary. You were assured defeat, until someone came alongside to help you fight your battle. This is the confidence that you have in Christ Jesus.

There is nothing that can come against you that He will not help you to walk in victory. Praise God for being your help. Honor Him for being your protector.

DECEMBER 17
Fulfill Your Calling!
ISAIAH 42:6

"I am God. I have called you to live right and well. I have taken responsibility for you, kept you safe. I have set you among my people to bind them to me, and provided you as a lighthouse to the nations, - The Message Translation

"I, the LORD, have called you to demonstrate my righteousness. I will guard and support you, for I have given you to my people as the personal confirmation of my covenant with them. And you will be a light to guide all nations to me." – New Living Translation

God has a job for you! You have an awesome responsibility. On your job, in your community – everywhere you go – you have the task of being a light shining in the midst of darkness. But, remember you are not alone. God is ever present with you.

Do not stress because you feel as though you don't have it all together. That is the beauty of God being with you. In your weakness, His strength is made perfect. He is the One upholding and keeping you. Do not allow distractions to throw you off course. The enemy would have you focus on the flesh, while God wants you to walk and see in the spirit.

Take every opportunity to draw men, women, boys and girls to a real relationship with the Father. Introduce them to Jesus Christ, the Son. Pray the power of the Holy Spirit upon them as He teaches, leads and guides them. Remember, you are not alone. Go and let your light shine and draw others to the Lord.

DECEMBER 18
Know The Word For Yourself!
TITUS 1:9

And have a good grip on the Message, knowing how to use the truth to either spur people on in knowledge or stop them in their tracks if they oppose it. – The Message Translation

Take every opportunity possible to study and learn God's Word. You will be positioned before people who will need the knowledge which you have gained. Also, there are some who are confused and you need to be scripturally sound in order to correct them and help them.

It's not good enough for you to declare to others what your pastor, your bishop, or your apostle said. You need to be able to say WHAT GOD SAID! You have a responsibility to know God's Word for yourself so that you may be an effective ambassador. Praise God for the spiritual leaders who speak into your life, but always remember God desires an intimate personal relationship with you. Yes, He will talk to you.

Don't be afraid or ashamed to share the good news of the kingdom. No matter where you are, learn to be a wealth of spiritual knowledge and information so others' lives are blessed. And when you hear error, in the spirit of love, learn to minister correction so others don't end up going down the wrong path. Just be a vessel of honor and allow God to use you!

DECEMBER 19

Is It A Godly Connect?
AMOS 3:3

Can two walk together, except they be agreed? – King James Version

Do two people walk hand in hand if they aren't going to the same place? – The Message Translation

Why do you insist on holding the hand and staying connected to someone who by their actions is not a part of your destiny? Talk is cheap. Smiles are temporal. Actions speak louder than words. Unless there is a spiritual agreement and connection (ordained by God) between two people, most often anything else is but a simple passing and a waste of time.

Understand that people are placed in your life for various purposes. There are those who will be lifelong companions. However, there are others whose purpose is fleeting. They are there for a season and that's all. When the season changes, release them and let them go!

Why do some people insist on forcing something that is designed to be seasonal into the perpetual category? The swimsuit was cute in July at the beach. However, the season has changed, it's December and the swimsuit has to go!

Pray and seek God's face. Ask God for direction. If you find yourself in an unhealthy relationship, seek God's face for the right answer. He has given you His Word. Trust Him and know that He wants your life and your relationships to be abundantly blessed.

If you really want to be free and have peace – let their hand go! Hold God's hand. If you hold God's hand and the other person holds God's hand you will find yourself walking in the right direction. However, if they are not connected to God as you are – what have you lost – nothing! But, if you are holding their hand and not God's, when they let go – what have you lost? Everything!

DECEMBER 20
Let The Light Shine!
ISAIAH 60:1

"Arise, shine, for your light has come, and the glory of the LORD rises upon you. – King James Version

"Get out of bed, Jerusalem! Wake up. Put your face in the sunlight. God's bright glory has risen for you. – The Message Translation

An investment was made in you prior to you entering the earth realm. Before you were formed in your mother's womb – God knew you and deposited destiny in you! God's glory and purpose are within you waiting to shine forth. As you accept Him as your Lord and Saviour, you are positioned to manifest His true glory.

All of the negative, bad, hurtful, tumultuous things that have taken place in your life have been turned around. And God has an awesome way of causing all those things to work together with the good things for your good. So, stop crying over "spilled milk". Yesterday is gone. Embrace the "new mercies" that God makes available for you.

No longer waste time in despair or depression! Even if you don't see the light at the end of the tunnel, that's okay. The light is within you! Yes, you have been on an exterior search for an interior solution. Let the light of Christ shine forth and illuminate your life and your atmosphere!

DECEMBER 21
For Seasoned Saints!
COLOSSIANS 2:7

Rooted and built up in him, and stablished in the faith, as ye have been taught, abounding therein with thanksgiving. – King James Version

You're deeply rooted in him. You're well constructed upon him. You know your way around the faith. Now do what you've been taught. School's out; quit studying the subject and start living it! And let your living spill over into thanksgiving. – The Message Translation

You didn't just get saved yesterday! You've been walking this walk for a while now. So, stop acting like you are confused and don't know what to do. As many messages as you have heard down through the years, you should be out winning souls.

That's right! You should be a living epistle. Stop just talking about it – and be about it! Show others how to trust God, believe God, honor God, worship God, praise God, and serve God in every aspect of your life. In your home, on your job, in the community and among strangers it's time to simply exemplify who God created you to be.

What are you waiting for? Don't allow setbacks and challenges change your actions. Your lips should be thanking and praising God for all things knowing that they are all working together for your good. You can do this. God has confidence in you. Now look in the mirror and have confidence in yourself. No more practice – it's game time! Go and live the abundant life!

DECEMBER 22

Serve Humanity

MATTHEW 25:40

And the King shall answer and say unto them, Verily I say unto you, Inasmuch as ye have done it unto one of the least of these my brethren, ye have done it unto me.

Take full advantage of your relationship with Christ. Practice doing those things that bring glory to His Name and please Him. Don't waste time in superficial and possible pretentious acts of piety. God loves praise. Praise is right. God welcomes worship. He allows you to commune with Him. However, there is a work in the earth realm that God expects His children to perform.

He wants you to impact the earth realm and usher in a season of change. Your light should shine so that others can see Him at work in you. You have been given the ministry of reconciliation to bring those disconnected from Him and His love into fellowship and union with Him. Mark 16:18 said that signs would follow believers.

God expects that you lay hands on the sick and see them recover. Visit those in prison and encourage them. Take notice of those who are hungry and provide them with a meal. Take those who are homeless and give them shelter. Aid and assist the motherless and the widows. Comfort and strengthen those who are bereaved. There is much work in the kingdom for you to do.

But, you must be kingdom minded. You must focus on exhibiting the characteristics and traits of your heavenly Father. You must manifest love. Your love must be sacrificial, unbiased, and pure. The danger in not doing the will of God is eternal separation from Him. Please God by serving others as though you were actually serving God Himself.

DECEMBER 23
Defeat Is Impossible
MATTHEW 16:18

And I say also unto thee, That thou art Peter, and upon this rock I will build my church; and the gates of hell shall not prevail against it. – King James Version

And now I'm going to tell you who you are, really are. You are Peter, a rock. This is the rock on which I will put together my church, a church so expansive with energy that not even the gates of hell will be able to keep it out. – The Message Translation

As a member of the Body of Christ you have an undeniable destiny! VICTORY! You may endure hardships and attacks, but it is impossible for the devil to defeat you.

You may get some bumps and bruises along the way. But, the devil cannot win in his battle against you. For in actuality, He is really not at war against you. But, his enemy is God! Because you belong to God and you are special to God, Satan launches his attack against you.

You must remain confident that God's Word is true. Your victory is not based on what you think or what you feel. Your status as an overcomer has nothing to do with your own power or might. You are victorious because God said so. Just that simple!

You will have challenges in this life. The Scriptures declare that the afflictions of the righteous are many, but God delivers you out of them all. So don't get distracted by health issues, financial issues, relationship issues, legal issues, job issues, or anything else – the devil can't win and YOU can't lose!

DECEMBER 24

Thank God For The Name

ISAIAH 9:6

For unto us a child is born, unto us a son is given: and the government shall be upon his shoulder: and his name shall be called Wonderful, Counselor, The mighty God, The everlasting Father, The Prince of Peace. – King James Version

For a child has been born - for us! the gift of a son - for us! He'll take over the running of the world. His names will be: Amazing Counselor, Strong God, Eternal Father, Prince of Wholeness. – The Message Translation

When a child is born family and friends are excited about the birth and new life that has been given. Parents in their minds and even verbally began to call the baby their little doctor, or their little lawyer – speaking positive things towards the child's destiny. They are expecting good things for the new baby.

When Christ was born – God, our Heavenly Father gave instructions to Joseph to name the baby Jesus. He decreed that the baby would save His people from their sins. There is only One name that has been given whereby men can be saved.

Today, as we invoke the Name of Jesus we have found the Name to have power! Sickness flees, demons tremble, prayers are answered, and men, women, boys, and girls are saved through that Name. It is a wonderful, glorious, awesome and anointed name. Celebrate the Name!

DECEMBER 25

A Messy Blessing!
LUKE 2:11-12

For unto you is born this day in the city of David a Saviour, which is Christ the Lord. And this shall be a sign unto you; Ye shall find the babe wrapped in swaddling clothes, lying in a manger.

God knows when and how to bless you. Don't get so wrapped up in outside appearances that you miss your blessing. When the Christ Child was born, he was not born in a castle or fancy hotel. But, he was born in a manger, a stable for the animals. Yet, He was the promised Messiah who came to save His people from their sins.

Today, God still works in mysterious ways. Don't attempt to "box God in" and determine how He is to bless you! Samuel encountered the same type problem when he visited Jesse to anoint one of His sons to be king. He considered all the other sons, but God had chosen David, the little shepherd boy. Your church may not be a crystal cathedral with chandeliers – but it is the blessed place where God has called you. Your spouse may not look like a fashion model – but they are the blessing that God has prepared to bless your life.

God can and will use anyone and anything He desires to be an agent of your blessing. Don't look down on people or mistreat people – they may be your blessing in disguise. Do not cater to people who seem to have power or influence – they may be the very ones standing in the way to hinder your progress. Always pray and be sensitive to the move of God. He often chooses the foolish things to confound those who think they are wise.

The manger may have been a messy place to give birth to a King. But the manger was the place chosen by God to be a blessing to mankind. Thank God for His blessing! As the old saints used to sing: "Anyway you bless me Lord, I'll be satisfied"!

DECEMBER 26
What Light Do You Have?
JOHN 3:19

And this is the condemnation, that light is come into the world, and men loved darkness rather than light, because their deeds were evil. – King James Version

"This is the crisis we're in: God-light streamed into the world, but men and women everywhere ran for the darkness. They went for the darkness because they were not really interested in pleasing God. – The Message Translation

Jesus is the light of the world. But, the Word of God said that the world was in darkness and rejected the light. This was shown in the Bible days from Herod attempting to kill the baby at birth all the way to the religious leaders who had Jesus crucified on Calvary some 33 years later.

Ask yourself the question: Am I rejecting the true light? Do not be fooled by the Christmas lights that adorn homes and trees. Those lights have nothing to do with the real celebration that should be taking place. Sometimes people get caught in the hustle and bustle of the "commercialized Christmas". And after the day is past and gone they are yet in darkness because the temporary lights of man's Christmas do not endure.

However, if you receive Jesus in your heart and allow Him to light up the dark areas of your life – your life will be forever changed. You will be a new creature. You will be filled with love, joy and peace. Your life will become a light that shines and men will see your good works and begin to give God the glory. That is the true Christmas light that you should have in your life.

DECEMBER 27
Freedom From Folk
PROVERBS 29:25

The fear of man bringeth a snare: but whoso putteth his trust in the LORD shall be safe. - King James Version

It is dangerous to be concerned with what others think of you, but if you trust the Lord, you are safe. – Good News Translation

Let the people talk! Let the haters hate! Don't be so moved by what "others" think about you, about your choices, about your decisions, and most importantly about your life overall. Your only concern should be – "What does GOD think?"

Being worried about people and their opinions is a trap. It is a trick of the enemy to defeat you. If you are not careful you will find yourself far away from your purpose, calling and destiny. You will find yourself living to please others. You will be miserable, unhappy and trapped. You will be spiritually and emotionally handicapped.

But, if you simply put your trust, faith, and confidence in God – He is a keeper! Yes, being totally dependent upon God will position you to be in a "safe place" away from the emotional or spiritual damage that can occur when others infiltrate your life. Free yourself! Today, walk in the liberty where God has made you free from NOUNS - "people, places, things or ideas". Yes! Live in the safety zone. Your only concern is pleasing God!

DECEMBER 28
Spiritual Rivals!
I TIMOTHY 6:8

Fight the good fight of faith, lay hold on eternal life, whereunto thou art also called, and hast professed a good profession before many witnesses. – King James Version

Run hard and fast in the faith. Seize the eternal life, the life you were called to, the life you so fervently embraced in the presence of so many witnesses. – The Message Translation

Real change will take place only when faith is activated. Mark 11:22 exhorts you to: *"Have faith in God"*. Faith and doubt contrast and contradict one another. There is an expression, "If you pray don't worry and if you worry don't pray"! Worry is a symptom (or by-product) of unbelief. And unbelief is a sibling to doubt.

Some have made the statement that faith and doubt cannot co-exist. That is not completely accurate. They can be present at the same time but they will not operate at their ultimate level when the other is present. Your level of reception diminishes when doubt tampers with the airwaves. The more you believe, the more you can receive. However, the more you doubt, the more you hinder what you really need from being made manifest. If the statement: "If you believe, you shall receive" is accurate. Then the converse must also be true: "If you do not believe, then you shall not receive".

This is why you must *"fight the good fight of faith"*. Your faith (belief) is under attack. If the devil can keep you from believing then he knows he can succeed in hindering you from receiving. For, if you don't believe that good things can happen for you then you won't look for or expect good things to happen for you. And sometimes blessings will pass right by you because you were not expecting them.

DECEMBER 29

Laugh With God!

PSALM 2:4

He that sitteth in the heavens shall laugh: the Lord shall have them in derision. – King James Version

Heaven-throned God breaks out laughing. At first he's amused at their presumption; - The Message Translation

Don't worry or stress over your enemies. They may plot, plan and scheme against you. But, understand that in truth they are not really fighting just against you. They are in a battle with the Lord. It is the anointing within you that most disturbs the enemy. And of course the devil will never win.

Smile at your enemies! They may be mean to you. They may say hurtful things to you and about you. But, pray for them and express the love of God towards them. God is watching not just their actions, but He is also watching your reaction!

God is tickled at their supposition that they can actually win over God or His people. God's Word promises that the gates of hell cannot prevail against the church. The enemy may come and make a lot of noise. He may even throw a few good punches. But it is all in vain. You and God will get the last laugh.

DECEMBER 30
Tonight May Be Too Late
JOHN 9:4

I must work the works of him that sent me, while it is day: the night cometh, when no man can work.

Do all you can while you can! This is a wise saying that urges you to seize the moment. Take advantage of the daylight hours of your life. Run while you have strength to do so. Speak while your voice is yet strong. Busy yourself with the activity of your hands while they are not feeble.

Many people waste precious time thinking and dreaming. They live in "one day" land. There comes a time to wake up and go and possess that which you have hoped for or longed for. You must activate your faith and mix what you say with what you do.

Do not miss your season of blessing. Do not tolerate laziness or slothfulness to hinder you. Do not allow fear to grip your heart or mind. Do not permit people to discourage you from making your dream a reality.

Go! Not tonight, but today! Embrace the vision. Seize your destiny. Now is the time. If not now, when???

DECEMBER 31
Take Time To Remember
PSALM 77:11

I will remember the works of the LORD: surely I will remember thy wonders of old. – King James Version

I will remember your great deeds, Lord; I will recall the wonders you did in the past. – Good News Translation

Once again I'll go over what God has done, lay out on the table the ancient wonders; - The Message Translation

Take a moment to look back over this year and more importantly your life! As you reflect and remember, you can't help but to declare that God has been better than good. He has been faithful to His Word. He has even blessed you at times when you were undeserving of His grace and mercy.

Take this hope and assurance as you prepare for a new year, a new month, a new day! God never changes. He is constantly good and gracious. So, plan to enter your tomorrow with confidence that God will continue to do for you what He has always done.

So as you remember – praise Him! Praise Him for the past and praise Him in advance for what is to come! God has been so good. God is still good. Always remember – and always keep Him on your mind!

BONUS 1
That Was Yesterday!
I CORINTHIANS 12:2

Ye know that ye were Gentiles, carried away unto these dumb idols, even as ye were led. – **King James Version**

Remember how you were when you didn't know God, led from one phony god to another, never knowing what you were doing, just doing it because everybody else did it? It's different in this life. God wants us to use our intelligence, to seek to understand as well as we can. – **The Message Translation**

As you develop your relationship with God things change. An old adage comes to mind: "When you know better, you ought to do better". No longer do you have to make the foolish mistakes of your youth over and over again. God will guide your feet and order your steps.

No longer do you have to wander aimlessly through life. But, God has given you His Spirit to lead, guide and direct you through life. It is simply your responsibility to hear the voice of God and then obey. Study His Word and allow your life to demonstrate the fruit of your study.

Yesterday is gone. Today is your present – an awesome gift that God has given you! Embrace the wisdom and knowledge that God has invested within you and makes available for you on a daily basis.

BONUS 2

Bread Of Heaven—Feed Me

MATTHEW 6:11

Give us this day our daily bread. – King James Version

The Scriptures declare that man does not live by bread alone, but by every word that proceeds from the mouth of God. Your daily prayer should be that God would speak a Word into the atmosphere for your existence. It is only by the power of God that you live, move and breathe. Alone you are nothing, but with God the impossible becomes possible. The invisible is clearly scene. And the intangible is touched and embraced.

Since faith comes by hearing, and hearing by the Word of God. Open your ears today and hear God as never before. For the Bible also says that the just shall live by faith. So, listen for a fresh Rhema from God (*a right now word*) that will address your present reality and thrust you into the divine destiny appointed for you. Read God's Word. Meditate on God's Word. Recite God's Word. Hear God's Word. And live the abundant life that God has promised you!

BONUS 3
God's Mercy Is Yours
PSALM 118:1

O give thanks unto the LORD; for He is good: because His mercy endureth for ever. – King James Version

Thank God because He's good, because His love never quits. – The Message Translation

When you awakened this morning, God had new mercies waiting just for you. He is just that good! No matter what challenges you faced yesterday – today is a new day. If you made a few mistakes, some wrong turns, or just couldn't get it together – stop stressing! God loves you enough to place yesterday in the history book and give you a gift called the "present".

Yes, He never stops loving you. He sent His Son to die for you before you ever thought about living for Him. And now He has blessed you with His Spirit to live within you to be an ever present reminder of His goodness, His graciousness, and His glory.

Embrace the mercy of God. His grace is greater than anything you have done or even thought about doing. Learn to forgive yourself and accept God's unconditional love for you. His mercy goes on and on. That's just how He operates – His mercy lasts forever!

BONUS 4

Compassion And Understanding

EPHESIANS 4:2

With all lowliness and meekness, with longsuffering, forbearing one another in love;

Believe it or not, there are some people who do not have it all together. Yes, some of your family, friends, co-workers and church members are individuals who are still struggling with areas you may have mastered in deliverance. Looking down on them or "discussing" them is not the appropriate action to take. But, you must learn to be like your Heavenly Father and demonstrate longsuffering towards them.

It may seem to be taking them a long time to "get it right", but you must recall that in some areas it took you maybe even longer. And if you are completely honest you would acknowledge that God is still working on you in other areas. Yes, you are a recipient of the longsuffering of God.

Now today, show patience, demonstrate agape, walk in forgiveness and understanding. Let the love of God be made manifest through your actions and attitude. Learn to live with compassion and understanding for others.

BONUS 5

Embrace Peace – Victory Is Yours!

JOHN 16:33

These things I have spoken unto you, that in me ye might have peace. In the world ye shall have tribulation: but be of good cheer; I have overcome the world. – King James Version

I've told you all this so that trusting me, you will be unshakable and assured, deeply at peace. In this godless world you will continue to experience difficulties. But take heart! I've conquered the world." – The Message Translation

Stop tripping over what you are going through and stay focused on what you are going to. Greater things and better days are ahead if you learn to endure. God's Word has already let you know that you will have challenges in life. Your job is to learn to grin and bear and keep trusting God.

Your assurance comes through your identification with Jesus Christ. The same victory that He achieved is the same victory that belongs to you. He suffered. You suffer. He sacrificed. You sacrifice. He lives and reigns. You live and reign. Your victory is settled so embrace the peace of God in your heart and mind.

BONUS 6

Don't Be Duped By The Devil!

ISAIAH 14:16

They that see thee shall narrowly look upon thee, and consider thee, saying, Is this the man that made the earth to tremble, that did shake kingdoms; - King James Version

People will stare and muse: "Can this be the one Who terrorized earth and its kingdoms, - The Message Translation

Many Christians have an unnecessary fear of the devil. You must remind yourself of what Jesus did for you! He conquered the enemy and gave the victory to you. When He declared that all power is in His hands and that He is giving that power to you – you should rejoice. The devil has no power or control over you.

He talks a big game! But, that's all he has is game. And his game is weak! When you really understand who and what he is you will operate differently. True he is an accuser. But his accusations are lies and twisted or perverted truth. Yes he can bring suggestions. But, you have the power to cast down imaginations and every high thing that exalts itself against the knowledge of God.

So, in actuality he is nothing! He won't let you know that. He wants you to remain fearful of him and his imps. But, you must remember that you have the Greater One living on the inside of you. So, keep walking in victory. He may steal, kill and destroy. But, remember he is not the winner – you are!

BONUS 7
You Won't Drown!

MATTHEW 14:30

But when he saw the wind boisterous, he was afraid; and beginning to sink, he cried, saying, Lord, save me. – King James Version

But when he looked down at the waves churning beneath his feet, he lost his nerve and started to sink. He cried, "Master, save me!" – The Message Translation

Walking by faith may not always be a piece of cake. You still face the challenges of life. The enemy will create circumstances that will encourage you to doubt. No matter what comes your way – don't be afraid to walk on the water.

God has already invested within you what you need to not only survive – but to be victorious. It is your faith. Don't allow your faith to fail. Even though, it is constantly under attack. When you see the blessings of the Lord – embrace them. The promises of God cannot and will not fail in your life. Keep persevering and pressing your way.

And when you feel overwhelmed or consumed by your circumstances – simply call God. He is ever present in your life. And not only is He ready and willing to help you – He is able! You won't perish. You won't drown!

BONUS 8
God Is Your Multiplier!
EPHESIANS 3:20

Now unto Him that is able to do exceeding abundantly above all that we ask or think, according to the power that worketh in us, - King James Version

God can do anything, you know - far more than you could ever imagine or guess or request in your wildest dreams! He does it not by pushing us around but by working within us, his Spirit deeply and gently within us. – The Message Translation

God is a multiplier. Go back to math class and multiply anything you want times zero. What is the sum? That's it – zero. Give God something to work with. Extend the faith that has been invested within you to believe for the impossible.

God Is Waiting On You!

Many times things don't happen because power is not activated. That means you have to "do" something. It's unfortunate that some Christians have this "sit back and let God attitude", not realizing that God actually works through people. If you expect God to do anything in the earth realm, you have to also expect Him to use you as a willing vessel.

When things don't happen, it's not because God can't do it, for the Word says He is able to do *"exceeding abundantly"*. Stop limiting God! When things don't happen, learn to unfold your arms while waiting on God. If His Word declares that He has given you all things that pertain to life and godliness you must begin by activating and releasing the power "your faith" that should be continuously working in you.

The miraculous working of God that is manifested in your life is in direct proportion to the amount of faith that you release. The Word said according to the power that *worketh* in you. The suffix –eth denotes a continuation of the primary word which is "work". That means that your faith must be a constant and deliberate action and not a sputtering on and off occurrence.

When thinking about the deliberateness of one's faith, consider a mighty river. No matter what rocks, valleys or turns are in its path it still flows. Your faith must continue to operate even in the midst of adversity, trials, tribulations and defeat.

BONUS 9
A Prayer Answering God
PSALM 116:1

I love the LORD, because he hath heard my voice and my supplications. – King James Version

I love the Lord, because he hears me; he listens to my prayers. – Good News Translation

It is a good feeling to know that someone listens to you and is concerned about what is important to you. God cares so much about you that it does not matter how big or small it is, He cares. He is a prayer hearing and even more importantly, a prayer answering God.

Express your appreciation to God with a praise! Early in the morning or even in the midnight hour, God is anxious to hear your heart and soul. He responds with His manifested presence in your situation. Take comfort in knowing that He is attending to your needs and even desires.

So keep crying out to God. He will show up – never late but always on time. Tell Him all about your situation because He cares. As the old saints used to say, "Have a little talk with Jesus, tell Him all about your troubles…" Can't help but to love God – He is awesome!

BONUS 10

Increase Is En Route!

ISAIAH 32:15

Until the Spirit be poured upon us from on high, and the wilderness be a fruitful field, and the fruitful field be counted for a forest. – King James Version

Yes, weep and grieve until the Spirit is poured down on us from above And the badlands desert grows crops and the fertile fields become forests. – The Message Translation

The Spirit of God will bring comfort as He promised. No longer struggle and stress over the past. Whatever didn't work – just didn't. Whatever failed – just failed. Whatever negative thing that took place – just happened. Stop looking around judging your tomorrow on the vision you see today.

Cry out in praise to your God. He is on the move and change is about to erupt. Abundance is on the way to your situation. Not just a little, but a lot. God is about to take your emptiness and barrenness and make it not just a fruitful and productive field – but a forest. Your blessings will replicate themselves.

Prepare for plenty. Position yourself to be a blessing to the nations. You will have more than enough because of the hand of God over your life.

O'NEAL STALLWORTH PORTER

Since 1989, **O'Neal Stallworth Porter** has served as the senior pastor of the Fellowship Church in Mobile, Alabama. Pastor Porter, a native Mobilian, is a graduate of the University of Alabama (Tuscaloosa) with a Bachelors of Arts degree in Communications and a graduate of the Alabama State University with a Masters of Education degree in Educational Administration. He is the CEO/Publisher of both Oh Kneel Publishing Co. and the Gulf Coast Christian Voice (a monthly Christian newsmagazine). He also serves as CEO/Director of the non-profit agency: REBOOT, Inc.

Pastor Porter is an anointed teacher, psalmist, composer, choral director, gospel music workshop clinician and speaker. One of the special areas that God has gifted him is to lead "Praise Into Worship" Seminars where he teaches praise teams, choirs and entire congregations biblical foundations and practical applications of entering into the presence of God. He is the author of two previous books: ***"Praise Is What I Do – No Other Option"*** and ***"God's Power In The Believer"***. Both publications are available on his website (www.onealporter.com) and on www.amazon.com. He is a proud parent of four wonderful children: Kymberly Dawnique, Brooke O'Neal, Morgan Char'les (son-in-love Timothy Martin Jr.), and Charles Van James; three granddaughters: Amber, MaKenzi and Madeline.

CONTACT INFO

Pastor Porter is a multi-gifted vessel in the Body of Christ. He brings a wealth of wisdom, knowledge and experience in the Word (teaching and preaching) Ministry as well as the Music (composing, directing, singing) Ministry. To secure him to come and be a blessing at a service or event you are planning, please utilize the following contact information…

Pastor O'Neal Porter

P.O. Box 13125

Eight Mile, Alabama 36633

www.onealporter.com - oporter1019@gmail.com

WEBSITE **EMAIL**

www.ingramcontent.com/pod-product-compliance
Lightning Source LLC
Chambersburg PA
CBHW060907300426
44112CB00011B/1372